LIVING ABROAD IN

Mexico

IRST EDITION

Ken Luboff

© Ken Luboff

AVALON
TRAVEL

CONTENTS

Resources

Preface

In preparing this new edition of *Living Abroad in Mexico,* Barbara and I have once again had the pleasure of traveling extensively throughout the country we have called home for the past 11 years. For six of those years, we lived in San Miguel de Allende in Mexico's central plateau. Another two were spent on the shores of Lake Chapala, near Guadalajara. We now live in a spectacularly beautiful spot, a remote area on the coast of Nayarit.

What a fine decision it was for us to move to Mexico! Yet, it has not always been easy. In this book, I hope to convey our enthusiasm for the life we live in Mexico, while giving a realistic portrait of the difficulties you may encounter living in this complex, often contradictory country. But first, the story of our move to Mexico a lifetime ago:

An ancient proverb says that the cup must be empty before it can begin to refill. Living in a different culture will help empty your cup. Time and openness will refill it with a new richness.

I was like most other people I knew—working hard in a stressed-out world while wistfully dreaming about the day I could stop and retire to some fantasy tropical beach or desert island. In recent years, so many friends had become ill or died that I began having visions of a coworker entering my office to find me with my feet pointed straight up in the air behind my desk, the rest of me dead on the floor.

Finally, at the ripe young age of 52, the opportunity arose to sell the company stock I owned. The moment had arrived! With great excitement and trepidation, my wife, Barbara, and I contemplated the reality of changing the life we had been leading. Would we have enough money? How would we keep from being bored? Where would we live? Would we drive each other crazy?

We decided to give ourselves a month or two away from home as a period of transition into our new life. A friend, Eve Muir, kindly offered us her house in San Miguel de Allende. We accepted and moved to Mexico. Our two-month stay became four months, four became six, and so on. Years later, we find ourselves still living in Mexico, in our own home, and loving every moment of it.

Few bordering countries in the world are as different from each other as Mexico and the United States. Mexicans think differently and view the world through a completely different set of lenses than Americans. You can see this contrast clearly as soon as you cross the border. Mexico's food, music, and architecture are unlike our own. Even the way the people look is strikingly different. These contrasts in themselves are an attraction—in Mexico, we are explorers discovering a new terrain as well as new ideas and points of view. A friend, Chris Smith, sent us a story that helps explain one of the differences in the two cultures beautifully:

An American businessman stood at the pier of a small coastal village in Mexico, when a small boat carrying a lone Mexican fisherman docked. Inside the small boat were several large yellowfin tuna. The American complimented the Mexican on the quality of his fish and asked how long it took to catch them. The fisherman replied, "Only a little while."

The American then asked, "If it took only a little while to catch these fine fish, why didn't you stay out longer and catch more fish?" The fisherman explained that this catch was enough to support his family's immediate needs.

The American then asked, "But what do you do with the rest of your time?"

The fisherman replied, "I sleep late, fish a little, play with my children, take a siesta with my wife, and stroll into the village each evening, where I sip wine and play guitar with my amigos. I have a full and busy life, señor."

The American scoffed, "I am a Harvard MBA and could help you. You should spend more time fishing and with the proceeds buy a bigger boat. With the proceeds from the bigger boat you could buy several boats. Eventually, you would have a fleet of fishing boats. Instead of selling your catch to a middleman you would sell directly to the processor, eventually opening your own cannery. You would control the product, processing, and distribution. You would need to leave this small coastal fishing village and move to Mexico City, then L.A., and eventually New York City, where you would run your expanding enterprise."

The fisherman asked, "But señor, how long will this all take?"

The American replied, "Fifteen to twenty years."

"But what then, señor?" inquired the Mexican. The American laughed and said, "That's the best part. When the time is right, you would announce an IPO and sell your company stock to the public and become very rich. You would make millions."

"Millions, señor? Then what?" asked the Mexican.

The American said, "Why, then you would retire, of course—move to a small coastal fishing village where you could sleep late, fish a little, play with your kids, take a siesta with your wife, and stroll into the village in the evenings, where you could sip wine and play your guitar with your amigos."

In this book, you will find detailed information about health care, money, housing, and working in Mexico, so that you will have a clear understanding of what it takes to make the move. Chapters on history and people will give you insight into the Mexican character and worldview.

Beginning in the Prime Living Locations chapter, I describe four distinct regions in Mexico, with profiled towns and cities where most newcomers to Mexico will wind up living—towns that new arrivals can ease into relatively effortlessly. Each location has a large and well-established expatriate community. Most have English-language newspapers, libraries, volunteer organizations, and clubs, and all have high-quality health and recreational facilities. Each has a unique character and a different mix of foreign residents. Also profiled in each region are several other very beautiful and remote towns and cities with small—sometimes very small—foreign populations. These descriptions may whet the appetites of the more adventurous among you.

But non-Mexicans live in every corner of the country. The towns and cities described here are only the tip of the iceberg. You might arrive at the most remote mountain villages only to run into residents from Europe, Canada, the States, and other parts of the world. A good friend, an American woman about 45 years old, lives happily on a 20-acre farm in the state of Michoacán with her French boyfriend. Another old friend and his wife are building a house on a remote beach in the state of Jalisco. Other artist friends live in the heart of Mexico City.

If you and your family are looking for an unparalleled cultural experience, or you want to escape the winter blues, Mexico is a superb choice.

Finally, I would like your input. Send me an update about a city I have included in the book. Maybe a new English bookstore has opened or great new library. Tell me about wonderful towns you have discovered. Maybe you have already moved there! My email is: bluboff@yogainmexico.com

–Ken Luboff

This book is dedicated to Liza.

© Jan Ambrose

Introduction

Welcome to Mexico

Mexico is one of the unknown wonders of the world—it is amazing how little people to the north know about their neighbor. Many Americans think of Mexico as having palm-studded beaches lined with mega-hotels and resorts, surrounding a vast, scary inland of baking cactus and unfriendly, if not hostile, Pancho Villa types.

This image couldn't be further from the truth. Mexico is filled with both natural and artificially constructed wonders—hot rivers, snow-capped mountains, magnificent colonial towns, charming Swiss-style villages, indigenous people wearing flamboyant costumes, exotic coffee plantations, art deco architectural fantasies in the jungle, and the generosity of a very warm people.

Foreigners living in Mexico defy any single classification. Many are snowbirds who return each winter to escape cooler climes; others come to study Spanish; still others to immerse their kids in the country's vibrant culture; some come to find work; and some to follow the sun and high surf.

In San Miguel a young family of four from Boulder, Colorado, spent a year in Mexico so that they could all learn Spanish and so that the two young children could gain a new perspective. The kids were enrolled in the local Waldorf school, where the majority of students are Mexican.

IS MEXICO RIGHT FOR YOU?

Mexico offers some obvious advantages over other countries. The foremost may be its location. Mexico is a breeze to reach from the United States. It has modern airports and a well-developed four-lane highway system. The trip by car from the U.S. border to most central Mexican cities takes only a day or two. Once at home in Mexico, you can keep in touch with friends and family back in the States using its modern telecommunications network. Phoning the United States is easy, but it is just as easy and less expensive to turn on your computer and stay connected by email and instant messaging.

> Foreigners living in Mexico have the opportunity to slow down, tune in to the subtleties of the culture, and discover the wonderful diversity of terrain within Mexico's borders.

Living in Mexico costs about one-third of what it costs to live in the States. Depending on where you make your home, it is possible to live very well in Mexico on $2000 per month—even less. After all, a pound of oranges costs about $.19, a dozen eggs $1.12, a dozen fresh long-stemmed roses $3, and a full-time maid $50 per week! Sure, in the fanciest areas of towns like San Miguel and Puerto Vallarta, higher rents drive monthly expenses up. But outside the ritzy areas—in the countryside and the smaller villages—houses rent for as little as $200 or $300 a month.

Those interested in buying a house in Mexico will find that laws make it easy for a foreigner to own property with a secure title. A few U.S. mortgage companies now offer mortgages on Mexican real estate at competitive rates. In many areas, homes and lots are covered by U.S. title insurance companies. Real estate is appreciating in popular areas, but bargains can still be found, and building costs are about one-third to one-half of those in the United States.

For the most part, Mexicans are sweet people who will go out of their way to help a friend or even a congenial acquaintance. You may go into shops for the first time and, because the shopkeepers cannot

Get a Life

Whenever my daughter (another Mexico "junkie") or I travel north and encounter close family members, the questions are always the same. "When do you think you'll come back?" "When are you going to come home and lead a normal life?" "How can you stand to be in a country with so much poverty?" "When are you going to get a real job?" "When are you going to come back to the real world and have a real life?" "How can you stand to be so far away from your family?"

One would think that—because out of the last 24 years of my life, I've spent about 21 in Mexico—they'd get used to the idea. Why can't they understand that I'm no longer enamored with commuting at least an hour each way every day to work on a freeway parking lot or having to "plug" my car into an electrical outlet on winter nights so that the block doesn't crack? I'm also not so crazy about going more than 30 days without seeing sunshine.

Why is the world north of the border perceived by many (especially those who live there) as the real one? Maybe because it's meaner and faster. My reality is living where people actually smile at each other, exchange pleasantries, take time to chat (in person, not on the cell phone), celebrate without guilt, and look after each other. The poverty of spirit that comes with the mad money and time chase and the isolating practice of communicating only by phone and computer in sound bytes is as debilitating in terms of "humanness" as spiritual scarcity.

Maybe my family would be easier to take if they didn't question my pleasure living at the edge of a culture (I know I'll never really be part of it, but that makes it all the easier to choose the parts of it I like) so different from the one in which I was raised.

As for a real job...this isn't a hobby, folks, but I love it just as much...well, almost.

Reprinted with permission by the author, Jeanne Chaussée, from the October 2–8, 2004 edition of the *Guadalajara Reporter*.

break your large bill, be told to return and pay later. Knowing at least a little Spanish, even if it is badly spoken, can make kindness like this more likely.

But can a country with a great sunny climate, friendly people, beautiful beaches, first-class recreational facilities, spectacular mountains, and low prices be perfect? That might be too much to ask. Like anywhere on earth, Mexico has its downsides. Among them are environmental degradation, poverty, and crime. Cultural differences, as well, are a source of frustration to some new arrivals. Government is not efficient by U.S. standards, and whereas computers are now ubiquitous, some offices still use old typewriters and carbon paper.

Most tourists come to Mexico to lie in the sun on a tropical beach, whoop it up in a border town over the weekend, or explore archaeological ruins and cathedrals. Foreigners living in Mexico, on the other hand, have the opportunity to slow down, tune in to the subtleties of the culture, and discover the wonderful diversity of terrain within Mexico's borders. As they meet and become friendly with Mexican people, foreign residents are often invited to weddings and other family celebrations, religious ceremonies, and community festivities. If they desire, they can leisurely explore the country—canoeing through a lush jungle lagoon in the morning, then sleeping in a high mountain pine forest that night. They might attend a first-rate opera in Guadalajara in the evening and spend the night in a quaint fishing village just 45 minutes away.

The contrasts in Mexico are astounding: the Stone Age and high technology stand side by side. An old man rides along the highway on his burro—a huge General Motors plant his backdrop—as a new Mercedes whizzes by. Poor families live in tin hovels back-to-back with fancy, high-speed cyber cafés. Your experiences in Mexico can be just as varied and sometimes just as striking.

Obviously, living in Mexico is not for everyone. As a foreign country, it can take some getting used to. For those who are stuck in their ways or not ready to experience some inconveniences, Mexico can be a real challenge. But if you are up for that challenge, you can meet amazing people with unique ideas. You can make good Mexican friends. You can even learn a new language. If you are adventurous and have a good sense of humor and a great deal of patience, living in Mexico can seem like the next best thing to paradise.

Lay of the Land

The Rio Grande defines more than half the border between the United States and Mexico. West of El Paso, no natural boundary exists; only an imaginary line divides Mexico from New Mexico, Arizona, and California. The entire border is closely guarded by the United States.

Narrowing from its 1,600-mile (2,575 km) northern border, Mexico measures just 125 miles (201 km) on its southern border at the Isthmus of Tehuantepec. The Pacific Ocean hugs the western and southern coasts; Guatemala, Belize, and the Caribbean Sea lie along the southeast border; and the Gulf of Mexico forms the eastern border. The peninsula of Baja California, about 800 miles (1,287 km) long, is separated from the mainland by the Gulf of California.

Mexico has more than 6,200 miles (9,978 km) of coastline: 4,400 miles (7,081 km) on the west and south coasts, 1,774 miles (2,855 km) on the east coast. The country covers an area of 760,000 square miles (1,968,400 square km). More than two-thirds of Mexico is mountainous, ranging from 3,000 to over 18,000 feet (912 to 5,472 meters) in altitude. The two principal mountain ranges, the Sierra Madre Occidental (West), which runs along the Pacific coast, and the Sierra Madre Oriental (East) join together as the country narrows south of Mexico City. This junction is an area of spectacular mountain peaks—many of them extinct volcanoes—with more than 22 peaks rising to 10,000 feet (3,040 meters) or higher. The two most famous peaks are Popocatepetl (which gushes smoke occasionally) and Iztaccihuatl. Both are over 17,000 feet (5,168 meters) and straddle the states of Mexico and Puebla. The highest peak of all is the majestic Pico de Orizaba, standing at 18,855 feet (5,732 meters) in the state of Veracruz. Between the two Sierra Madre ranges lies a vast high plateau, home to the majority of Mexico's 100 million inhabitants. The plateau itself is crisscrossed by a series of valleys and mountain slopes.

Mexico is the world's most populous Spanish-speaking country, with a rapidly expanding population. More than 40 percent of its people are under 25 years old. The overall population density is about 125 people per square mile. Compare that to the United States, with its overall density of about 70 people per square mile. However, the countryside feels empty because Mexicans tend to live close to family and friends in villages and cities. Mexico City, with a population of about 26 million, is the world's largest city. In some areas, its population density reaches more than 40,000 people per square mile. The second largest city in Mexico is Guadalajara, with five million inhabitants. In area, Mexico is the world's 13th largest country, slightly less than three times the size of Texas.

COUNTRY DIVISIONS

The United States of Mexico has 31 states and one federal district known as DF, much like our Washington, D.C. The states are Aguascalientes, Baja California, Baja California Sur, Campeche, Chiapas, Chihuahua, Coahuila, Colima, Durango, Guanajuato, Guerrero, Hidalgo, Jalisco,

Mexico, Michoacán, Morelos, Nayarit, Nuevo León, Oaxaca, Puebla, Querétaro, Quintana Roo, San Luis Potosí, Sinaloa, Sonora, Tabasco, Tamaulipas, Tlaxcala, Veracruz, Yucatán, and Zacatecas.

WEATHER

For many people north of the border the weather in Mexico is a surprise. Folks living in New York City, Chicago, and other cities that are boiling hot in summer find it hard to imagine that at the same time of year most central Mexican cities are very cool. In most of Mexico, summer is the start of the rainy season. Add to the rains a few thousand feet of elevation and you get sweater-cool summer nights. The rains generally fall for a few hours every afternoon between June and October. On the coast of Mexico, even with the rains, August and September are usually very hot and sticky.

Generally, the coldest months are January and February, with snow in the north. South of the city of Zacatecas, however, it rarely freezes. Mexico City and other high-elevation towns definitely require a sweater or jacket during these months.

April, May, and part of June—the last months before the rainy season—can be hot, dry, and dusty in the central part of the country. This is a good time to visit the west coast, where it is cool, breezy, and bug free.

Driving through the Mexican countryside can be an experience much like touring the farming areas in the rolling hills of central Pennsylvania, the forested mountains of New England, the high savannah in Kenya, Alpine lake regions, and the foothills of the Himalayas!

FLORA AND FAUNA

Many Americans imagine Mexico to be a stark cactus-covered desert. It is true that Baja California and a large portion of northern Mexico are desert, but there are areas in northern Mexico with lush green valleys that support huge dairy farms and orchards. The majority of the country is surprisingly green and diverse. As a matter of fact, Mexico is one of the most ecologically diverse countries in the world, ranking fourth in bio-diversity. The landscape includes jungles, forests, deserts, basins, and valleys, which encompass many diverse ecosystems. Approximately half of Mexico lies above 3,200 feet (973 meters) in elevation, and there are six major mountain ranges and two minor ones. Mexico is extremely rich in bird, animal, and plant life, and more than 800 species are endemic.

The states that surround Mexico City have millions of acres of pine forests and deciduous forests. The western coastal states of Nayarit, Jalisco, Colima, and Michoacán, have a mixture of tropical forests, sugar cane fields, vast coconut palm plantations, and fruit orchards. The eastern coastal state of Veracruz has coffee and tea plantations as well as native tropical forests. Driving through the Mexican countryside can be an experience much like touring the farming areas in the rolling hills of central Pennsylvania, the forested mountains of New England, the high Savannah in Kenya, Alpine lake regions, and the foothills of the Himalayas! Many of the forests are home to ocelots, jaguars, bears, wild boar, wolves, and deer. The coastal areas host iguanas, mapaches (small raccoon-like mammals), and of course small rodents. The diversity of the flora attracts a huge variety of birds, both native and migratory, making Mexico a bird-watcher's paradise. Each winter in the state of Michoacán, a butterfly preserve welcomes millions of Monarch butterflies, many having flown from as far as 5,000 miles (8,047 km) away! One November evening, while driving through San Angelo, Texas, on our way to Mexico, Barbara and I decided to stretch our legs and take a walk along a river. All of a sudden we were surrounded by thousands of Monarchs that were settling into a tree for the night, surely on their way to Michoacán—just like us!

Unfortunately, population pressures, pollution, and a lack of environmental protection have created a situation where the exceptional native flora and fauna are threatened in many regions. About 30 percent of the wildlife is endangered and a high percentage is considered threatened; 23 species are believed to be extinct.

Social Climate

Like the United States and Canada, Mexico is part of North America, a fact that makes it difficult for us "foreigners from North America" to label ourselves appropriately while in Mexico. *Los Estadounidenses* (people from the United States) would probably be the most politically correct name—if we could even pronounce it. Some Mexicans call us *de Los Estados Unidos* (from the United States). But, for the most part, Mexicans call us *Norteamericanos* or just *Americanos*. On rare occasions, we are called *gringos,* a term for Anglos who come from (or just look like they come from) the United States. In the past, this was a derogatory term, but these days, many Mexicans use it simply to describe anyone from the north. There are several explanations for the origin of the term gringo. One theory holds that "gringo" derives from "green," the color of the U.S. army uniform seen during U.S. invasions of Mexico. Another theory relates the word to the U.S. "greenback." An accepted academic version traces the word's origin to *griego*, Spanish for Greek. A dictionary written in 1765 by Jesuit Spaniard Esteban Terror y Pando says that, "In Malaga they call gringos foreigners who have a certain kind of accent...." *Gringa* is not only a young Anglo girl, but also a very tasty type of stuffed taco prepared in some parts of the country.

In general, Mexicans are polite and reserved when dealing with foreigners from the north. Newcomers from the States often take this treatment as friendliness, but it is far more complicated than that. Mexicans and other inhabitants of Latin America often wear masks that cover their true feelings. Nevertheless, common courtesy is part of every interaction in Mexico, as is formality. This formality appears unexpectedly at times. For instance, you may get used to being greeted with *"Buenos días"* or *"Buenas tardes"* by the gas station attendant or a stranger on the street and to being called *Señor* or *Señora* by a shopkeeper, but it might surprise you when a total stranger in a restaurant says, *"Buen provecho"* (good appetite) or *"Con permiso"* (excuse me) when passing your table. It is a good idea to learn as many of these formal expressions as possible. Using them can bring you a new measure of respect in the eyes of Mexicans. And, with time and some effort, they can help you to make good Mexican friends.

THE UNIQUE MEXICAN EXPERIENCE

The unique Mexican worldview can produce some funny, bizarre, and Fellini-esque experiences. Many times you will see or hear something that causes you to shake your head in amazement. For example, on the saint's day of construction workers, wandering bands serenade construction sites, occupied or nonoccupied. They make their rounds usually between 4 and 6 A.M. It is one thing to hear a lover serenade his lady on her balcony at sunset and quite another to be awakened at 4:30 A.M. by a booming tuba, blaring trumpet, and thunderous drums, having no clue as to what is going on. These phenomena are wonderful because they remind you just how foreign the Mexican culture is—and enhance your sense of adventure in such an exotic land. One of Mexico's more endearing attractions is the element of surprise. There is innocence in the way teenagers giggle together or play with their families unembarrassed.

National Holidays and Celebrations

January 1—Año Nuevo (New Year's Day)

January 6—Día de los Reyes Magos (Three Kings' Day; children receive gifts on this day rather than on Christmas)

February 2—Día de la Candelária (candlelight processions and dancing)

February 5—Día de la Constitución (Constitution Day)

February 24—Día de la Bandera (Flag Day)

Late February or early March—Carnaval (marking the beginning of Lent)

March 21—Día de Nacimiento de Benito Juárez (birthday of Benito Juárez)

March or April—Semana Santa (Holy Week; the week beginning on Palm Sunday and ending on Easter)

May 1—Día del Trabajo (Labor Day)

May 5—Cinco de Mayo (celebration of Mexico's victory over the French army at Puebla in 1862)

May 10—Día de la Madre (Mother's Day)

September 16—Día de la Independéncia (Independence Day; commemorating Mexico's war of independence from Spain)

October 12—Día de la Raza (Day of the Race; commemorating Columbus's discovery of the New World and the founding of the *mestizo*—Mexican people)

November 1—Informe Presidenciál (president's State of the Nation address to the legislature)

November 1—Día de Todos Santos (All Saints' Day)

November 2—Día de los Muertos (Day of the Dead; people bring food, drink, and flowers to cemeteries to commune with the departed)

November 20—Día de la Revolución (anniversary of the Mexican Revolution of 1910)

December 12—Día de Nuestra Señora de Guadalupe (Day of Our Lady of Guadalupe, Mexico's national patroness)

December 24—La Noche Buena (Christmas Eve)

December 16–24—Posadas (parades that commemorate the journey of Mary and Joseph to Bethlehem)

December 25—Día de Navidad (Christmas Day)

Mexicans love a fiesta. It may take the form of a party, parade, celebration organized by the town, or an impromptu gathering. Mexicans have a saint for every day of the year and one for every neighborhood. They celebrate major religious holidays like Easter (*Semana Santa*), Virgin of Guadalupe Day, and Christmas. They hold dozens of political rallies and observe national holidays like Independence Day and El Cinco de Mayo. All of these events are celebrated in their own way, some more uniquely than others, and you never know when you are going to encounter something really odd. You may round a corner and bump into a crowd of costumed dancers in absurd homemade chicken or bull dog masks, or in store-bought rubber heads of Laurel and Hardy, Bill Clinton, Carlos Salinas de Gotari, Mickey Mouse, or George Bush. You may see a parade of Aztecs walking shoulder to shoulder with soldiers in Civil War dress, priests, and people in space suits—all preceded by an oompahpah band. In San Miguel de Allende, decorated taxis parade on their saint's day.

It is not unusual to be startled awake at 5 A.M. by the sound of rockets exploding in the sky. Then there are the ubiquitous church bells, roosters, barking dogs, and loud truck mufflers. On weekends and holidays, a neighbor may decide to play his stereo at full volume, or music at the city park may be loud enough to feel like a mild earthquake. Most incomprehensible to non-Mexicans are the occasional town celebrations in which two bandstands are set up next to each other with speakers the size of Buicks. Two bands then play simultaneously—completely different ear-shattering music—until late into the night. Meanwhile, the crowd in the street below dances, seemingly impervious to the noise, loving every high-decibel moment of it.

On Day of the Dead (around Halloween), people visit cemeteries with flowers and candles. They bring food, wine, and booze or wear a dead loved one's favorite hat. Some stay all night talking to the dead, playing music, singing, and not paying too much attention to the priest chanting in the background. Mexicans say that on this night the veil between the living and the dead is at its thinnest, and the dead can hear and appear to their loved ones. The day before Day of the Dead is dedicated to young children who have died. For a week or so leading up to these days, stands around town sell sugar candy shaped and painted like skulls, skeletons, and caskets. Some candies are exquisitely carved. Many people set up altars in their homes—some quite large and elaborate—dedicated to one or more dearly departed. The altars hold flowers, candles, and photos of the dead, of course, but also anything else that the dearly departed might enjoy, like a pack of cigarettes, a bottle of tequila, guitar strings, paintbrushes, or a hammer and nails.

Mexican shops can and do sell many strange combinations of goods. Imagine a small store in the United States that carried booze alongside children's toys! Shops might sell jewelry and Tupperware and have a launderette in the back selling souvenir masks and crosses. "No way!" you might say. But in Mexico, anything goes.

In most shops in Mexico, prices are fixed and bargaining is a thing of the past. But look for outdoor arts and crafts markets, called *tianguis,* where bargaining is still accepted and expected. Almost all Mexican towns have a market day when farmers and craftspeople from surrounding towns come together to sell their wares. On this day, you can hone your haggling skills and walk away with a bargain.

You might do some of your best bargaining from the comfort of a beach chair, with a margarita in hand. A constant flow of beach peddlers move from tourist to tourist all day long, hustling jewelry, wood carvings, rugs, T-shirts, and clothing. Bargaining is so expected that if you were to say yes to the first price given, the salesperson would probably faint from shock. We have bought some wonderful items at great prices on the beach. This kind of bargaining can be fun, but also quite time- and energy-consuming. You can easily find yourself surrounded by 10 insistent sales people.

Be aware that Mexicans are reluctant to say, "I don't know." When you ask for directions, you will most certainly be given directions—although the direction-giver may have no idea where the street or town you seek is located. When you ask what day a job will be completed, you will always get a specific completion date. The plumber will say, "I will be there tomorrow at 10 A.M." Whether or not he comes is up to the gods. You are likely to be told what you want to be told. Such responses stem from the fact that Mexicans sincerely want to help and oblige—not from meanness.

Mexicans really mean it when they say *mi casa es tu casa.* One day, Barbara was walking our dog in the country and encountered a poor woman who, without too much ado, asked Barbara how old she was and if she had knee problems (which, it turned out, the woman herself had). After a little chat, the woman gave Barbara directions to her home and said she should visit any time—that her home was always open. She said she was poor and that her house was very humble, but she would be honored by Barbara's visit. Another time, in San Miguel, we were invited to a Christmas *posada* at a Mexican's home. The party spilled out into the street, where a piñata for the children was strung between two houses. A couple of American tourists wandered down the street to see what the commotion was. The hostess happened to be outside and asked them if they had eaten or had a drink yet. They kind of sputtered, "Well… we were just passing by, we weren't invited." The hostess looked at them like they were half crazed—she had just invited them! To be asked into a stranger's home is not out of the ordinary.

History, Government, and Economy

ncient Mexico may have fallen, but it is not buried. Even today it is evident in almost all aspects of contemporary society. Prehistoric and ancient Mesoamerica remain very much part of the heartbeat of the 21st century, a profound ingredient of Mexico's soul. The past is fused inexorably with the present, for Mexico's most ancient inhabitants have left a legacy that continues to contribute to the art and culture as well as the physical characteristics of the Mexican people.

History

One of the oldest societies on earth, Mexico had established several great civilizations long before the appearance of modern people in

Europe. Archaeologists have identified more than 10,000 ancient Mesoamerican building sites and cities. Evidence indicates that this land may have been populated for more than 30,000 years. The most widely accepted theory is that nomadic tribes from Asia crossed into the Western Hemisphere before or during the last ice age, via a land bridge that connected Siberia to Alaska. The tribes migrated south through Alaska, Canada, and the United States into what is now the Republic of Mexico.

Composed of fishermen, hunters, and fruit gatherers, the tribes remained nomadic until they discovered wild corn. At that time, the small plant's one meager ear contained just a few grains, but between 5000 and 3000 B.C., farmers improved this primitive plant, producing corn as we know it today. With the advent of cultivated corn, wandering prehistoric tribes were able to settle in scattered communities.

PRE-COLUMBIAN RESIDENTS

The most acclaimed pre-Columbian tribes included the Aztecs, Maya, Mixtecs, Olmecs, Teotihuacanos, Toltecs, and Zapotecs. The powerful Olmecs, who lived in the dense jungles of southern Veracruz and northern Tabasco, can be traced to 2000 B.C. Although they left few architectural remains, a great wealth of their stone sculpture and pottery has survived. These artifacts show us the astonishing extent of the Olmecs' cultural evolution. They originated a numbering system, hieroglyphics, an almost perfect calendar, and astronomical observations that are amazingly accurate. They were also adventurous, colonizing many areas and widely influencing other tribes.

It was the Mayans who introduced the mathematical concept of zero--unknown even to the Roman Empire. Their mathematical system was based on the number 20 rather than 10, and through advanced calculations, the Mayans were able to pinpoint eclipses with remarkable accuracy.

In fact, the Olmecs contributed to the development of other civilizations, especially the Teotihuacanos, who erected the imposing Pyramids of the Sun and Moon in their vast city of Teotihuacán, 25 miles (40 km) northeast of what is now Mexico City. These pyramids took 10,000 people a period of 20 years to construct. Talented urban planners, the Teotihuacanos continued to build until around A.D. 650, when they began to decline, eventually abandoning their city some 150 years later. (Some archaeologists claim that the Toltecs destroyed Teotihuacán.) As Teotihuacán began to fall, the Zapotecan cities of Monte Alban and

Mitla were becoming prominent in Oaxaca. Again, the Olmec influence can be seen in the Zapotecs' hieroglyphs, their sophisticated 52-week calendar, and their bar-and-dot mathematical system.

In Oaxaca, where both Zapotecs and Mixtecs developed large urban centers, archaeologists are still uncovering abundant and wondrous artifacts. Oaxaca is one of Mexico's principal crafts centers, and although many materials have been modified and modernized, many crafts found in the region are a continuation of ancient traditions.

The Mayans, in southeastern Mexico and reaching into Guatemala and Honduras, were also influenced by the Olmecs. Architectural geniuses, the Mayans built some of the greatest cities in Mesoamerica, including Chichén Itzá, Palenque, Tikal, Uxmal, and Yaxchilan. A mind-blowing fact: These enormous cities were built without the aid of the wheel. Contrary to popular belief, the Mayans knew about the wheel, but they did not use it because they had no animals large enough to pull it, and pulling it themselves would have degraded them.

The Mayans refined the Olmec calendar further. Based on a solar year of 365.242 days, it was more accurate than the calendar used in Europe at that time. It was the Mayans who introduced the mathematical concept of zero—unknown even to the Roman Empire. Their mathematical system was based on the number 20 rather than 10, and through advanced calculations, the Mayans were able to pinpoint eclipses with remarkable accuracy.

The great Mayan cities, for still-obscure reasons, were abandoned beginning in the 15th century, about 50 years before Columbus set out from Spain. Rebellion against ruling priests, natural disasters, and the forecasting of intrusion by barbarians from the north are some of the theories regarding the decline of this incredible civilization.

Astronomical observations played a pivotal role in Mesoamerican life. Astrology and religion were firmly linked, and the sun and moon were worshipped as deities. Almost every Mesoamerican city was built in strict accordance with celestial movements, and ceremonies and sports were planned around the activity of stars and planets. Rituals to appease the gods were performed to prevent droughts, floods, and earthquakes. Gods of the sun, moon, wind, rain, fire, and earth predominated, and human sacrifice was considered absolutely vital—especially among the Aztecs, who believed that without sacrifices the sun would be extinguished and all life would perish. This belief ultimately caused the Aztecs to lose their country to a handful of invading Spaniards.

THE AZTECS AND THE SPANISH INVASION

It was the Aztecs whom Hernán Cortés and his men discovered in November 1519. Some historians claim that the Aztecs were called Mexicans, thus the name Mexico. But whatever their name, this tribe was the fiercest and most powerful of all. The Aztecs arrived from the north and invaded the Valley of Mexico toward the end of the 12th century. A series of islands on a vast lake, the region was then divided into several city-states, none of which were dominant. It was not until an Aztec priest saw an omen—an eagle perched on a cactus with a rattlesnake in its beak—that the Aztecs began to overthrow the smaller cities and build the mighty city of Tenochtitlán, now Mexico City. They built causeways to link their capital on the largest island with the mainland. They planted gardens on floating reed islands, which provided both food for the city and safeguard from attacks.

As they grew in strength and numbers, the Aztecs forged alliances with the powerful states of Texcoco and Tlacopan and began to conquer and brutally suppress other tribes. Each conquered tribe was heavily taxed. Increasingly, the only way these vanquished tribes could pay was in human life—sacrifices that the Aztecs needed to keep the sun rising. Hundreds of thousands of captives were sacrificed. The Aztecs' city flourished rapidly. By the time the Spaniards arrived, the Aztecs, although relative newcomers, were undoubtedly the most authoritative and feared of all tribes.

In April 1519, just 27 years after Columbus reached the New World, Hernán Cortés and about 700 men dropped anchor off the coast of Veracruz. Cortés, on horseback, had no trouble overpowering the indigenous people. Horses were unknown in the New World, and the sight of fair-skinned beings astride these huge beasts terrified all those who encountered them. Cortés enlisted the aid of Jeronimo de Aguilar to act as an interpreter. A Spanish priest shipwrecked several years earlier, he had been living among the indigenous people in peace. Cortés was quick to advise the native population about the importance of Christianity and the greatness of King Carlos V of Spain. The people of that region were peaceful, and they listened attentively.

Cortés and his expedition searched for what was described to them as a city filled with "towers floating on water." When they arrived at the pass between the mountains of Popocatepetl and Iztaccihuatl, they were not prepared for the astounding sight that lay below them in the Valley of Mexico. Tenochtitlán, home to 100,000 people, was at

Sports

Futbol (soccer) is Mexico's most popular sport. In 1986, Mexico City proudly hosted the World Cup. Six years later, Mexico suffered a huge defeat both on the field and to the nation's pride, when on Monday, June 17, 2002, it lost to the United States and was eliminated from the World Cup. But really, that was nothing compared to the price of defeat in Aztec times.

During the time of the Aztecs, ball courts were shaped like a capital "I." Temples stood at both ends, and banks of seating ran along the sides, atop 12-foot-high walls. In the middle of each opposing wall were stone or wooden rings. The ball was a solid rubber sphere about six inches in diameter. To protect themselves against injuries from the heavy ball, the players (usually nobles and a sprinkling of professionals) wore helmets, wide belts of hard wood and leather, hip pads, knee pads, and a single glove.

After the ball was thrown into play, players had to pass it to their teammates using their hips, elbows, or legs, without letting it run into the opposing team's end of the court, which would count as a point against them. The excited crowd would bet "gold, turquoise, slaves, rich mantles, even cornfields and houses" on the outcome, according to a Spanish chronicler. Star players were the ones who could hit the ball up through the ring on the side of the court, thereby winning the game.

Here's the payoff: The victorious side had the right to grab the clothes and jewelry of any spectators who couldn't get away fast enough. And because the game had religious significance—in fact, omens were read from the movement of the ball and the nature of the victory—the losing team sometimes paid the ultimate price for defeat, decapitation as a sacrifice to the gods. Sculptural reliefs found next to many ball courts depict this gruesome end.

the height of its glory. Given that they were also at the height of their barbarous power, it is amazing how quickly the Aztecs succumbed to Cortés and his men.

According to Aztec belief, 1519 was the year in which the god-king Quetzalcoatl, disguised as the plumed serpent, was to return to claim his throne. Legend has it that the night Cortés arrived, a brilliant comet appeared in the sky and at the same time lightning struck a temple. Montezuma, the Aztec emperor, instantly mistook the white men on horseback for gods—heralded by the comet and the flash of lightning. Having never seen horses before, the Aztecs thought each animal and rider were one unearthly being. In fact, there were only 16 horses with Cortés, but that was enough to awe the Aztecs.

When Cortés rode down into Tenochtitlán, he was greeted as a god and housed in the former palace of Axayacatl, Montezuma's father. Soon the Aztec emperor began having doubts as to Cortés's godliness, and for a few months Montezuma kept his distance, keeping Cortés virtually imprisoned in the palace. Pressured by his people, who insisted that Cortés was indeed a god, Montezuma finally agreed to meet him. Cortés, a fearless and a masterful organizer, tied the emperor in psychological knots and ended by saying, "Either we take you prisoner, or you die by your own sword." Montezuma, now convinced Cortés was a god, willingly became a prisoner.

Soon after, the Spaniards began the wholesale destruction of the city. Aztecs watched in horror as the Spaniards destroyed their temples and idols. Montezuma, from his luxurious prison, could do nothing. The Aztec bows and arrows, clubs, stones, and darts were no match for the Spaniards' steel, artillery, and muskets. Within a short time, Cortés and his force of less than 700 men were in full command of the immense city. When Cortés heard that a second Spanish fleet, led by Panfilo de Navaez, had arrived on the coast, he left 140 men under the command of his lieutenant, Alvarado, and raced off to meet the fleet.

During Cortés's absence, Alvarado had 200 Aztec nobles killed. When Cortés returned with an enlarged army, the city was rioting and Montezuma was once again in command. While trying to pacify the city, Montezuma was killed by one of his own men when he stepped onto the roof of his palace to address the people. With no leader to control them, the Aztecs rose up fiercely against the Spaniards, who were forced to flee the city. It is said that the Spaniards escaped by using bridges comprised of the dead and dying between the causeways. They found safety at Tlaxcala, where the tribal leaders had been impressed by the Spaniards' bravery against the Aztecs.

The battle continued. The Aztecs' indigenous enemies joined Cortés, swelling the ranks of the Spaniards. Now reinforced, the Spaniards steadily managed to obliterate Tenochtitlán with cannons. By August 1521, the defenders were worn down and resistance ended. Spanish rule began, and Mexico was declared a territory of Spain. By 1575, there were 60,000 Spanish in Mexico. While as a group they were the elite, not all were powerful or rich. Some even resorted to begging.

SPANISH RULE

The administration of New Spain was a hodgepodge of powers and subdivisions, with much infighting. Spain's two main objectives were

a colonial church

to convert every last indigenous person to Catholicism and to appropriate the riches of Mexico, notably gold and silver, which were discovered in unimaginable quantities. To eliminate pure indigenous races,
impregnation and intermarriage were encouraged. Catholicism was
enforced—often brutally. Hundreds of thousands of native people died
of smallpox, and the tribes managed only sporadic opposition to the
Spanish, who had already spread and conquered territories from the
Gulf of Mexico to Guatemala, the Yucatán, and Honduras.

From 1570 to 1821, silver was mined in Mexico in such vast amounts
that the world supply doubled. One-fifth of all silver mined belonged to
the Spanish Crown, but much of it never reached Spain. This was the
era of pirating, and British and Dutch pirates even won titles for preying
upon the treasure-laden Spanish galleons. For 200 years, the escapades of
Walter Raleigh, Francis Drake, Thomas Cavandish, and other celebrated
pirates made them heroes in their homelands, fiends abroad, and objects
of romantic fiction. Greed was rampant, and the beginning of Mexico's
continuing acquaintance with corruption was founded.

By 1800, education was completely dominated by the Catholic
Church and was the exclusive property of the privileged classes. The

masses were deliberately denied education, impoverished, and taught to fear the church. With these conditions, rebellion was inevitable, although the elite didn't imagine that the downtrodden would even entertain such a notion. The *ejido* system, whereby families were granted small land holdings, was failing as large haciendas absorbed the small farms. The church was the biggest landholder of all; at the close of the colonial era, it owned more than half of Mexico's land and buildings and was exempt from taxation. Spain had forbidden Mexico to trade with any country other than itself, bringing to near collapse an economic system that could no longer survive the rage of the people.

The American Revolution of 1776 had started the first small rumblings, but it was the French Revolution shortly afterward that brought Mexicans to the point of actually discussing independence from Spain. Subversive talk and the distribution of revolutionary literature were swiftly and cruelly punished, but as conditions for the vast majority grew steadily worse, there was no stopping the inevitable.

INDEPENDENCE

On the night of September 15, 1810, Father Miguel Hidalgo y Costilla, a lowly parish priest in the town of Dolores, Guanajuato, joined by Ignacio Allende, commander of the local militia, rang the church bells to assemble the villagers. There he raised his famous cry, *El Grito* (The Shout), which is reenacted all around the country each year on September 15, Mexican Independence Day. Hidalgo was not a military man, and no preparations had been made to arm or feed the 50,000 indigenous and mestizo people who arrived within the first week alone. Armed only with machetes, slingshots, clubs, crude spears, and a terrible rage against the Spanish, the ragtag army swept through the countryside looting, burning, and acquiring large numbers of enthusiastic recruits. On November 2, they won their greatest victory at Las Cruces in the state of Mexico. The *Guerra de Independencia* (War of Independence) was under way. The battle was gory and protracted, lasting until 1821, when Colonel Agustín Iturbide finally took the capital. Mexico, after terrible bloodshed, had won its independence. The Spanish flag was taken down forever, and the Mexican flag—with an eagle on a cactus devouring a serpent—was erected.

With the advent of independence, Mexico was in complete chaos. No native-born Mexican had experience in government, and during the war a new class, the military, had come into being. Military generals, virtually all corrupt and caring nothing for the lower classes, ran the country for the next hundred years. With the leaders' exorbitant payrolls, the national treasury was in constant bankruptcy. During this period, Mexico had two self-proclaimed emperors—Colonel Agustín Iturbide and Maximilian of France—40 presidents, the 35-year dictatorship of Porfirio Díaz, and a number of provisional governments. Between 1830 and 1850, Mexico lost Texas, Arizona, New Mexico, and California to the United States and was invaded by the French and the Americans 14 times.

Nothing changed for the lower classes, who were as repressed and destitute as before independence. Large landholdings were given to preeminent families and friends of presidents. By 1910, 1,000 families owned 90 percent of the country, and 95 percent of the rural population was landless. Ferocious bandits roamed the hills inciting riots, and Mexico had again arrived at a state of insurrection. "Land for the landless" was one of the most stirring cries of the era.

REVOLUTION

In 1910, violent revolution started. There was no one leader. Instead, many factions fought with and against each other, depending on their needs and shifting political affiliations. Never had a more confusing battle taken place. Pancho Villa and Emiliano Zapata admired each other and often helped one another, only to then fight against each other. Presidents came and went; political assassinations were rife; the church was forcibly closed then reopened. Intellectuals joined in the struggle ostensibly to help the workers and downtrodden, but often worked only to forward their own ideals. Promises were made, then broken; bills were drawn up, signed, and then ignored. Censorship became a way of life. Hundreds of thousands of civilians were killed, and priests and nuns went into hiding. The battle seemed to take on a murderous lifeblood of its own. Mexicans had started something they could not control, let alone stop. The conflict would have a lasting effect upon the working and farming classes; to this day, most are reluctant to protest against inequitable conditions.

Although a new constitution in 1917 declared an end to the hacienda system and returned land to the people, little changed. Modern Mexico is said to have started in 1921, when General Obregon, then president, finally took decisive steps to put the constitution into effect. Although people got their land back, political havoc

Diego Rivera

Diego Rivera was one of the greatest Mexican muralists of the 20th century who used his art to express his social and political revolutionary conscience. Unique for their clean lines, simplicity, and bright colors, his paintings captured important events in Mexican history through images of ordinary people and political figures. He symbolically depicted Mexican society and thought after Mexico's bloody revolution, which raged from 1910 to 1920.

Rivera was born on December 8, 1886, in the city of Guanajuato, about an hour and a half from San Miguel de Allende. In 1892, his family moved to Mexico City. By the time he was 10 years old, he was taking art classes, and he had his first exhibition in 1906, when he was 20.

During his travels in Europe in the early part of the century, Diego was influenced by cubism and postmodernism techniques. He also developed an interest in Russia and Marxism that would be expressed in many of his later works. In Europe, he continued to paint and showed his work in a number of exhibitions. He also met a Russian painter, Angelina Belhoff, whom he stayed with until his return to Mexico in 1921.

After returning to Mexico, Rivera became involved with the muralist movement along with other artists, like Jose Clemente Orozco and David Siqueiros. The idea was to make art large and available to the common people. The style is reminiscent of socialist Russian art of the period. In 1922, he participated in founding the Revolutionary Union of Technical Workers, Painters and Sculptors, and also joined the Mexican Communist Party. That same year, he married his second wife, Lupe Marin.

In 1929, Diego married Frida Kahlo. Both were artists, revolutionaries, and passionate people. They stayed together for many years in a loving yet often rocky marriage, which lasted until 1954, three years before his death.

Rivera painted several murals in the States during visits in the 1930s and '40s. In 1933, he caused a commotion when he painted Lenin into his famous mural, *Man at the Crossroads*, in Radio City Music Hall at New York City's Rockefeller Center. In 1934, the wall and mural were destroyed.

Rivera's childhood home in Guanajuato, now a museum, is worth the visit.

continued, with presidents and other leaders, including Obregon, being assassinated.

The 1920s brought a certain amount of peace and economic recovery to the devastated country. Until 1934, however, when General Lazaro Cárdenas took office, Mexico was governed by veterans of the revolution, all power hungry and all well entrenched in corruption. Although a veteran of the revolution himself, Cárdenas recognized that unless the needs of the people were met, another battle would ensue. He took education and land distribution seriously and also nationalized the petroleum industry, announcing to the nation and the world that Mexico, and Mexico alone, was the sole owner and leader of its oil industry. All foreign interest in this enterprise was expelled, and the country lauded him. The world was impressed with Mexico's authority.

Mexico entered the 20th century as a country in disarray. With its entrance into the 21st century, despite economic and political problems, modern Mexico has a more stable identity. Much of this stability is due to the Mexican character and its people's ability to live in the present while embracing the ways of their ancient ancestors. Were the Mexicans less cheerful and quixotic, it could be a very different story.

Government

The Mexican government is made up of three parts: executive, legislative, and judiciary. The executive branch is the most powerful part of the government and includes the president and his hand-picked cabinet. The president is elected for only one six-year term.

The Chamber of Deputies and the Senate make up the legislature. Members of the 500-member Chamber of Deputies are elected for three-year terms. The 128-member Senate is elected every six years, two from each state and the Federal District, for a total of 64. The other 64 are elected on the basis of the number of votes cast for each party. Members of the legislature may be reelected, but not in consecutive terms.

The Supreme Court is appointed by the president with the approval of two-thirds of the Senate. The court rarely invalidates or shapes laws through judicial precedent, as the U.S. Supreme Court does. The decisions of the court usually follow the policies of the president and the executive branch. Thus the court has far less influence than the U.S. Supreme Court.

Occasionally, people I meet express concern that living in Mexico may be dangerous because the country could descend into political chaos. To this I answer that Mexico is one of the most politically stable countries in the hemisphere. Its constitution is based on democratic principles, such as freedom of speech, religion, and the press. On the other hand, almost every Mexican institution has long been rife with corruption and payoffs. The country clearly has political problems, especially among the large indigenous population. Nevertheless, in many ways politics in Mexico is in its best shape in years, especially after the 2000 election swept Vicente Fox and his conservative PAN political party into office, the first really democratically elected president in more than 70 years.

For the decades between the end of the Mexican Revolution and the election of Vicente Fox, the Revolutionary Institutional Party (PRI) dominated the political scene. The PRI always handpicked each president and controlled Congress, creating a one-party system. In recent years, Mexican politics began to change. Two strong opposition parties emerged—the conservative, pro-business National Action Party (PAN) and the left-leaning Party of the Democratic Revolution (PRD). Each party made strong showings in the 1997 midterm federal elections, leading for the first time ever to a federal Chamber of Deputies in which no party had an absolute majority. After Fox's unexpected and resounding win (even though the Chamber of Deputies remained split), most Mexicans believe that finally democracy is alive and well in Mexico.

President Fox, a former Coca-Cola executive, has failed to live up to his extremely ambitious agenda. This is due mostly to an entrenched opposition in congress, but also to the attacks of September 11, 2001, which changed the economic and political landscape for the worse. By his fourth year in office, Fox finally began pushing through a few of his programs. Mexicans have mixed feelings about the future. While inflation is fairly low by Mexican standards (about 5 percent), wages are also low, and jobs are hard to find.

For foreign residents interested in politics, following the political scenes in both Mexico and the United States is like reading two overly dramatic tragi-comedies. Most of the characters are full of themselves and are either uninteresting or infuriating. Discussing Mexican politics with friends is one thing, but, until recently, actively participating in politics was another. It could get you arrested and deported. Vicente Fox loosened this rule and now foreigners can legally participate in political rallies, like the massive Zapatista march from the state of Chiapas to Mexico City in 2004.

Economy

Mexico's economy has traditionally been driven by oil and gas production, tourism, industrial production, textiles and clothing, and agriculture, and by money sent back from Mexicans working in the States. Amazingly, in 2003, Mexicans working in the United States sent home more than $14.5 billion, equaling oil exports for the first time as Mexico's top source of income. Mexico has 20 percent of the world's oil reserves but badly needs outside investment in its oil industry, which is restricted by the country's constitution. After NAFTA (North American Free Trade Agreement), hundreds of North American companies built factories in Mexico to take advantage of low-cost labor and relaxed labor rules. In 2003, a few of these companies moved from Mexico to China, looking for a less expensive and more highly educated work force. Some Mexicans are concerned that this portends an outflow of jobs like the United States is experiencing. Many feel that the United States and Canada should work with Mexico to develop an investment plan for the country's infrastructure and for the education of its workers. They reason that a stable and prosperous country on its border would be in the United States's best interest.

> *Amazingly, in 2003, Mexicans working in the United States sent home more than $14.5 billion, equaling oil exports for the first time as Mexico's top source of income.*

In the years since the devastating devaluation of the peso in 1995, the economy has improved and has registered fairly high growth rates. The year 2000 proved to be a banner year for the Mexican economy, with a growth rate of 5.5 percent. Experts say that such a rate of growth will not be matched in the near future. The growth rate in 2003 was 3.4 percent. This economic improvement has helped to expand the Mexican middle class, but there is still vast poverty in the country. Mexicans complain bitterly about how hard it is to make ends meet. Wages for most people are still very low. In the relatively well-off state of Jalisco, for example, about 55 percent of the population live on 30–60 pesos ($2.65–5.31) a day. The minimum wage in the country is less than $130 a month, and almost half of the working population earns less than $250 a month. Even with relatively low inflation, prices are still rising, keeping a large mass of the population poor. According to the

World Bank, some 20 million Mexicans subsist on less than a dollar per day, and 42 million live in extreme poverty. Poverty is a state of life in Mexico, despite the fact that it also has a disproportionate number of enormously affluent people by world standards.

The birth rate in Mexico has fallen significantly. Between 1950 and 1970, the birth rate averaged 3.2 percent. By the early 90s it had dropped to 2.1 percent. Mexico's family planning programs continue to be a model to the rest of the world. In the villages, however, the *campesinos* (farmers and country folk) continue to have extremely large families. Often, 12 or more children, many ill, live with their parents in a one- or two-room shack with no running water, and, in many cases, no electricity. Many of these children don't go to school and thereby continue the cycle of poverty and illiteracy.

Each year, thousands of *campesinos,* in a desperate endeavor to better their living conditions, move to Mexico City, usually with disastrous results. The city is now the largest in the world and cannot support more people fleeing the *campo.* The influx is a growing problem, and one for which the government has not managed to arrive at a realistic solution.

© Ken Luboff

People and Culture

Perhaps more than any other country, Mexico requires an understanding of its history before you can begin to grasp the character of its people. The combination of indigenous and Spanish blood resulted in a highly complex caste system. During the 2nd century of Spanish rule, authorities counted a total of 16 different racial categories, classifications that helped solidify a distinct class system. At the lowest end of the social ladder were the indigenous people; at the top were the pure Spanish. Those in between ranged from various *mestizos* (of mixed blood) to Mexican-born Spaniards. The system was further complicated by the importation of black slaves, who produced yet another class of people. Today, more than 80 percent of Mexicans are mestizos, with skin color ranging from light to quite dark. For Mexicans, class remains an important social issue, built into their psyche and reflected in every aspect of society, from marriage to hiring.

Mennonites in Mexico

One of the most reliable installers of high-speed satellite Internet and other communications systems in Mexico is a Mexican Mennonite named John. It may seem strange to meet a Mexican citizen with fair skin, blond hair, and blue eyes who speaks fluent Spanish, German, and accented English, but Mennonites are fairly well known in Mexico. There are about 50,000 Mennonites living in the country, most in the vicinity of Cuauhtémoc, which is located about 65 miles (105 km) west of Chihuahua. They are known throughout Mexico for the wheat, corn, and oats that they grow, as well as the cheeses they produce.

Driving through many of Mexico's cities, you will see, from time to time, young Mennonite men, wearing black wide-brimmed hats and white shirts with black suspenders. The young women wear bonnets and long, wide skirts, and are often seen standing at a busy intersection selling kilo blocks of Mennonite cheese. This is one of the tastiest cheeses made in Mexico, and there are many!

Mennonites trace their history here to the migration of 8,000 men, women, and children who left Eastern Europe in 1874. They settled in Western Canada in an attempt to escape the influence of the secular world on their society. In Canada, they were promised the freedom to operate their own schools as well as exemption from military service.

But government regulations changed in 1916 in response to a growing nationalism accompanying World War I. The new regulations required mandatory school attendance and English-only instruction. Mennonites faced additional pressures with the passing of the Conscription Act in 1917. As a result, the churches began discussing emigration to Latin America.

In 1920, the Mennonites purchased 155,000 acres in the state of Chihuahua, Mexico. The Mexican government granted them military exemption as well as the freedom to operate their own schools. More than 6,000 Mennonites left Manitoba and Saskatchewan and settled in Mexico in 1922. This also worked out well for the Mexican government, which needed farmers to settle the land following the Mexican Revolution.

John is a modern Mennonite who wears blue jeans and a baseball cap and drives a pickup truck rather than a black horse-drawn carriage.

Ethnicity and Class

It was not until the end of the Mexican Revolution of 1910–1921 that the mestizos recognized that they were the overwhelming majority. They were even advanced as a new race by philosopher-writer José Vasconcelos, who became education minister in the new revolutionary government. He named mestizos as *la raza* (the race) and asserted their superiority based on their blend of the best qualities of indigenous and Spanish people.

The mestizos are simply and proudly Mexicans, all of them. However, even today most Mexicans carry self-doubt as to their ancestry and status. Many families, usually those living in Mexico City, will proudly tell you that they have pure Spanish blood going back seven generations with no intermarriage with anyone of mixed blood. Rather than questioning this claim, I have found that a nod or respectful smile works better in promoting cordial relations (and, ultimately, an understanding of Mexican sensibilities) than a discussion on racism.

The subject of race is a sensitive one, and foreigners cannot easily ask Mexicans about their racial heritage. At a dinner party we once had, a friend visiting from the States asked another friend, a Mexican lawyer and a man of sophistication, what percentage of indigenous blood he had. For just a moment we saw our lawyer friend's protective facial cloak—his mask—come down. Knowing he had lost face, he reached for a bottle of wine and replied in a forced, offhanded manner that his family was old and pure Spanish. But a palpable heaviness hung over the table, and as soon as was decently possible, he left. When we saw each other a few days later, the incident was not mentioned, and our friendship remains intact.

Many Mexicans are skilled at wearing masklike expressions, making it difficult for foreigners to understand what people are really thinking. Often, how Mexicans react *inside* to a situation or statement is sharply incongruent with their outward response. Newcomers usually find Mexicans to be polite, formal, congenial, and even friendly. Only with time do foreigners begin to understand that the Mexican character is subtle and complex. It takes time to begin to understand Mexican etiquette. Until then, just be polite. Mexicans are gracious, aware that foreigners don't understand their ways, and they will forgive many of our transgressions as long as we are polite.

Mexican friends explain that in general Mexicans are fatalistic, remarkably patient, proud (often to the point of arrogance), mystical, strangely evasive, and impassive. At the same time, many Mexicans display a love of music and dance, a readiness for a fiesta, and a warm and extraordinarily cheerful disposition. All these traits are coupled with a machismo that often goes way beyond the machismo displayed in other countries.

One thing few Mexicans—even the most humble of *campesinos*, man or woman—will tolerate is loss of face. Foreigners have to learn this fact immediately. For many generations, Mexicans were subjugated and had control over only their personal dignity. For this reason, many have developed a sense of pride that can be formidable and is not something to be messed with.

Customs and Etiquette

Coming from a relatively classless society, certainly a country of less rigid or conspicuous classes, we Americans are often bewildered by the overt class structure in Mexico. And it takes time to learn the finer points. Just accept that the system exists and treat all Mexicans with respect, including the bus driver and the checkout person at the grocery store. Use *usted* (the formal "you") until a Mexican uses *tú* (the informal "you") with you. Note that people who work for you will almost never use *tú* when addressing you, and you should not encourage this practice—to do so would make them extremely uncomfortable. I say "almost never" because this had not happened to us until Barbara and I moved to a remote area of the Nayarit coast. There we hired a young woman from a nearby village to do some housecleaning and cooking. Within a week she surprised us by calling us by our first names. This was fine with us, and we continued on a first-name basis until she left us about one year later. We attributed this informality to the fact that we were now living in a rural area of small, relaxed farming and fishing villages far from the more formal ways of the city. The next woman we hired addressed us as *usted* for about a week and than shyly asked Barbara if she should continue to use *usted* or if *tú* would be okay. Barbara said *tú* would be fine. She works for us to this day.

To unknowingly treat an equal as an inferior must be carefully avoided. Hence, until status is firmly established, Mexicans are formal with each other—to a degree of politeness that has long disappeared from the United States. Always address people with respect. Use titles in formal circumstances: *licenciado(a)* for lawyers or anyone else with a university degree, *doctor(a)* for doctors, *arquitecto(a)* for architects, and *profesor(a)* for all teachers. Address a plumber, electrician, carpenter, or other skilled tradesman as *maestro*. Adding *Don* or *Doña* to a first name is useful, such as Don Pedro, Doña Maria, or Don Alberto. You will be addressed as *Señor* or *Señora*, and you should use these titles with everyone you meet—until or unless they invite you to use their names.

Arturo

Our neighbor's gardener, Arturo, is an immensely likable man. Each day, he travels many miles on a rickety bicycle to town, where he takes care of several gardens. And each year, he announces that the rains will start on May 28. That they usually start before or after—but never on this specific day—doesn't faze him one bit. This year, after May 28 had come and gone and still the rains had not arrived, I teased him. He shrugged, then grinned and said the rains were late because it was raining heavily in a faraway country like Turkey. He had seen this news on television.

Two of Arturo's brothers died of alcoholism and three of poverty-related illnesses. So he allows himself just one beer each Saturday after work and plans to have no more than three children. It's unlikely his wife will contest him in this matter, even though the church and her family might not approve of so few children.

Arturo is deeply loyal to our neighbor because he sees that she respects and trusts him totally. She can joke with him about his ways and he about hers. Recently, Arturo made a mistake, feeding the roses too much fertilizer and killing them. He took full responsibility and asked to have his pay docked. Instead, our friend told him that the fertilizer was *basura* (rubbish) and that she wouldn't buy it again. He looked at our friend, then grinned and said, "Well, it's made in the United States and therefore not correct for Mexican soil."

"What about me?" our friend asked. "I was made in the United States. Does that make me not fit for Mexican soil?" "You, señora," replied Arturo, doffing his hat, "you are an honor to have in our country."

If you ever need to correct a Mexican—the most humble of workers included—never do it in front of anyone else. Take the worker aside, explain that you're not satisfied with his or her work, and suggest a different way. Stress that a misunderstanding has occurred, that it is not the worker's fault (unless it blatantly is), and that you are used to different methods. The more educated the Mexican, the easier this situation will be, but even so, handle it with tact. Sometimes the problem can be greater, and the worker less agreeable, if you are a woman and he is an uneducated man.

If you live in a city rather than a small pueblo, you will inevitably meet many middle- and upper-class Mexicans. Ultimately, you will make some good friends among them. Here, too, be sure to follow proper etiquette: Always use *usted* until they use *tú*. Even if you are with good Mexican friends, don't criticize the politics of their country, even though they may criticize it loudly themselves. (Many Mexicans

Mordida—The Bite

Hector Ulloa, former editor of *Atención San Miguel* (a weekly English-language newspaper), offers his observations about *mordida*, a national custom:

> Perhaps the most extended (and accepted) form of corruption in Mexico is bribery—although most Mexicans do not see it as bribery but as a "tip" or "gift." The name itself suggests a share of something—*una mordida, a bite. Would you like a bite of my apple?* Although this kind of bribery is practiced all over the world, it has become both an art and a nuisance in Mexico. It is a fact of life—and as difficult to get rid of as cockroaches.

The line between bribery and tipping is a thin one. If you drive into a gas station, the attendant will smile, fill your tank, clean your windshield, and check your oil—alas, not for free. Along with the cost of the gas, he will expect a small tip. If the tip is not to his liking, he will frown, and you may see him in the rearview mirror grumbling to another attendant. Tips have always been common in restaurants; now they're common everywhere. Smiles can be bought, and people expect you to buy them.

One morning you show up at a government office, ask to see the topmost official, and smile. The person behind the desk, most often a young woman, will smile back and say, "He's not here yet." Then, nothing else matters. It doesn't matter if you see the official walk in. The clerk will bluntly deny that he's in or will say he's busy, even if you can peek through the partially open door and see the official looking out the window. It doesn't matter if you say you are the official's best friend. It doesn't matter if you say the building is on fire. The clerk will smile and continue filing her fingernails, saying "Can't you see he's not here?"

are perplexed to hear gringos criticize the United States. They find it greatly disloyal, even if they themselves have little love for the States.) Once you have lived in Mexico for a while, you may feel comfortable enough around friends to add your opinions on Mexican politics. But, until then, be prudent. Also realize that some Mexicans—often academics and intellectuals—have a longstanding gripe with the United States and are not eager to mix with gringos. But they are well worth getting to know, if you can, for they have long and lively debates on all subjects, including literature, the arts, politics, religion, sexual conventions—just about everything. Most speak several languages.

Too often, poverty is mistakenly attributed to laziness. Mexicans are not lazy; in fact, many are very hard workers. However, their work

Next comes the magic. You smile and, with apparent naiveté, say, "Is there some way I could see him right away?" and flash a 20-peso note that you immediately hide inside a folded newspaper. Then she will definitely smile back and say, "I'll see what can be done," as she grabs the newspaper and pretends to be interested in the latest news about Pakistan. Is this a tip? Is it bribery? Or is it simply "buying" your way around?

There are more obvious situations, like skipping a red light and paying off the traffic cop. The officer will never say the payment is bribery, of course. It is a "gift" or a "fee" for his time. The longer it takes you to understand that you must pay, the higher the fee. First the officer will give a long explanation about how you broke the law and how he wants to help save you valuable time. Second, he will offer a simple arithmetic problem: "If the fine is 100 pesos and half the fine is 50 pesos, how much money do you have with you?" Third, he leaves the penalty "up to you" and abides by whatever "your will is." Fourth attempt—if nothing has worked so far—he will threaten to impound your car and put you in jail.

Any advice, you ask me? It is probably easiest to play the game. Smile and tell the officer that you understand you broke the law and ask him for your ticket. Then take mental note of his badge number and squad car or motorcycle number. As soon as you are on safe ground, report him.

To this, Barbara and I add some practical advice from a foreigner's point of view: If the *mordida* seems reasonable, or if you live in a small town where you and the cop will be seeing each other again, pay it and forget the whole matter. Reporting the bribe is not worth the potential bureaucratic hassle. We would report the incident only if there was no infraction and the whole thing was just highway robbery.

ethic is different from ours, and this situation is slow to change (except among professionals). For many generations, Mexicans were ruled by brutal and authoritarian bosses and were not encouraged to think for themselves. Today, if a group of workers is not well supervised, they will often all work independently without consulting their fellow workers. The result can be a completely disorganized job that will take forever. (I have seen this happen in the States as well.)

Then there is the concept of time. Mexicans do not conceive time as linear as we do. Keeping a precise time schedule is not viewed as important—work can always be done later, *mañana*. Besides, working like a robot or adhering to a rigid schedule is seen as taking the spice out of life. We have witnessed this attitude clearly with our excellent carpenter, Gabriel. He will agree to a job, like building a door by the first of the month. He intends to finish the door on time, but other jobs will come his way. He will take on each of them and work on them all, at the same time. When we ask about our door, he will put it on top of the pile and move ahead with it. But when we ordered it, we already accepted the fact that the door would not be built on time. Workers who are more used to dealing with foreigners will try to maintain a schedule. This same ethic can be seen clearly from the opposite point of view when you arrive at a mechanic's shop with a broken car and he drops everything he has been doing to give you a hand.

If plumbers—or any tradespeople—say they will be at your place tomorrow morning, never take that as a given. They may arrive in the morning, or maybe not. Believe me, you'll get used to it, and if you don't, then Mexico is not for you. For most of us who have moved here, the mañana attitude has entered our thinking, too. Often when we return to the States, we have to snap to and get back into the routine of punctuality.

Mexicans live and work in the here and now, not for tomorrow or the day after—which is the distant future for most of them. Foreigners usually learn the hard way. You may invite some Mexicans to dinner at 7:30, only to have them roll up at way past 9, by which time the dinner is spoiled. You can try saying, "7:30 gringo time" or "7:30 *en punto*" (on the dot), but even that is usually ignored. Or your guests may not arrive at all. When Mexicans receive an invitation, they will always accept, even if they know they will not be able to make it. To say no would be an insult. We have learned to do the same thing. On occasion, when invited to a party at a Mexican's home, we have accepted graciously, then not shown up.

We have a friend, José, a highly successful businessman, who arrives not just a few hours late but days late. In business, he is on time; socially, rarely. When we first moved to Mexico, José said he would take us out for dinner to celebrate Barbara's birthday. We asked what time to expect him, and he muttered eight o'clock. At eight we were ready. No José. At nine o'clock, hungry, we had a snack. At 10, Barbara had another snack, then went to bed. Around 11, José arrived. Barbara came out with her arms folded in mock anger. José laughed. "Excuse me, but that's how it's done here. Go on, get dressed." We did, and had a wonderful evening, during which José went to great lengths to explain to us this *mañana* concept. On another occasion, he said he'd arrive on Friday to take us to an old Spanish hacienda. In fact, he arrived the following Tuesday, four days late (this is extreme, even for Mexico). So, you may ask, isn't that downright rude? What's all this about Mexican politeness? But being late in Mexico is not considered rude. Bus and flight schedules, however, are exceptions to this pattern of lateness. Flights always depart on time, and buses almost always depart on time. Professionals, such as doctors and lawyers, also expect you to arrive on time for your appointments.

Life is not dull in this country. It is sometimes highly frustrating, but never dull. And it does teach you to live in the here and now. Spontaneity is a way of life here, both in social situations and at work, and it offers a good lesson to most *norteamericanos.* You learn to loosen up and live in the moment. If you don't, you're not too likely to make many Mexican friends or, for that matter, make it in Mexico at all. However, don't worry too much about fitting in. You are likely to live among many other foreigners, and Mexicans who live around large numbers of gringos are more likely to be on time. More or less—you never know.

> *Spontaneity is a way of life here.... You learn to loosen up and live in the moment.*

Reading some of the very rich literature of Mexico will give you good insight into the Mexican character. Laura Esquivel's novel *Like Water for Chocolate* and the movie of the same name will probably give you more insight into the Mexican character than hours of studying nonfiction. That the book is set in another era means nothing; the same psychology prevails today.

Mexican people have been downtrodden for centuries, have been ruled by many cruel dictators, and have lost much to invading forces—including the United States. Yet they are warm and loving to foreign residents. Once you have made friends with some Mexicans, and you have gained their trust and respect, you will find that they will turn themselves inside out to help you, make you laugh, and comfort you when you are sad.

Sure, modern Mexicans wear jeans like their American counterparts, but they are not the same as Americans. They adhere to family and ancestral traditions deeply; some are extremely influenced by the church; most are fiercely patriotic, and while many may outwardly emulate *norteamericanos,* most have absolutely no aspirations to be like us. We have heard Mexicans express pity for us—that our family structures are so weakened, that we must follow a strict schedule, that we place far too much importance on money and too little on spiritual matters, that we are not able to enjoy life or be spontaneous, that the clock is such a tyrant in our lives ... the list is long.

Here is yet another dichotomy in the culture: Mexicans, usually the men, can curse like no one else can. And they do. However, this habit doesn't mean that we foreigners can take up cursing—although it's tempting, as many curses are quite funny and colorful. My advice is to avoid imitating Mexican profanities until you are really a part of this country. Cursing will not make you "one of the boys." Rather, it will shock Mexicans profoundly.

A small but important point that can be startling to people from the north: The Mexican handshake, especially that of *campesinos* (country folks) and the poor, is not strong like the hearty American grasp. The first time I shook a Mexican's hand, I was shocked. It felt like shaking a moist towel. Except when dealing with the upper class and well-traveled businesspeople, you will find yourself shaking rather limp hands. Accept this fact and make your handshake equally sensitive. It's the Mexican way.

Gender Roles

In the last three decades, Mexican women have increased their level of education and have entered the job market and the political arena in greater numbers. There have been a number of high-profile women on the political scene in recent years, the most well known being Marta Sahagunde Fox, the wife of Mexico's president Vicente Fox. Women's emergence is due in large part to better health care services as well as increased access to birth control and family planning, which has made it possible for women to postpone and control their fertility. Nevertheless, the number of women in decision-making positions in business and in the Mexican parliament is still very low, and women's salaries are far below those of men for equivalent jobs.

For the most part, women in Mexico are expected to fill traditional family roles. When asked about the role of women in Mexico, Bertha, our 46-year-old Mexican friend, was quick to point out that women are expected to have a male child, and that they will keep having babies until a male is born. She also talked freely about abuse she received from her late husband and the strong machismo present among Mexican men. Bertha is from a small, fairly remote farming town on the coast of

Nayarit, but she said that her experiences are common at almost every economic level in the country.

Gay and Lesbian Culture

Mexico is an extremely Catholic and family-centered culture. In spite of this, gay life is present in all parts of Mexico. Because family life and children are so integral to Mexican culture, many gay men and lesbians, especially in non-urban areas, marry and have children, or else they move to cities where they can live more openly.

Most cities of a million or more residents have at least one gay bar or disco. Though it may only be open for one or two nights a week, it provides a meeting place for gay men and lesbians. In Mexico City and Guadalajara, there are numerous bars, cantinas, and discos catering to gay men. But many of them have cover charges, which keep less affluent Mexican gay men from patronizing them. This economic and class stratification also is apparent in the number of gay men and lesbians who can live openly without marrying. Wealthier and more educated gay men and lesbians have a much easier time living a nontraditional lifestyle, and can more easily live openly with their partners away from the family. Poorer Mexicans, however, may be expected to continue to live with their families, even as unmarried adults.

There are alternatives to the bars and discos. The traditional *zócalos* (public squares) provide opportunities for gay men to meet discreetly when bars and discos aren't available or finances preclude such activities. Bath houses, although rarely strictly gay, also provide places to meet, especially for gay men who live with parents or who are married.

Although not totally accepted in this conservative culture, gay men have an open presence in the society. Films like *Doña Herlinda and Her Son* and *Y Tu Mamá También* feature themes and scenes that would be unthinkable in big studio American films. Gay men are often characters in Mexican *telenovelas* (soap operas), which are the major TV entertainment for the masses. There are large Gay Pride Parades in Mexico City and in Guadalajara, with thousands of participants and onlookers. In sophisticated urban areas, such as Mexico City, there are gay theater groups and dance companies. Drag shows, called *Travesti* are a part of the gay scene and are surprisingly popular, even beyond the urban gay and lesbian culture.

Support groups for gay men and lesbians are beginning to surface in certain urban areas. These groups focus primarily on the concerns of gay men. In Mexico's strictly sex-role-defined culture, lesbianism is something mysterious and hidden for the vast majority. Motherhood and marriage are sanctified as the ultimate goal for women. To deviate from this norm is very difficult.

Gay and lesbian foreign residents generally have no difficulty adapting to life in Mexico. The foreigner's culture is usually so different from that of the average Mexican that differences in sexual orientation and lifestyle are usually considered just another inexplicable difference. What is most important in relationships between people is the creation of an atmosphere of respect and mutual consideration.

For tourists and residents alike, the gay-positive areas like Puerto Vallarta, Acapulco, and Mexico City are meccas for entertainment, meeting people, and developing a sense of community. Puerto Vallarta, for example, has so many gay-oriented businesses that it has a Gay Business Association. The gay nightlife in Mexico City rivals that in any other big city anywhere.

Religion

Mexico remains primarily a Catholic country. The traditions of the church have been woven into the cultural fabric for centuries. Pre-Hispanic societies also placed great emphasis on rituals, celebrating the milestones of the life of the individual from birth to death. While the conquistadores forced the indigenous people of Latin America to convert to Christianity, many native people skillfully managed to maintain their religious traditions by incorporating their pantheon of deities in camouflaged form into the hierarchy of Christian saints.

Historically, Mexico's fight for independence has at times placed the politics of the nation in opposition to the church, leading to separation of church and state. Generally, the more strict and conservative tenets of the church are less rigidly practiced by Mexican Catholics in comparison to the Catholics of other countries. For many, church and family are the foundation stones of life, and signs of deeply expressed devotion are everywhere.

In the 16th century, the religious believed that the Virgin of Guadalupe appeared to an indigenous peasant as a manifestation of the Virgin Mary, who came expressly to protect the poor indigenous people. The Virgin of Guadalupe, *La Virgen Morena* (the Brown Virgin) or the Mother of Mexico, is omnipresent. More than a million pilgrims honor the Virgin every December 12th by attending her Basilica in Mexico City. The symbols of the Virgin Mary have extraordinary power and influence, more so than in most western countries. People of all ages make arduous pilgrimages to specific churches known to house statues of the Virgin whose legends are considered especially sacred. These pilgrimages often require that people walk hundreds of miles, sleeping outdoors with only crude provisions. Aged and disabled pilgrims often lead the mass parades. People honor promises to the Virgin after receiving her blessings and miracles, or they come to give thanks and show their devotion.

> Mexicans are very spiritual people, and to them, it's not so important what religion someone follows, but rather that they are believers.

Local communities are organized around their parish churches. The patron saint of each church is honored with grand celebration and ritual. Fireworks are lit in the wee hours of the night to make sure that God is awake to witness the celebrations. Parades and reenactments of biblical stories are common.

There is a large Evangelical Christian movement in Mexico, as in all of Latin America. Jehovah's Witnesses and Pentecostal groups have extensive recruitment campaigns yielding many followers. Mormon missionaries have also made consistent outreach efforts here with relative success.

Jewish immigrants and refugees throughout the years have established isolated footholds in Mexico, especially the prosperous community of Polanco in Mexico City. Recently, workshops on various forms of Buddhism and meditation have been offered in select locations. Most religious traditions can be found alive and well somewhere in the country. Mexicans are very spiritual people and to them it's not so important what religion someone follows, but rather that they are believers.

However, the power of ritual traditions remains, even among those loosely affiliated with the church, primary in Mexican society.

The Arts

Mexican art has its roots in the extraordinary Mesoamerican civilizations of the Aztecs, Mayans, Olmecs, and Toltecs. These cultures, with their celebrations of massive forms, monumental architectural statements, the spiritual world, and animistic powers, have fascinated and inspired Mexican artists for hundreds of years. They are the primal forces of Mexican art.

But these early civilizations were conquered in the 16th century and dominated by the Hispanic culture for more than four hundred years. Modern Mexican culture has struggled to resolve the dilemma of being in the midst of both indigenous and European worlds. The great art of Mexico almost always celebrates the grandeur and power of the pre-Colombian civilizations, and also expresses the issues arising from a European consciousness. The work of visual artists, especially the post-revolutionary muralists like Diego Rivera, Jose Clemente Orozco, and David Alfaro Siquerros, reflects both the pre-Hispanic history of Mexico and a political criticism of modern social issues. This self-analysis causes Mexican artists to return to themes reflecting their indigenous origins as well as their struggle to find their voice as a nation of blended indigenous and European cultures.

This dialogue finds its distinctive form in works that explore the vibrant colors and celebrations of the indigenous cultures, the magical realism of the spirit world, and the centuries of human struggle during the periods of wars and revolution. This attempt at reconciliation has created a distinctive stylistic vision, unlike any other in the world. Cubism, surrealism, or abstract expressionism may influence artists, but these influences are sifted through the Mexican sensibility to emerge as distinctively Mexican.

Popular music in Mexico has a similar history. Much of the mariachi, *ranchera,* and *norteña* music, so beloved by the masses, has elements of North American and European popular music, but these elements are melded with strong ethnic and folkloric traditions to create distinctively Mexican sounds and rhythms. Once again, Mexican artists have kept their traditions, creating an artistic vision tied to historical origins.

Today, unique artistic expression finds its centers all over Mexico, including the *norteña* music of Sinaloa, the vibrant painting and architecture of Monterrey, and the eclectic indigenous and contemporary art of Oaxaca. Yet, the true center of the modern Mexican art world is in Mexico City. Here you will find a schedule of theatrical performances as full as that of New York or London; multiple symphony orchestras; astonishing museums; a thriving film industry led by directors like Alejandro Gonzalex Inarritu (*Amores Perros*) and Alfonso Cuaron (*Y Tu Mamá También*); and a contemporary art scene that has captured the attention of collectors from around the world.

The history of Mexican art is long, and the creative artistic impulse remains a primary force in Mexican life and culture today.

Cuisine

If you think the food in Mexico will resemble the fare at Taco Bell or a Mexican restaurant in the States, you're in for a wonderful surprise. Sure, there are tacos, enchiladas, and fajitas in Mexico, plenty of them, but the cuisine of Mexico has so much more. There are regional specialties and sauces that would make any gourmand's head spin, but what makes Mexican cuisine stand out is the great variety of fresh fruits, vegetables, and fish.

A common myth holds that the food is hot, hotter, or hottest, but in fact, most of the food is mild. On tables in restaurants, along with the salt, pepper, and napkins, you'll find different types of bottled hot sauces and a bowl or two of homemade *picante* sauce (salsa). From an eating point of view, traveling in Mexico is a joy compared to the United States. Even in the middle of nowhere, you can find a good homemade meal, and you won't have to resort to McDonald's or Denny's. As a rule, you'll find more varied menus and international specialties in the tourist areas and large cities—just as in the States. But Mexico is full of culinary surprises. Friends once found an outstanding Japanese restaurant on a hill overlooking a spectacular beach halfway between nowhere and outer nowhere. Another found a Polish restaurant in the small beach town of Bucerías!

Occasionally, restaurants along the roads and in very small towns don't have menus. When you ask what's available, the staff may ask you what you want. Be careful! Ask for something simple like eggs. Once, many years ago in a small restaurant, after going back and forth through the "What would you like?" "What do you have?" dance, Barbara and I decided on chicken. A short while after ordering, we saw a small child run out of the back of the restaurant. A half hour later, the small child ran back clutching a squawking chicken. Need I go on? The chicken was delicious and, of course, very fresh! But eating in that restaurant was an all-day affair.

Most restaurants want very much to please their customers and will bend over backward to do so. A short time ago, in a lovely upscale restaurant in San Miguel, a Mexican friend ordered lasagna, which he wasn't happy with. He asked his wife to taste it, but before she could, two waiters descended. They had seen the sour look on our friend's face when he first tried it. They took the lasagna away and brought the specialty of the house, a delicious *arrachera*-style steak (marinated in a special, slightly hot sauce).

In Mexico you are going to have to change your eating habits, unless you are in areas where there are lots of gringos. The most important thing to remember is that the main (and heaviest) meal of the day, the *comida,* is eaten between 2 and 4 P.M.—a most sensible custom! Once you get used to this schedule, it will take a few days to adjust when you are back in the States. For the evening meal, many Mexicans just snack at home or buy a couple of tacos or tamales at a stand. Many poor Mexican women set up little taco or *gordita* stands in their doorways in the evening (especially on weekends), where strolling neighbors can pick up a fresh, usually deep-fried, goody.

Generally speaking, the average restaurant outside of tourist areas will serve the following breakfast: fresh orange or carrot juice, eggs any way you like, and either fresh hot tortillas, *bolillos* (bo-lee-yos, crusty French bread–style Mexican rolls), or *Bimbo* (white bread). Usually, we opt for tortillas. But if we're in the mood for bread, we're sure to ask for *bolillos.* Coffee is often instant, but for some reason Nescafé in Mexico tastes about 100 times better than Nescafé in the States. Some restaurants serve *café de olla,* a delicious home-brewed coffee made with cinnamon. *Te negro* (black tea) and *te de manzanilla* (chamomile) are always available. If eggs aren't your thing, usually *avena* (oatmeal) is available, or pancakes from a mix.

For your *comida,* if you are not looking for anything fancy, try the *comida corrida* (running meal), or special of the day. It is the least expensive meal on the menu, you don't have to think about what you want, it's easy to order if you don't know Spanish, and it will be served fast. It usually consists of a soup—generally a cream-based vegetable soup—a main course of simply prepared chicken, beef, or pork, steamed fresh vegetables, rice, beans, and sometimes a small "salad"—a couple of tomato and onion slices and a few lettuce leaves. Dessert is generally flan, Jell-O, or pudding. The meal is served with a refreshing homemade *agua* (water-based fruit drink), and tea or coffee is served afterward. This meal will put you back 23–45 pesos ($3–5) and will rarely be memorable, but it should be quite satisfactory and filling. If you want a soft drink or beer with your *comida*, you will have to pay a bit extra. *Cena,* the light evening meal, often consists of things like tacos, tostados, or fajitas, but if you're hungry, restaurants also serve a wonderful variety of entrées.

Do not be afraid to experiment. Restaurants serve many wonderful dishes that you won't find anywhere but in Mexico, and you don't have to worry about getting anything weird or disgusting like sautéed chicken beaks or stewed puppy feet. Perhaps the nastiest item on the menu by gringo standards would be tripe, which in Mexico is called *menudo* and which quite a few people actually like. Some of the strangest (but most delicious) things are *tuna* (not the fish but a type of cactus fruit) ice cream, *huitlacoche* (a black fungus that grows on corn) crepes, and *cabrito* (baby goat). One fabulous Mexican specialty, *chiles en nogada,* is a green chile stuffed with ground beef and smothered in a tamarind-walnut cream sauce with pomegranate seeds sprinkled on top. *Sopa Azteca* (Aztec soup) appears on almost every menu. It is prepared in several ways, but usually is a clear tomato- or chicken-based broth with crisp tortilla strips, avocado, onions, cheese, *chipotle* chile (a smoky, not-too-hot chile), and chicken. At the beach, be sure to treat yourself to fresh fish.

Some of the best meals anywhere in the world are found at beachfront *palapas* (palm-frond shacks with no flooring). There's nothing like digging your feet into the sand, watching waves pound the beach and palm trees sway in the breeze, and eating fresh fish with garlic-butter sauce running down your chin—or maybe *camarones a la diabla* (shrimp smothered in a hot sauce). Add a hot tortilla or two and a cold beer, and you know you've landed in paradise. In the state of Nayarit (north of Puerto Vallarta), fish is barbecued *sarandeado* style. Some sophisticated New York friends said they could not get fish at *any* price in Manhattan that could compare. Cost: about $20.

If you are a vegetarian or a vegan, unless you are in a large city, tourist area, or place with lots of expats, your choices will be limited at restaurants. But don't worry—you won't starve. Keep in mind that the markets are full of incredible vegetables and fruits. And most restaurants want to make their customers happy. Many will gladly fix you something special—like *sopa de arroz* (a plate of rice) with steamed *verduras* (veggies). Or ask for rice and some veggies in a fresh, piping-hot tortilla with a little hot sauce sprinkled on top. Voilá—a wonderful vegan taco! All restaurants serve quesadillas (cheese-filled tortillas); many serve sautéed mushrooms in garlic sauce; and there's usually guacamole. The beans are usually, but not always, cooked with a bit of lard—ask to be sure. Granola and yogurt are available everywhere, as well as nuts and seeds. There are many fruit and juice stands, so you can always get a *licuado,* basically a smoothie with any combination of fruits and water or milk. (Just point to the fruits you want if you don't know the Spanish words.)

All restaurants now serve only purified water and ice cubes. They usually purify their vegetables well. *Absolutely* wash your hands before eating, and if you want to take a little extra precaution, squeeze lemon juice (a natural disinfectant) over your food. A small plate of halved lemons or limes is served with every meal. If not, ask the waiter for *limones.*

© Ken Luboff

Prime Living
Locations

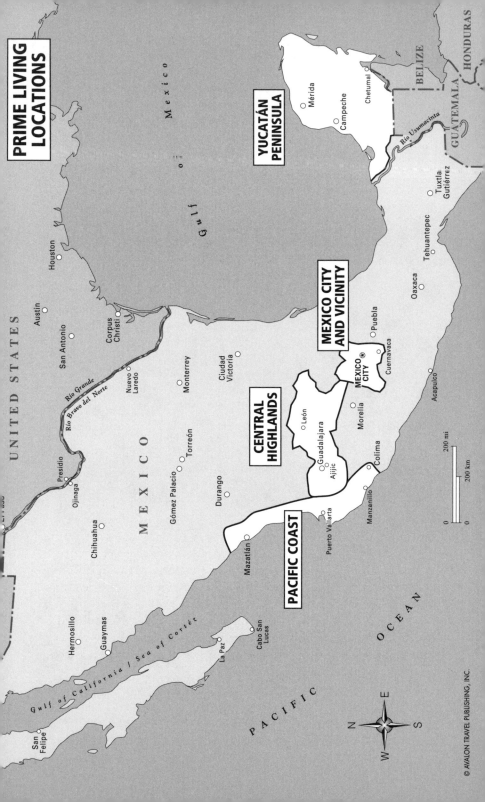

Overview

Choosing a new place to live takes some serious consideration of the kind of environment and lifestyle you are seeking. This section will help with descriptions of four very different regions in Mexico, and with profiles of several cities within each region.

Think about whether you would rather live by the sea, or in the drier mountain air? Would you prefer to be in a big city, with a myriad of cultural, entertainment, and employment options, or in a quiet village with a strong European atmosphere? On a farm, or in a gated community? And what about money? Do you need to work? Can you afford to buy a house, or a condo, or will you be renting? How is your Spanish? Maybe living in proximity to a Spanish school or near a university is important. How critical is it that you live close to an airport, a school for the kids, or a hospital?

The following profiles explore some of the principal living locations within four distinct regions in Mexico: The Central Highlands, The Pacific Coast, Mexico City and vicinity, and the Yucatán Peninsula.

Each region is unique in terms of climate, terrain, culture, and lifestyle. The cities in these regions have been chosen because U.S. "escapees" to Mexico are most likely to land in one of them. Although each city has a relatively large group of foreign residents, proportionally they make up a minority of the total population. Each city has a different and uniquely Mexican character. These cities make for a relatively easy transition into a new culture for those who have little previous experience with Mexico or those who do not speak Spanish. Because they have welcomed generations of tourists and expats, these locales each have well-established infrastructures for foreign residents. Most have English-language newspapers, libraries, schools for kids, Spanish classes, English-language cable TV, theaters, art galleries, and modern communications and banking services.

Included within each region are short profiles on characterful towns that have a small foreign presence. After a few years of living in one of the Prime Living Locations, learning enough Spanish and becoming comfortable in the culture, the most adventurous among you may want to relocate to one of these more remote locations.

CENTRAL HIGHLANDS

In many ways, this area is the heart of old Mexico. In the central part of this region, known as the Bajio, vast amounts of silver were mined for 250 years. The resulting wealth built the colonial cities of Guanajuato, San Miguel de Allende, Morelia, Querétaro, San Luis Potosí, and Zacatecas. In these and other cities in the central region of the country, such as Guadalajara, grand cathedrals, huge haciendas, and romantic, cobbled streets reveal the romance and splendor of the Spanish colonial period. In this area, one can witness more traditional rituals and fiestas than anywhere else in the country. This is also an area of enormous historical significance. In San Miguel de Allende and surrounding towns, including Dolores Hidalgo, independence from Spanish rule was declared in 1810, and the ten-year fight for independence began.

The Central Highlands is primarily a high desert environment, with most cities located at 5,000–6,000 feet (1,520–1,824 meters) above sea level. This is also the bread-basket of Mexico. In the States of Guanajuato and Jalisco, large areas of desert have been reclaimed and planted with crops like broccoli, corn, alfalfa, sugar cane, beans, and agave for making tequila. Here the year is divided into the rainy and dry seasons. A "good" rainy season means an abundant harvest for farmers and spectacular gardens for residents. In dry years, everyone conserves water and worries about the future.

Central highland cities, like Leon, Querétaro, and Guadalajara, have become major commercial and industrial centers. Others, like San Miguel de Allende, Guanajuato, and Pátzcuaro, have managed to preserve much of their colonial past. Still others, like the towns along Lake Chapala, are renowned for their tranquility and charm.

Lake Chapala is a huge shimmering mirror that intensifies the colors of the surrounding hills with reflecting sun and moonlight. The area has the feel of a high mountain lake area in Italy. But unlike Italy, the weather here is perfect year-round. Foreigners are charmed by Lake Chapala's beauty, tranquility, and its large and hospitable expatriate community. This area is especially attractive to retirees because of its low prices, easy access to an international airport, and proximity to Guadalajara. In recent years, younger people have moved into the lakeside communities, but the area remains a haven for retirees. It is worth checking out if you are looking for small-town living and clear mountain air at about 5,000 feet (1,520 meters).

> *It is an experience to walk through San Miguel's narrow, cobbled, busy downtown streets. This romantic and friendly city boasts high culture and high energy.*

San Miguel is unique in Mexico. It is a stunningly beautiful Mexican colonial tourist town, but also home to a large and cosmopolitan expatriate community, including many Europeans and South Americans. A high desert town of about 100,000 people, San Miguel features art and language schools, ancient churches, theaters, a great library, and fine restaurants. It is an experience to walk through San Miguel's narrow, cobbled, busy downtown streets. This romantic and friendly city boasts high culture and high energy.

Guadalajara, Jalisco, Mexico's second largest city, has grown into a city of more than five million people. Throughout the city, there are still grand colonial homes, cathedrals, and other buildings that evoke the romance and charm of Guadalajara's history. This beautiful city of wide, tree-lined boulevards, colonial plazas, and majestic fountains has a perfect climate year-round. Additionally, Guadalajara is a major electronics, manufacturing, and arts and crafts center. It is a modern and sophisticated city with art, culture, museums, universities, fancy shopping malls, and a foreign population of at least 20,000 residents.

Guanajuato and San Miguel de Allende are only about 50 miles (81 km) apart, but they are about as different from one another as two small colonial cities can be. Guanajuato is the capital of the state of Guanajuato and one of the most beautiful colonial towns in Mexico. Unlike San Miguel, Guanajuato has a very small population of permanent foreign residents. However, it does have a constant but small stream of foreign students studying at the University of Guanajuato. With less foreign influence, this town seems more authentically Mexican than San Miguel.

Because of Pátzcuaro's Tarascan heritage, the architecture and the feel of this town is unlike that of any other colonial city in Mexico. Pátzcuaro is truly picturesque, with its beautiful plazas surrounded by red-tiled, one-story adobe buildings with white painted walls. The town sits on the shore of Lake Pátzcuaro, at over 7,000 feet (2,128 meters), and is surrounded by pine forests. Due to its high elevation, Pátzcuaro can be chilly, especially in the winter months. Pátzcauro is about one hour south of the city of Morelia, a colonial city and the capital of the state of Michoacán. A small number of foreigners live in Pátzcuaro and the nearby towns.

PACIFIC COAST

The Sierra Mountains run from Canada, down the west coast of the United States, and into Mexico. In Mexico, they are called the Sierra Madre Occidental. This range separates Mexico's central highlands from its Pacific coastal plane. Along some parts of the coast, the mountains come right to the ocean, creating spectacularly dramatic scenery. In other areas, the mountains form a backdrop many miles inland from the ocean. This is true at Mazatlán, the most northerly large city on a coastline that continues south for more than 850 miles (1,368 km) and is known as the Mexican Riviera. And what an impressive coastline it is, with palm trees growing along hundreds of miles of relatively unexplored beaches, great surf breaks, large resort cities, shipping ports, huge areas of fertile farmland, plantations of mangos, bananas, coconuts, and coffee, and major tourist and fishing industries. Along this coast are some of the best beachfront retirement and living locations in the world.

In many ways Mazatlán is more real than the glitzier Puerto Vallarta. Just leave the main tourist strip with its onslaught of noisy "love boat" tourists during the winter, and you move into quiet, clean, village-like residential areas and the somewhat tattered colonial downtown. This is not a city of grand buildings or great cultural activity, but one that appeals as a nice, inexpensive place to live.

Foreigners living in Mazatlán come mainly for the beach, the fishing, the golf, the low cost of living, the relatively easy 735-mile drive to the U.S. border, and the quiet life. Many come down only for the winter months, put off by summer heat and humidity. But the ones living here year-round love the place. This is a place to check out if you like the idea of living in a small-town U.S. atmosphere plunked down into a large Mexican city on the sea.

Over the past 30 years Puerto Vallarta has become a tourist mecca. Yet, in spite of its growth and crowds, it is still an attractive place to live. Quiet neighborhoods and quaint nearby villages offer oceanside living apart from the huge tourist scene. During the very short shoulder season, cobblestoned downtown Vallarta is wonderful, feeling somewhat as it did before it was "discovered." Puerto Vallarta is in a perfect setting, with mountains sloping down to Banderas Bay and creating a misty and exotic sunset backdrop. Mountain villages also offer a cool escape from Vallarta's late-summer high temperatures and humidity.

Puerto Vallarta has a large and friendly foreign community, probably larger than any other on the Mexican coast with the exception of Acapulco. Expatriates love living in Vallarta, with its easy access to shopping, schools, theaters, restaurants, fishing, surfing, and cultural events, although many prefer living in one of the villages along the coast to the north of Vallarta.

Manzanillo is a port town, with a kind of honky-tonk feel. This is a working town, not a slick tourist center like Puerto Vallarta. It does have some incredibly fancy tourist resorts and hotels, but they are located along the beaches to the north of town. The main *zócalo* (town square), which faces the bay, is unpretentiously pretty, with a relaxed and open atmosphere. The cost of living and buying real estate here is much less than it is in the more glamorous towns along the coast.

MEXICO CITY AND VICINITY

It is no wonder that the Aztecs settled in the valley of Mexico. The high-mountain and fertile-valley terrain around present-day Mexico City is some of the richest and most dramatic in the country. The states of Mexico and Morelos adjacent to Mexico City have spectacular high plateaus, lush valleys, and rivers, all set in a perfect climate. Many of the villages and small cities in these states are so picturesque that you can easily image that you have somehow stepped back in time to the 17th or 18th centuries

Mexico City itself is both beauty and beast. With more than 22 million people, the city can have horrendous traffic and air pollution. Crime and poverty are serious problems. Yet, once you get to know it, you find that the city is actually like a series of small villages knitted together, many of them very beautiful and elegant. Mexico City is a center of both ancient and modern arts, culture, and finance. It is also a place where people live with an amazing degree of politeness and formality.

Cuernavaca is no longer the perfect vacation retreat village it was when the first expats arrived after World War II. Since the 1980s, it has grown into a large city of more than a million people, many of them wealthy Mexicans who escaped Mexico City after the devastating earthquake of 1986. People have continued to be drawn by the exceptional weather and spectacularly beautiful location, under the imposing, giant Mount Popocatepetl volcano. The city now has the usual problems associated with growth, traffic, crime, and days of far less than perfect air quality. Nevertheless, Cuernavaca's community of foreign residents enthusiastically embraces the city. They praise its relaxed, elegant lifestyle, the wide variety of cultural activities, museums, shops, and restaurants, and the openness of the Mexican community to outsiders.

YUCATÁN PENINSULA

The Yucatán Peninsula was the first part of Mexico discovered by the Spaniards. A Spanish ship sailing from Darien (Panama) for the island of Española (Santo Domingo) accidentally landed on its coast in the year 1511. Stranded by a hurricane in the *Las Viboras* (the Vipers) bays in front of the Islands of Jamaica, the boat was pulled to the coast of the peninsula by strong currents, landing on what is today the state of Quintana Roo.

The Yucatán Peninsula is made up of three states, Campeche to the west, Yucatán on the north, and Quintana Roo to the south and east. Altogether there are approximately 1,659,000 inhabitants. It is impossible to guess how many of them are full-time foreign residents and how many are snowbirds. But what is clear is that the number of foreigners from the United States and Canada buying property in the Yucatán is growing.

The peninsula's terrain is almost flat, comprising limestone shelf with a covering of dense, scrubby, desert-like trees in a semi-tropical climate. During the rainy season (May–October), water seeps into limestone crevices and creates underground rivers and sink holes. These water stores allowed early Mayans to survive on the harsh terrain.

Until 1974, when Cancún was built from scratch, only the most intrepid and adventurous travelers explored the wonders of this region. These were primarily archaeology and anthropology buffs following the Mayan trail and exploring the area's fabulous ruins. Today, Cancún is the most popular tourist destination in Mexico, with more than three million tourists a year visiting its glitzy hotels, palm-lined, white, coral sand beaches, and turquoise Caribbean waters. Most vacationers to Cancún—if they explore the Yucatán at all—take day trips 60 miles (97 km) south along the Quintana Roo coast (now know as the Mayan Riviera) to the Mayan ruin at Tulum. The other, grander, and more extensive sites, such as Chichén Itzá, Cobá, and Uxmal, are left to more intrepid travelers.

Until 1974, when Cancún was built from scratch, only the most intrepid and adventurous travelers explored the wonders of this region.

Apart from Cancún and vicinity, the largest cities in the Yucatán are Mérida and Campeche. Both cities have colonial roots and beautiful architecture, and both have permanent communities of foreigners, though the one in Mérida in larger and more active.

Planning Your Fact-Finding Trip

I f you are intrigued by the idea of living in Mexico and have never been here, it is time to plan your first trip. Visiting any one area of the country is a breeze, but if you want to see it all, you face a great challenge. Mexico is a large country with a culturally diverse population and geographical extremes. Although all Mexicans speak the same language, people in different parts of the country have different accents, customs, and cuisines. Rather than trying to experience the entire country on the first trip, it is better to sample the representative parts that most appeal to you.

Before leaving home, read as many books about traveling and living in Mexico as you can, read the chapters in this book devoted to the cities on your itinerary, and surf the Internet (see the recommended reading list and recommended general information websites in the Resources chapter). These cities all have informative websites.

Preparing to Leave

WHAT TO BRING

Pack lightly for your first trip to investigate Mexico, especially if you are flying or plan to take buses. Unless they are attending a night at the opera or a fancy dinner party, Mexicans and foreigners living in Mexico normally dress very casually. The exceptions are Mexican businesspeople, executives, and fashion plates in the larger cities. You can easily have clothes washed. Most hotels have laundry service or can point you in the direction of a nearby launderette.

Be aware of Mexican sensibilities. Women should avoid going braless or wearing see-through tops. Wear short-shorts only at beach resorts. These days, some Mexican men have taken to wearing short pants in hot climates, but they are still very much in the minority. Most Mexicans are poor and dress in whatever clothes are available, although middle-class Mexican kids often dress like they just stepped out of a Calvin Klein commercial.

For travel to Puerto Vallarta or any of the other coastal towns, pack lightweight clothing. On the coast, men should pack their favorite Hawaiian shirts, cotton slacks, shorts, a swimsuit, lots of T-shirts, and a cool hat. Women should pack a light cotton dress or two, cotton slacks, a sarong, and their own version of a Hawaiian shirt. Bring sandals (or flip-flops) and a light sweater or jacket for cooler evenings, especially in winter.

Mexico is large, with varying topography. Climatic conditions in one part of the country can be the complete opposite of those in another part.

Inland, even in summer, it can be cool at night almost anywhere in the country, so a light sweater is a necessity. If you are traveling to San Miguel de Allende or another high-elevation town in winter, be prepared for warm days in the low 70s and very cool nights, with temperatures sometimes dropping into the mid-30s. In April and May, temperatures in these towns can reach into the 90s during the day. Wherever you are going, you will need good walking shoes and a hat (you might want to wait and buy a good-looking Mexican sombrero). Check the weather on the Internet before your trip.

Mexico is large, with varying topography. Climatic conditions in one part of the country can be the complete opposite of those in another part. For instance, in August during the rainy season, the coast can be stiflingly hot and humid, while inland at higher elevations you can feel chilled to the bone. With this in mind, the optimal months to travel extensively throughout the country are mid-October, November, and December.

Name-brand toiletries and cosmetics are widely available. If you run out of your favorite body lotion, don't worry. Mexican and foreign-made cosmetics are sold everywhere; many are high quality and very inexpensive.

People who need special medications will want to pack enough for the entire trip. Many medications available in the United States are not sold in Mexico, but substitutions can usually be found. Officially, prescriptions are required for narcotic painkillers, sleeping pills, and the like, though a few pharmacies sell restricted medications without a prescription. Most pharmacists can recommend a nearby doctor who will write a prescription. Antibiotics, stomach remedies, and many other medications can be bought at any pharmacy without a prescription.

To stay healthy on this trip, take the same precautions you would while traveling in the States. If you are planning to walk around in the hot sun, wear a hat and use sun block. While Mexican food, drink, and ice cubes, especially in tourist areas, are entirely safe, it is recommended that you wash your hands at every opportunity. It helps to pack a bottle of antibacterial hand lotion in case you can't get to a sink before eating.

If you have the space, pack your swimming goggles and a light pair of binoculars to view distant sights and Mexico's exceptionally diverse bird population (Mexico is a birder's paradise).

If you don't speak Spanish, bring along a small dictionary. If you are preparing to shop (which is almost impossible to resist), pack a light-weight empty luggage bag.

Currency

The only reasons to bring traveler's checks to Mexico is because they are replaceable if you are robbed, or you intend to make some very large purchases. Whether or not you bring traveler's checks, it is wise to bring some U.S. dollars to start with and for emergencies. The rest of the cash you need you can get from ATMs, which take all U.S. credit and debit cards. With these machines, you get a better exchange rate than with many banks and money changers. It is a good idea to call your bank or credit card company before you leave and increase the daily limit for withdrawals. Occasionally, during a fiesta or in times of extra-heavy usage, an ATM may run out of cash, so always keep some cash in reserve. Note that although ATMs are ubiquitous in cities, in the sticks finding one is as easy as finding a rabbi.

By now you surely know that the currency in Mexico is the peso. Bills come in denominations of 20, 50, 100, 200, and 500 pesos. Coins range from 10 centavos to 20 pesos. Coins are each a different size, although the one- and two-peso coins are close in size and often confused, even by Mexicans. Occasionally, you may see N$ written before a price. This is an archaic symbol referring to the "new peso," which came into existence several devaluations ago. These days, pesos are written with a single-bar dollar sign before the number. For the exchange rate, check your nearest big-city newspaper, go on line, or call a large bank.

Arriving in Mexico

If your fantasy is to live on a palm-studded, semitropical beach, you can fly into a Pacific coast city like Puerto Vallarta, Mazatlán, or Manzanillo, rent a car, and check out the nearby coastal villages. Or arrive in Cancún and explore what is now being called the Mayan Riviera or one of the other fabulous and more remote Yucatán beaches. If you are attracted to a more European ambiance, fly directly into the Leon, Guanajuato, airport, and begin exploring San Miguel de Allende, Guanajuato, Morelia, Zacatecas, and the rest of colonial Mexico. And don't forget somewhere along the way you might just unpack your bags and set up housekeeping.

Below are three separate itineraries, each for a different region of the country. The two coastal itineraries, one for the Pacific and one for the Yucatán, are each seven days long. The itinerary for Central Mexico is fourteen days long and includes Mexico City, Guadalajara, and some of colonial Mexico. These itineraries are intended to introduce you to the prime living areas in that region. If you have limited time, choose the itinerary for the area you most want to see. If you have two weeks or more, choose two itineraries, and so on. Try to be flexible. Do not plan everything down to the minute. You may find

Just the Facts

Not everyone has what it takes to live in a foreign land. Many people would feel insecure trying to learn a new alphabet that goes from bottom to top and from right to left. And that is nothing compared to trying to figure out the laws and customs of some foreign countries. Do you shake hands or bow? Do you bribe a cop and go to jail, or not bribe a cop and go to jail? Just keeping track of which way to look for traffic may be too much for some people.

Fortunately, Mexico operates with the same alphabet as us (give or take a few letters), and the words are fairly easy to pronounce. More difficult is Mexico's adherence to the Napoleonic code of law, which says basically that every person is considered guilty until proven innocent.

What it comes down to are the FACTS for living in a foreign country. That is to say:

F for flexibility, both mentally and emotionally, to go where the culture takes you.

A for adventurous. Take chances. Try new foods and dances. Learn the language.

C for calm and courteous. Be polite, listen, and learn. Don't react.

T for tolerance. Accept differences. You are in the minority here.

S for sensitivity. Develop the consciousness and awareness to live with contentment in new circumstances.

There they are. Just the FACTS, ma'am! Just the FACTS.

that you want to extend your stay for an extra night or two. In this chapter is a short list of hotels to get you started. Check other sources for more extensive listings.

Spend as much time as possible in the cities that make you feel most at home. Amble through the streets to get an idea of what it would be like to live there. Most importantly, be open to talking with local people, both foreign and Mexican, anywhere you can. Many Mexicans speak some English and will graciously answer any politely asked question. Ask foreign residents what attracts them to the town, where they shop, what kinds of foods and supplies are available, what they do for entertainment, and how much they spend each month. Most people enjoy talking about the town they live in. You can always make contact with foreigners at the library, Internet provider, or local English newspaper office.

When you arrive in town, buy a copy of the local English-language newspaper. It will offer insights into the character (and characters) of the town. A scan of the real estate sections should give you a pretty good idea of the cost of living there. If you have time, hire a car and driver (or rent a car) and explore the nearby villages.

Keep in mind that this is a fact-finding trip, not a vacation. Really, it's more like a working vacation. As such, these itineraries will keep you on the move. It may also stretch your finances, especially if you put together two or three itineraries. Covering that much territory by air or rental car will not be inexpensive.

Sample Itineraries

PACIFIC COAST

Note: Mazatlán, one of the Prime Living Locations, is located about 700 miles (1,127 km) south of the U.S. border on the west coast of Mexico and 286 miles (460 km) north of Puerto Vallarta. The seven-day itinerary below can start in either Mazatlán or Puerta Vallarta.

Day 1: Fly into Mazatlán and find a hotel in the Zona Dorado. This is the part of town where the majority of tourist hotels are located. It is also the end of town where most foreign residents live. Walk in the area, then hire a taxi to give you a tour of the residential areas of Las Gaviotas and Sabalo Country Club (not really a country club), the marina, and the El Cid Resort, the largest residential and commercial development in town.

Day 2: In the morning, tour Mazatlán's old town (where once-crumbling old colonials are being beautifully renovated) and the curvy streets of Mazatlán's only two hills. Fly to Puerto Vallarta in the afternoon. The drive by car takes five and a half hours. By bus, it is seven hours. For a traditional Mexican-style meal and beautiful views, eat dinner at Los Arbolitos.

Day 3: Explore old town and south of the Rio Cuale to Olas Altos in the morning. This is a charming area with sidewalk coffee shops and restaurants, perfect for a cup of coffee and a roll. After breakfast, meander up Basilio Badillo, then over to the Rizo Grocery store. Rizo's is a large, old-fashioned grocery. The store has one of the best bulletin boards in town—a good place to find a house or apartment for rent or a car for sale. If you are there at lunchtime, eat at the restaurant across the street to the south or at one of the sidewalk *camarone* (shrimp) stands.

For *la cena* (dinner), try a restaurant on Basilio Badillo. If you like Indian cuisine, go to Dasan, a small, inexpensive place serving good food. Or try the restaurant at the Hotel Posado Rio Cuale. It has been there for years and has the best Steak Diane in town, which they prepare at your table.

Day 4: Rent a car from your hotel (you save the 15-percent airport tax). Be sure to check out every ding and dent so you don't become responsible for them later. Drive north to Bucerías and spend some time exploring this town with its thriving little foreign community and local English newspaper. Have a seafood lunch at one of the restaurants on the beach, or head to a wonderful little place called We Be Sausage. The restaurant, run by an American who brought his expertise to Bucerías several years ago, offers fabulous hamburgers and homemade sausages. The fries and pickled vegetables aren't bad either. It seems to be somewhat of a local hangout for Buceríans.

Hop back in the car and head north to Punta Mita. Ten years ago, there was little sign of development here. Now it's hot property, especially since the opening of the Four Seasons Hotel and Golf Resort. A Rosewood Hotel is soon to open here as well. The drive is still lovely, with new fancy developments cropping up along the way. While checking out Punta de Mita, ask someone about the condition of the back road to the village of Sayulita. You can find an English-speaking person in any real estate office. Usually the road has many potholes, so take it slow.

Day 5: Spend the night in Sayulita. Don't let Sayulita's dirt streets fool you; it has definitely been discovered. New boutiques are springing up as fast as the real estate prices. For an afternoon snack, Don Pedro's on the beach is a good, but pricey, spot for watching the surfers and sunbathers. The other restaurants on the beach are good but not as trendy. Spend the night at Villa Amor on the beach, 329/291-3018, or one of the many other hotels and guesthouses that can be rented through the website www.sayulitalife.com.

Day 6: Drive twenty minutes north to San Francisco (better known by its nickname, San Pancho). From the main street, Avenida Tercer Mundo (Third World Avenue), follow signs toward the Costa Azul Resort. Continue past the resort and you will begin seeing the beautiful hillside and beach homes of American snowbirds and expats. Back in town are excellent little restaurants for breakfast. Take a walk on the beach and swim, then return to Puerto Vallarta for the night. If you have the money, try another restaurant on the Rio Cuale. The River Café and Le Bistro both have good jazz groups and even better food.

Walking down the streets of any town, such as this one in Cuernavaca, will give you a feel for the life of the place.

Day 7: Fly home.

You can also fly from Puerto Vallarta to Guadalajara in 45 minutes. I recommend the drive. The highway takes you through the lava flow of the Ceboruco Volcano, past blue-green fields of agave (used to make tequila), hills of sugar cane, and mountain passes—a nice slice through the diversity of Mexico's landscape.

CENTRAL MEXICO

Central Mexico includes the country's largest and second largest cities and its colonial cities. It is a huge area, and one too rich in culture and diversity to experience in one week or even ten days. Therefore, this is a 14-day itinerary. If you only have ten days, it is recommended that you choose to visit either Mexico City and Cuernavaca or Guadalajara and Ajijic after seeing San Miguel de Allende and Guanajuato.

Day 1: Fly into the Del Bajio Airport in León, Guanajuato. Take a taxi to San Miguel de Allende, about one and a half hours away. In San Miguel, you have an extensive choice of hotels and bed-and-breakfasts in all price ranges. In the evening, take a long walk around San

Miguel's romantic streets. Find a good spot to sit on the *jardín* (main plaza) and people-watch. Have dinner at El Pegaso, near the *jardín*, the romantic Buganvilea (established back in the '40s and still under the same management!), or enjoy the lovely outdoor garden dining in the more expensive Casa Sierra Nevada en el Parque (on the park).

Day 2: Enjoy San Miguel on foot, starting at the plaza area and the cathedral. Walk to the Parque Juarez, the market, and the *biblioteca* (library). While at the library, pick up a copy of *Atención,* the city's English-language newspaper. Tour the various *colonias* (neighborhoods) adjacent to *centro* (downtown). These neighborhoods may offer the last of the real-estate bargains.

Day 3: Rent a car and explore the towns around San Miguel. Start with the nearby subdivision of Los Frailes and El Mirador. Drive to Pozos, about one and a half hours away. Pozos is a resurrected mining town that now has a small foreign community of mostly artistic people who have given up on the more trendy and expensive San Miguel scene. A trip to the ruined hacienda on the hill is worthwhile. La Casa Mexicana hotel, 449/293-0014, pozosmex@yahoo.com, has nice rooms for about $75/night for 2 people and a good restaurant in a pleasant garden.

From Pozos, drive to Guanajuato by way of Dolores Hidalgo, a town primarily renowned for its colorful, Italianate ceramics. From Dolores, the road winds for about one hour through the Santa Rosa mountains to Guanajuato. Spend the night in downtown Guanajuato at one of the colonial hotels on the plaza opposite the old opera house or at La Casa de Espiritu Alegres (The House of the Happy Spirits), a restored 18th-century ex-hacienda in the area of town called Marfil.

Day 4: Guanajuato boasts numerous museums, as well as a major university. Tour the town on foot. Don't miss the opera house or the Diego Rivera house and museum. In the afternoon return directly to San Miguel, one hour away.

Day 5: Take the first-class bus from San Miguel to Mexico City (or if you prefer to skip Mexico City this trip, jump to Day 10 and fly to Guadalajara instead). You will arrive at the Terminal de Autobuses Norte. Take a taxi to the Centro Historico. Check into the Hotel Gillow or the Hotel Cathedral. Both are reasonably priced and close to the *zócalo.* The new, upscale Sheraton Centro Historico is near the Alameda.

If you have never visited Mexico City, the place to start is the Centro Historico, the oldest part of town. The huge central plaza (known as the *zócalo*) is where the Aztecs erected their main temples and the Spanish conquerors established their new empire. Traces of ancient ruins can be seen right next to the colonial-era government buildings.

Inside the Palacio Nacional (presidential palace) are colorful murals depicting the entire history of Mexico, painted by one of the country's most famous artists, Diego Rivera. (You will need a photo ID to enter the Palacio Nacional.) On the north side of the *zócalo* stands the massive Cathedral Metropolitana, the center of Mexican Catholicism, the construction of which began in 1573. Between the Palacio and the Cathedral, you will find the ruins of the Aztec Templo Mayor. On most days, you will see and hear groups of *conchero* dancers in front wearing feathered Aztec headdresses.

Day 6: From the *zócalo*, walk down Avenida 5 de Mayo or Avenida Madero toward the Alameda, a lovely green park dating back to colonial times, when it was reserved for the Spanish elite. Instead of walking, you might hire one of the bicycle taxis seen all around the *zócalo* for around 50 pesos ($4.50), depending on the number of people and the exact destination.

The Alameda can be a delightful and soothing oasis in the midst of the urban chaos and a good place to sit and watch people. It is especially beautiful just as the sun is setting and the light shines through its many fountains.

The area around the park has several noteworthy tourist sites. Visit the Palacio de Bellas Artes, the city's main opera and concert hall. If you are there on a Wednesday or Sunday, you can see performances of the Ballet Folklorico, a colorful spectacle of Mexican music and dance. Diagonally across the street from Bellas Artes is the Torre Latinoamerica, until recently the tallest building in Latin America. The *mirador* (observation deck) on the 44th floor has amazing views of the valley of Mexico if the skies are clear enough. A block north of Bellas Artes is the Correo Mayor (main post office), whose recently refurbished cast-iron interior is worth a look. Stop for lunch at the Casa de Azulejos (the house of tiles), one block from Bellas Artes between 5 de Mayo and Madero. Dating from 1596, it is completely covered in beautiful Puebla-style tiles. The former home of the Marques del Valle de Orizaba, it is now owned by Sanborns, a chain of restaurant/stores found all over Mexico. The central patio dining room is a beautiful place to eat, with classic Mexican dishes well prepared.

They are also famous for their chocolates, available at a counter just outside the dining room. Sanborns is also a good place to find a clean public restroom. Other highlights of the Alameda area include the Museo Nacional de Arte and the Museo Franz Mayer, both of which specialize in Mexican art.

A good dining option in the area is the Cafe Tacuba (Tacuba 28), an old-time favorite with a beautiful interior and strolling musicians. Just a block south of the *zócalo* on 5 de Mayo is Jugos Canada, a great place to stop for refreshing (and safe) fruit and vegetable drinks. Try the *apio* (celery) and lime combination for something different.

Day 7: Explore the city. In the morning, take a taxi to Culiacán and visit Frida Kahlo's house and museum, and, a few block away, Leon Trotsky's house and museum. In the afternoon, take a taxi tour of the residential areas of Polanco, Condesa, and nearby Roma. Have dinner at the restaurant in the Palacio de Bellas Artes.

Day 8: Take a taxi to the Terminal de Autobuses Sur. From there take a bus to Cuernavaca, one and a half hours away. Check into a hotel in Cuernavaca. Go downtown and walk around and check out the sights. Go to the Museo Robert Brady. An American artist and collector, Brady assembled some incredible pieces in his home, now a museum, including an amazing (and valuable) self-portrait of Frida Kahlo. For dinner, try one of Cuernavaca's wonderful restaurants. One possibility is Gaia, a lovely place located on the square in a house once owned by Cantinflas, one of Mexico's most famous and beloved actors.

Day 9: In the morning, hire a taxi to take you on a tour from the upper to the lower ends of town. Ask the driver to show you the best residential neighborhoods, many of which will be gated. Then take a taxi to Tepotzlan, a small town with an eccentric foreign community, situated at the upper end of a valley. On the main square are the Iglesia (church) de San Francisco Javier and a number of shops and restaurants. Try Café de Colores, a lively place with traditional Mexican food. Surprisingly, many of the shops carry Indonesian and Thai furnishings and clothes! Back in Cuernavaca, be sure to go to Las Mananitas, a spectacular hotel, for a drink or dinner. Spend the night in Cuernavaca.

(Optional) Hire a taxi to take you to Malinalco, about one hour from Cuernavaca. This town, also at the upper end of a valley, has become a weekend getaway for wealthy Mexico City folks, as well as home to a few foreign residents. A well-preserved Aztec temple sits on a cliff above the town.

Day 10: Return to the Mexico City airport by bus and/or taxi. (Optional: Fly to Oaxaca for one night, then back to Mexico City. Enjoy sitting on the *zócalo,* observing the energy of life passing by). Fly to Guadalajara. Drive it in five hours or take a luxury bus (7–8 hours). Stay in a downtown hotel in Guadalajara, like the Hotel de Mendoza near the cathedral or the San Francisco Plaza. From either one you can simply explore the area on foot. Visit the vast San Juan de Dios (also known as Libertad) market, where there is even a section on witchcraft. Female visitors can buy, among many other things, dried hummingbirds to stick in their bra for good luck. Nearby is the Hospicio Cabanas museum, home of the Orozco murals. That evening, stop at the nearby El Toreador bar and restaurant, or take a taxi to Ma Come No, a very nice Italian restaurant.

Day 11: Hire a car to show you all around the city. Rauol Negrete is a taxi driver who knows Guadalajara very well and speaks English. You can reach him at 333/604-0699 or 333/119-7473. He is generally available for a day's guided tour. Be sure to stop by the American Society for inside information about living in Guadalajara, then visit Talaquepaque and Tonola.

Day 12: Take a taxi or bus, or rent a car and drive one hour to Ajijic on Lake Chapala. Walk around town, and stop in at the Lake Chapala Society, the main meeting place for the foreign community. Here you will find information and insights into making the move to this part of Mexico. Spend the night at the beautiful and relaxing Los Artistas B&B, 376/766-1027, Artistas@laguna.com.mx, owned by our friends Kent and Linda. Have dinner and/or a margarita a few blocks away on the patio at the Nueva Posada Hotel.

Day 13: By car or taxi explore as many of the other lakeside villages as possible. Each has a unique character. A local realtor will be happy to give you a tour, especially in the off-season. One or two of the realty companies hold weekly house tours. Spend the night in Ajijic.

Day 14: Fly home from Guadalajara's Don Miguel Hidalgo International Airport.

(Optional) Drive (about two and one half hours by car) or take the bus to Morelia. There are very few foreigners living in Morelia, yet its colonial beauty warrants a visit. In the heart of downtown Morelia are the main cathedral and the central plaza, a huge park-like square surrounded by colonial buildings. Morelia has become a large, bustling city, with a major university. The nicest place to stay in town is the

Hotel Virrey de Mendoza, the converted mansion of the first viceroy of Mexico. The rooms are decorated with colonial furniture and chandeliers and are very reasonably priced.

As an alternative, drive to Pátzcuaro, less than one hour from Morelia, and check into the Best Western Don Vasco, a hacienda-style hotel. Walk through Pátzcuaro's narrow streets and its two main plazas. Take an afternoon drive through the beautiful Michoacan countryside to the nearby village of Tocuaro, 10 km (6 miles) outside of Pátzcuaro and home to Mexico's best mask makers. Drive 20 km (12 mils) south of Pátzcuaro to Santa Clara del Cobre (also called Villa Escalante). This former copper mining town is the copper arts center of Mexico. Here you will see both utilitarian and art quality copper work that is uniquely beautiful and affordable. Not far away is Tingambata, ruins from A.D. 450–900, which include a ball court, temple pyramids, and an underground tomb.

YUCATÁN PENINSULA

Day 1: Arrive in Mérida (on a Saturday, if possible)—likely on an evening flight—and check into your hotel in the historical center of the city. Freshen up a little and then walk up to Noche Mexicana. This city entertainment is held every Saturday night at the beginning of Paseo de Montejo (Montejo at Calle 47). It includes an interesting craft fair, kiosks selling food and drinks, and a stage with song and dance from various parts of Mérida. While a popular Saturday night meeting place for the expat community, Noche Mexican draws primarily Mexicans enjoying their Saturday night family outing.

When you have seen and heard enough, take a *calesa* (a horse-drawn buggy) along Calle 60 and around the main plaza. The streets here are closed to traffic Saturday night and there is live entertainment everywhere. Sit outside in one of the many cafés and restaurants and have a meal, snack, or a drink. Relax and soak up the atmosphere.

Day 2: This is a perfect day for an orientation of Mérida. The streets around the main plaza and along Calle 60 to Santa Lucia are blocked to vehicles, and traffic in the rest of the city is lighter on Sunday than on other days. There is a flea market at Parque Santa Lucia and a craft fair along Calle 60 to the main plaza. Take your time and stroll around the main plaza, checking out the crafts for sale. Visit the cathedral on the main plaza, one of the oldest buildings on the continent.

For a good tour of the city, catch a small open-air bus at Calle 60 and 55, directly across from Parque Santa Lucia. For 75 pesos per person, the two-hour tour offers a good opportunity to see Mérida's various neighborhoods and housing styles.

Have lunch in one of the many cafés and restaurants on the sidewalks and streets near the main plaza. Visit the Palacio de Gobierno (Governor's Palace) and go upstairs to see the striking paintings depicting the history of the Maya and their treatment by the Spanish conquistadors. It is open daily and there is no charge.

By now you might want to head back to your hotel for a siesta or swim and then freshen up before going out for dinner. Have dinner at the Hacienda Xkanatun, just north of Mérida. Xkanatun is a beautifully restored hacienda that is now a hotel with a wonderful restaurant.

Day 3: The first stop today is the Mérida English Library on Calle 53 between Calle 66 and 68. Here you will meet many English-speaking people who have made Mérida their home. Visit the Yucatán Museum of Contemporary Art (Museo de Arte Contemporáneo Ateneo de Yucatán, or MACAY), Pasaje de la Revolución #58–60 in Mérida. Open Wednesday–Monday, 10 A.M.–5:30 P.M. Free admission.

On Monday nights, the Mérida English Library hosts a conversation group between 7:00 and 9:00 P.M. This is not a formal class but an opportunity for Mexicans to practice their English and for the English-speaking community to practice their Spanish. It provides a good opportunity to meet the expat community and some of the local Mexicans too. There is no charge and no Spanish is required.

Day 4: The city of Campeche in the state of Campeche is about a two-hour drive from Mérida. Rent a car or take a bus and head out early because there is a lot to see. Plan to stay overnight. Campeche is a very different city than Mérida.

Arrive in the city and check into the Frances Drake Hotel, a well-run, moderately priced, centrally located establishment. Walk over to the main square, check out the cathedral, and then take a trolley-bus tour of Campeche. This will give you a good idea of the downtown areas. Then stop for lunch at one of the famous seafood restaurants. La Pigua, at 129 Miguel Aleman, is a good choice.

In the afternoon, take a trip out to see Edzna, a beautiful Mayan site. If you're up for it, climb the five-story pyramid for a worthwhile view. This quiet site has very few tourists. Sunset would be a good time to take a stroll along the malecón. This is a port city and it has a lovely walkway along the harbor, with parks and sculptures along the way. Although located in the heart of a busy city, the walk is very peaceful. Have dinner at a restaurant on the main square, where you can people-watch as the locals come out to use the park.

Day 5: Before heading back to Mérida, take a walking tour of the city center. The colonial center is surrounded by a wall built in the 1600s to protect the inhabitants from the pirates in the area. Seven *baluartes* (forts) still remain along this wall and there are parts of the wall that you can still walk on. Amble through the center of the old city and visit the little museums in the forts. The buildings here in the center have been restored and provide some of the best examples of colonial architecture anywhere.

Head back to Mérida, check into your hotel, then have lunch. This afternoon, shop, see some of the things you missed, talk to real estate agents, or just relax.

Day 6: It is time now to start out for the Caribbean coast. I suggest an early start for your drive or bus ride to the most famous Maya site, Chichén Itzá. If you leave Mérida by 8:00 A.M., you should arrive around 10:00 A.M. Take a guided tour of Chichen Itza and see all the highlights. Climb the pyramid, Kukulkan, and look out over this incredible site. Spend some time exploring Chichén Itzá on your own, then break for lunch. Have lunch at the Hacienda Chichén Itzá, once a working hacienda and later the site's earliest archaeologist bungalows. It has been beautifully restored and is well run with an excellent menu.

Leave for Playa del Carmen. It will take about three hours by bus or car, so if you leave by 3:00 P.M. you should arrive in daylight. Check into a hotel and then take a stroll on the beach. Walk through the town and pick out a place for dinner. There are many good restaurants.

Day 7: These last two days will give you a taste of the Cancún side of the Yucatán peninsula. It has a very different feel. Spend a morning on the beach, then take the passenger ferry to Cozumel for the day. Take the bus and go to Puerto Morelos, just a half hour away. This smaller, quieter community has a number of expats living there. The English bookstore on the main square is a good place to browse and meet expats.

Optional: There are other places to check out: Isla Mujeres, Cancún, Akumal, and more. However, if you spend some time in Playa del Carmen, Cozumel, and Puerto Morelos, you should have a good idea whether this part of the Yucatán is for you.

If these itineraries make your head spin a little, you're not alone. Don't worry. You will have time to do it all. Adjust the itinerary to fit your pocketbook and travel schedule. You may save money by flying both in and out of the same city, paying more in domestic travel. If available, a rental car gives you the most flexibility and the best view of the countryside, but rental drop-off fees are high. Unlike the States, first-class bus travel in Mexico is very comfortable and relatively inexpensive, and you will get to meet and talk with more people along the way.

If you have unlimited time, choose whichever city works best for you and use it as a base. From there, you can plan and take trips to other parts of the country. Or tack all three itineraries together. Those of you who enjoy long drives should consider a driving trip from the States to Mexico. Driving will give you an interesting cultural experience. You will be challenged to deal with everyday activities like buying gas, ordering meals in Spanish, changing money, and navigating the Mexican highway system (see the Travel & Transportation section of the Daily Life chapter for more information about driving in Mexico.)

Practicalities

The following is a short list of hotels and restaurants in the cities covered in the book. Price categories are included for restaurants. Generally, budget means under US $10 for an entire meal (drinks, dessert, etc.), moderate is US $10–20, and expensive is US $20 and up. Most accommodations listings give the web address or phone number so you can check their current rates. For more extensive listings, check with AAA, city websites, or one of the many Mexico guidebooks.

LAKE CHAPALA AREA

Accommodations
Los Artistas B&B
This bed-and-breakfast is owned by our friends Kent and Linda. A beautiful parklike setting and a wonderful breakfast make this our top choice.

Constitucion #105, Ajijic
tel. 376/766-1027
fax 376/766-1762
www.losartistas.com

La Nueva Posada
Right on the lake, this hotel has old-world charm even though it is fairly new. The rooms are large and comfortable. It has a very nice restaurant with outside seating in a garden overlooking the lake.
Donato Guerra #9, Ajijic
tel. 376/766-1344
nuevaposada@laguna.com.mx

Swan Inn Ajijic B&B
This bed-and-breakfast is conveniently located right next to the library and near the plaza.
16 de Septiembre #18, Ajijic
tel. 376/766-0917 or 376/766-2354
www.swaninnajijic.com

Inn of the Plumed Serpent
This is a unique bed-and-breakfast in Chapala. Although expensive, it's worth visiting. Each suite is a completely a different work of art, and the gardens are breathtaking. D. H. Lawrence lived here when he wrote his novel, *The Plumed Serpent.*
Calle Zaragoza #307
tel. 376/765-3653
fax 376/765-3444
www.accommodationslakechapala.com

Restaurants
Pedro's
At the corner of Aquiles Serdan and Avenida Ocampo, this is the "hottest" new restaurant at lakeside. It has both indoor and outdoor garden seating and serves both Mexican and international food. Moderate.
Corner of Aquiles Serdan and Avenida Ocampo, Ajijic

La Bodega
This is a nice, small garden restaurant and a favorite with expats. Live dinner music. Moderate.
16 de Septiembre #124, Ajijic
tel. 376/766-1002

La Nueva Posada
The garden with its twinkling lights and view of Lake Chapala is a very romantic place to dine. Moderate/Expensive.
Donato Guerra #9, Ajijic
tel. 376/766-1444

GUADALAJARA

Accommodations
Hotel San Francisco Plaza
This is an inexpensive colonial hotel in downtown, with a regal beauty and a decent restaurant.
Degollado #267
tel. 333/613-8954 or 333/613-3256
fax 333/613-3257

Camino Real
Camino Real is more a fancy country-club resort than a hotel. It has four pools, a putting green, gym, tennis courts—you get the picture.
Avenida Vallarta #5005
tel. 333/134-2425
fax 333/134-2425
www.camino-real-reservations.com

Hotel de Mendoza
This hotel is a former convent and offers very nice rooms in the historical center of town.
Calle Venustiano Carranza #16
tel. 333/942-5151
fax 333/613-7310
www.demendoza.com.mx

Hotel Francés
Another downtown jewel.
Maestranza #35
tel. 333/613-1190
fax 333/658-1703
www.hotelfrances.com

Restaurants
Ma Come No
This restaurant has some of the best Italian food, and the best salad bar, in the Americas in a beautiful old hacienda-style building. Moderate/Expensive.
Avenida de las Americas #302
tel. 333/615-4952

Casa Fuerte
In Tlaquepaque, this is the place to eat in the garden of a magnificent ex-hacienda. Moderate/Expensive.
Independencia #224, Tlaquepaque
tel. 333/639-6481

SAN MIGUEL DE ALLENDE

Accommodations
Hotel Mansion Virreyes
Downtown on the main plaza, this hotel has reasonable rates.
tel. 415/152-3355
fax 415/152-3865
mansionvirreyes@prodigy.net.mx

Casa Carmen
This is more a pension than a hotel. Small and charming, it is located near the *jardín* (main plaza).
Correo #31
tel. 415/152-0844
ccarmen@unisono.net.mx

La Puertecita Boutique Hotel
This hotel is small and very pretty, with beautiful grounds.

Santo Domingo #75
tel. 800/336-6776 or 415/152-5011
lapuertecita@lapuertecita.com

Casa Luna B&B
Casa Luna is a small bed-and-breakfast with wonderfully and uniquely
decorated rooms. It now has two locations, Casa Luna Pila Seca and
Casa Luna Quebrada.
Pila Seca #1
tel. 415/152-1117
Quebrada #17
www.casaluna.com

Puesta del Sol
This is a beautiful bed-and-breakfast on a hill above downtown. With
incredible sunset views, it's one of our favorites!
Fuentes #12
tel. 415/152-0220
www.casapuestadelsol.com

Restaurants
El Pegaso
This restaurant has both Mexican and Euro-American specialties with great
desserts. Busy and a bit noisy, but extremely friendly waiters. Moderate.
Corregidora 6 (corner of Correo) across from the Post Office

Buganvilla
This place has been in operation since the 1940s. It has a lovely setting
in the courtyard of an old colonial building. They serve mostly Mexican
gourmet specialties. Moderate/Expensive.
On Calle Hidalgo two blocks north of the *jardín*

Casa Sierra Nevada en el Parque
Dine here and enjoy the beautiful gardens, good Mexican food, and a
peaceful, romantic atmosphere. Moderate/Expensive.
Santa Elena #2 next to the Parque Juarez

GUANAJUATO AND POZOS

Accommodations
La Casa de Los Espiritus Alegres
This House of the Happy Spirits is a very charming bed-and-breakfast in a 17th century colonial hacienda. Each room is colorfully decorated with a different motif.
Ex-Hacienda la Trinidad #1, Guanajuato
tel. 473/733-1013

Posada Santa Fe
Posada Santa Fe is located in a colonial building on a romantic square with outdoor restaurants and strolling musicians.
Jardín Unió #12, Guanajuato
tel. 473/732-0084
www.posadasantafe.com

Casa Estrella de la Valenciana
This hotel has magnificent panoramic views of Guanajuato and the surrounding mountains from every room.
Callejon Jalisco #10, Valenciana
tel. 473/732-1784
www.MexicanInns.com

Real de Minas
This is the largest hotel in town, with a pool, restaurant, tennis courts, a nightclub, and all the trimmings.
Nejayote #17, Guanajuato
tel. 473/732-1460

Restaurants
La Casa Mexicana Hotel
The small restaurant on the main square serves delicious and creative food in their peaceful garden. Moderate/Expensive.
Main square, Pozos

Café de Colores
In Tepotzlan, this place is colorful (of course!) and you won't be able to miss it in its main street location. They serve delicious traditional Mexican cuisine. Moderate.

PÁTZCUARO

Accommodations
Posada Don Vasco/Best Western
A colonial-style hotel with pool, tennis courts, and more.
Avenida Lazaro Cadenas #450
tel. 434/342-0227
fax 434/342-0262
bwposada@prodigy.net.mx

La Casa Encantada Bed & Breakfast
This bed-and-breakfast is in an elegantly restored 18th-century mansion.
Dr. Coss #15
tel. 434/342-3492
www.lacasaencantada.com

MAZATLÁN

Accommodations
Fiesta Inn
This inn offers nice rooms overlooking the beach at reasonable prices.
Avenida Cameron Sabalo #1927
tel. 669/989-0100

Pueblo Bonito
This place features large rooms and suites on the beach.
Avenida Cameron Sabalo #2121
tel. 669/989-0525
www.pueblobonito.com

Motel Los Arcos
A little gem right on the beach with a wonderful staff. Each room has a kitchen, living room, bedroom, and appliances. Very clean and quaint, it has security and parking. Our personal favorite.

Avenida Playa Gaviotas #214
tel. 669/913-5066
www.motellosarcos.com

Restaurants
La Costa Marinera
Located on the beach between the Oceano Palace Hotel and the Luna
Palace, this place has firmly established itself as the premier seafood
restaurant in Mazatlán. On your way in, check out the holding tanks
with fish, lobster and turtles. Moderate.

Terraza Playa
Another beachfront restaurant, this place has music and dancing
nightly and a fireworks display on Sundays! Excellent food and service. Moderate.
Avenida Playa Gaviotas #202

Mango's Restaurant and Bar
It's loud, but oh, those mango margaritas! The coconut shrimp and
seafood platter are also not bad! Moderate.
Rudolfo T. Loasa #404
tel. 536/916-0044

PUERTO VALLARTA

Accommodations
Hotel Molino de Agua
A nice downtown hotel with a great location and fabulous gardens.
Phone ahead.
Ignacio L. Vallarta #130
tel. 322/222-1907 or 322/222-1957
www.molinodeagua.com

Villa Mercedes
A lovely bed-and-breakfast in the "romantic" zone of Puerto Vallarta.
Amapas #175
tel. 322/222-2148
www.villamercedes.com

Hotel Rosita
This was one of the first hotels in Vallarta. With its great location right on the beach, it is still popular.
Díaz Ordaz #901
tel. 333/223-2000
www.hotelrosita.com

Hacienda Mosaico Bed and Breakfast
Off the beaten track in the Versalles neighborhood, but worth it for the comfortable rooms, nice pool, and reasonable prices. Owner, friend, and artist Sandy "Sam" Leonard has created a whimsical and warm environment.
Calle Milan #274
tel. 322/225-8296
www.haciendamosaico.com

Restaurants
Los Arbolitos
Located in the 2nd and 3rd stories of a home overlooking the tree-lined Río Cuale. Moderate.
Camino de la Rivera #184

El Calamar Adventurero
They have a counter to enjoy the delicious fish tacos and a small dining area with more fish and shellfish choices—even sushi. Budget/Moderate.
Corner of Aquiles Serdan and Insurgentes

Le Bistro
This is a very romantic place in a beautiful setting with a creative menu. Expensive.
Isla Río Cuale #16A

The River Café
In an open-air setting on the Río Cuale with friendly service and excellent live music. Expensive.
Isla Río Cuale #4
tel. 322/223-0788
www.rivercafe.com.mx

Le Gourmet
This restaurant, located in the small hotel Posada Río Cuale, has an extensive menu with excellent food and hospitable and gracious service. Moderate.
Aquiles Serdan #242
tel. 322/222-0914

We Be Sausage
This is where many of the local expats gather. It has great sausage! Moderate.
Carretera a Puerto Vallarta, Bucerias
tel. 329/208-0954

Don Pedro's
Don Pedro's is romantic and right on the beach. Head downstairs for the bar with snacks, upstairs for dining. Expensive.
Marlin #2, Sayulita
tel. 329/291-3153

OAXACA

Accommodations
Hotel Victoria
This hotel is located on a hill overlooking the city. It has nice gardens, a pool, and tennis courts.
Alto de Centro del Fortin
tel. 951/515-2633
www.hotelvictoriaoax.com.mx

Camino Real
Located four blocks from the main square (the *zócalo*) in the 400-year-old former convent Santa Catalina, this is a luxury hotel with all the frills.
tel. 951/516-0611
www.camino-real-oaxaca.com

Hostal de La Noria
This hotel is located two blocks from the main square in a colorfully and beautifully decorated colonial building.
tel. 951/514-7844
www.hotel-lanoria-oaxaca.com

MEXICO CITY

Accommodations
Hotel Gillow
This hotel has moderate prices and is located on a colonial tree-lined street in the historic center, very close to the *zócalo*.
Isabel La Católica #17
tel. 555/518-1440 or 555/510-2636
www.hotelgillow.com

Hotel Catedral
Also located on a beautiful colonial street. Behind the main cathedral, it's close to the Government Palace and the Templo Mayor.
Donceles #95
tel. 555/518-5232 or 555/521-6183
www.hotelcatedral.com

Sheraton Centro Historico
A luxury hotel within walking distance of museums and a few minutes from the financial and business district.
Avenida Juaraz #70
tel. 555/130-5300
www.sheraton.com/centrohistorico

Restaurants
Sanborn's Casa de Azulejos (House of Tiles)
Located downtown, it is one of *the* places to go. The tiled exterior walls are something to see! Great food and service. Moderate.
Madero #4

Café Tacuba
It's an old favorite, with a beautiful old-style interior and strolling musicians serving continental food and standard Mexican favorites. Budget.
Calle Tacuba #28

CUERNAVACA

Accommodations

Suites Paraiso
An inexpensive hotel with clean, adequate rooms set in a lovely garden.
Avendia Domingo Diez #1099
tel. 777/313-2408
www.suitesparaiso.com.mx

Las Mañanitas
This is one of the most desirable and beautiful small hotels in Cuernavaca. Book early for this one.
Ricardo Linaares #107
tel. 777/314-1466
www.lasmananitas.com.mx

Posada María Cristina
A beautiful old hacienda-style hotel located south of the main plaza. The rooms are among the most spectacular I have ever seen, and the hotel features lush grounds and a great restaurant.
Boulevard Benito Juarez #300
tel. 777/318-5767

Las Campanas de San Jeronimo
This bed-and-breakfast is set on gorgeous grounds.
San Jeronimo #410-A
tel. 777/313-9494

Restaurants

Las Mañanitas
This is the restaurant in the hotel of the same name. They have wonderful food and a gorgeous setting. Expensive.
Calle Ricardo Linares #107
tel. 777/314-1466

Gaia
Gaia is in a beautifully decorated old home that was once owned by the famous Mexican actor, Cantinflas. Moderate/Expensive.
Boulevard Benito Juárez #102
tel. 777/312-3656

PLAYA DEL CARMEN

Acommodations
Taninah
This hotel is on 10 fenced and gated acres in an exclusive and environmentally friendly, private jungle enclave just a few miles south of Playa del Carmen.
Esquina de 5a Avenida y Calle 8
tel. 984/873-0040 or 984/876-2460
www.taninah.com

Hotel Lunata
This is a charming hacienda-style hotel located in the heart and soul of Playa Del Carmen, just steps away from the white-sand beaches.
5a Avenida between Calle 6 and 8
tel. 984/873-0884
www.lunata.com

Hotel Fiesta Banana
This is a small luxury hotel with 23 beautifully decorated rooms, each with balcony or terrace.
5a Avenida Norte, Esquina Calle 32
tel. 984/803-0201
www.fiestabanana.com

MÉRIDA

Accommodations
Casa Esperanza
Ideally located within walking distance of Santa Lucia and Mejorada Parks, as well as Plaza Grande, the main square.
Calle 54 #476
tel. 999/923-4711
www.casaesperanza.com

Gran Hotel
One of the most beautiful and elegant buildings in downtown, built in 1901, it recalls Mexico's Belle Epoque.

Calle 60 #496
tel. 999/924-7730 or 999/923-8163
www.granhoteldemerida.com.mx

Restaurants
Los Almendros
Serves authentic Yucatecan food and is a large, fun, and comfortable restaurant. Moderate.
Calle 50 #493
tel. 999/928-5459

Casa de Piedra (House of Rock)
An elegant restaurant located in Hacienda Xcanatun, a small luxury hotel. Expensive.
Carretera Merida-Progreso, km 12
tel. 999/941-0273

CAMPECHE

Accommodations
Frances Drake Hotel
With its ideal location in the fortified historic downtown, it has 24 luxurious rooms.
Calle 12 #207
tel. 981/811-5626 or 981/811-5627
www.hotelfrancisdrake.com

Restaurants
Marganzo
Located in one of Campeche's colorful colonial buildings, they serve good regional food. Moderate.
Calle 8 #267

La Pigua
It's right on the gulf and is the place in Campeche for seafood. Moderate.
Malecón Miguel Alemôn #197A

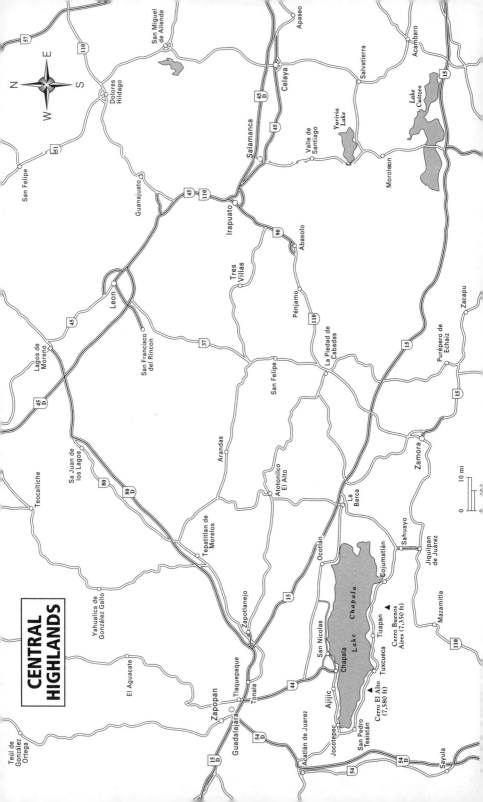

© Ken Lubcff

Central Highlands

Lake Chapala, Mexico's largest lake, is in the center of one of the most strikingly beautiful areas in the country, the Central Highlands. The lake is more than 45 miles (72 km) long and averages six miles in width. Surrounded by mountains, it gives the villages along its shores a sense of remoteness that belies their proximity to Guadalajara, Mexico's second largest city. Looking at the lake's rugged coastline from one of the surrounding hills far to the east of the town of Chapala, you may feel like you have been beamed up to the northern California coast.

With the exception of Jocotepec, the villages on the north side of the lake (where the majority of foreign residents live) are quaint and tranquil, with the mellow feeling of old, well-established European mountain resort towns. Each village—Ajijic (ah-HEE-heek), San Antonio, La Floresta, Chula Vista, San Juan Cosala, and El Chanté—has its own unique character. Chapala is larger and more commercial, but it also retains an old-world charm.

Lush gardens are everywhere in Mexico.

Along the narrow, cobbled streets of the older parts of these villages grow a remarkable variety of colorful flowers and trees—bougainvilleas of every hue, giant mango trees laden with fruit in late summer, flowering vines accenting old stone and brightly painted walls. Hidden behind the walls are homes with lawns, pools, and lush gardens. The modest front gate of many a home opens on to a surprisingly large garden, with mature trees and flower-lined stone paths. Some of these gardens rival small city parks in the States. Along the same street may be larger homes, more modest homes, or even very small homes. It is appealing to have an economic mix of people, rather than a separation of rich and poor into enclaves. These towns are very safe and the neighbors get along well with one another.

A number of gated communities have developed in the hills overlooking the lake. Homes in these communities come in all sizes and price ranges and usually have great views of the lake and adjacent mountains.

Lakeside residents are blessed with a nearly perfect climate, with a year-round high temperature averaging 77.4°F (25.2°C), lows averaging 58.3°F (14.6°C), and average rainfall of 31.9 inches (81 cm). The coldest months are December and January; the hottest and driest are April and May—before the start of the rainy season. There is little humidity, probably due to the lake's relatively high altitude of 5,200 feet (1,581 meters). But there's enough moisture so that you don't have to slather on copious amounts of body lotion the way you might in higher and drier locales.

Another obvious attraction is the lake's proximity to Guadalajara, a city of five million people, just 45 minutes away. Guadalajara may be large, but it is still easy enough to get around. It provides big-city energy and sophistication in direct contrast to the laid-back life in towns along the lake. Guadalajara has a wonderful variety of good restaurants, first-class medical care, museums, cultural events, and enough goods and merchandise to make serious shoppers break into a sweat. But Guadalajara's proximity to the lake is also a disadvantage on weekends, when thousands of *Tapatios* (Guadalajarans) crowd lakeside villages and create traffic jams on the lakeside's main highway. Prior to 2004, the water level of the lake was so low that docks and piers were a quarter mile from the water's edge and people could not take their boats out on the lake. However, as a result of the lake's high water levels these days, weekend tourism has increased the amount of traffic on the lakeside's main road.

Lake Chapala Area

About 100,000 people live along the shores of Lake Chapala. Included among them are about 4,000–6,000 permanent foreign residents. Most are from the United States, with a growing number of Canadians and a few Europeans. The numbers more or less double during winter with the influx of snowbirds escaping cold weather to the north.

The relaxed pace of life in the lakeside villages is in sync with the senior age of the majority of foreign residents. Most are retired and in their 60s, 70s, and older. Many of the area's early expats, who arrived in the 1960s and 1970s, still live in the lakeside communities. Very few foreigners living by the lake make an attempt to learn more than the minimum amount of Spanish needed to get by. It is sad because the inability to communicate in Spanish denies foreign residents access to the richness of the Mexican culture.

Some old-timers say the average age is beginning to drop, as a new and younger generation have discovered the area. These days, an equal number of people from the United States and Canada are moving in— some younger with small children. But there are very few college-aged people among the foreign community, as there are in other Mexican cities with large foreign populations. This is largely due to the lack of universities and language and art schools (plentiful in Guadalajara) or places for young people to hang out lakeside.

Much of the lakeside social activity revolves around the Lake Chapala Society in Ajijic, a nonprofit charitable organization that has been a gathering place for expats for almost 50 years. In 2003, the LCS hit a membership high of around 2,400. With beautiful gardens, a library, and video rental shop, it is a place for people to meet with friends or join one of the ongoing groups or clubs. These include groups of writers, investors, gardeners, Spanish-language students, bridge players, computer hackers, and ham radio enthusiasts to name a few. LCS acts as an information clearinghouse, with regular visits from U.S. consulate and Social Security personnel to help U.S. citizens solve passport and other problems.

Local English-language newspapers, magazines, and billboards announce a wide variety of free gatherings and activities open to the public. Any number of groups and activities might be listed in the weekly announcements: Alcoholics Anonymous, the Axixic Masonic Lodge, Gamblers Anonymous, mixed volleyball, Tai-Chi and yoga, the Rotary Club, British Society, Canadian Club, German Club, exercise and art classes, art society shows, theater group rehearsals, Gurdjieff discussion groups, save the lake groups, and calls for volunteers to assist the Mexican Red Cross in raising funds for people with serious health problems. And there are many other volunteer organizations competing for people's time and money.

The largest and perhaps most interesting diversion for lakeside residents is Guadalajara. Guadalajara-bound buses run often along the lakeside highway.

History

Historians argue that Chapala may have been a pre-Hispanic village, settled by the Nahuatl sometime before the 12th century. What is known is that a tribe called the Cocas settled for a while near the site of the town of San Juan Cosala.

In 1524, five years after Hernán Cortés landed in Mexico, Spanish soldiers and priests entered the area. The town of Chapala was officially founded in 1538. For the next three centuries, mainly indigenous people and Franciscan missionaries inhabited the area.

In the years of Mexico's fight for independence from Spain, Mezcala Island, one of two islands in the lake, served as the base for a band of insurgents who held out against repeated attacks from the royalist army. Several structures built by the insurgents stand today and can be visited via boat.

It was not until the end of the 19th century that Mexicans began living near the lake. At the turn of the century, a parish priest described Chapala as a small fisherman's village with neoclassical Mediterranean-style summer residences. The remaining 19th-century buildings include the Arzapalo Hotel, the Casa Braniff (now the Cazadores Restaurant), the old Hotel Palmera, and Hotel Niza (now the Hotel Nido). The *palacio municipal* (town hall) and the old railroad station were built between 1913 and 1930.

The now-defunct railroad connecting Chapala with Guadalajara and then Mexico City enabled Guadalajara's high society to spend weekends and the Easter and Christmas holidays at the lake. The trip from Guadalajara by rail took only three hours, as opposed to 12 hours by stagecoach (and 45 minutes today by car).

Foreigners have been coming to the lake for a hundred years; some of the most famous have included D. H. Lawrence and W. Somerset Maugham. The first large wave of expats from the United States arrived in the 1950s and early 1960s, in the form of young, artistic men and women. The area soon developed a reputation as an art colony. During the 1970s, there was a large influx of retired military people to the area, especially to the town of Chapala.

WHERE TO LIVE

The majority of people living on Lake Chapala, including almost all of the foreigners, reside in or near one of the small towns on the lake's north shore. The largest concentration of foreign residents is in Ajijic and Chapala. Of all the lakeside towns, Ajijic has the most expensive real estate, though there are many high-priced residences in high-end developments on the hills overlooking the lake. In other lakeside towns, many just as—or more—beautiful than Ajijic, real estate can cost as much as 50 percent less. In general, a house on the lake or one with views will cost more than one in town.

The number of gated real estate developments in the area continues to grow. Older developments are expanding where they have the space. So far, new real estate projects have not greatly damaged the natural beauty or "Old Mexico" look and feel of the area, but some of the north shore hillsides are becoming more densely packed.

The best way to see how the locals live is to sign up for the weekly home tour, which operates every Thursday from November through April. Tickets are sold at the Nueva Posada Hotel in Ajijic.

Ajijic

Ajijic, because of its beauty and its history as an art colony, is the most popular town among foreign residents. Its name derives from a spring called Eye of the Water, found at the foot of the mountains that slope gently uphill from the lake.

The town itself is divided in two by the highway that runs from Chapala to Jocotepec, 15 miles (24 km) to the west. The part of town above the road is called, appropriately, Upper Ajijic. Below is the Village of Ajijic. The distance from the lakefront to the road is about five long blocks (at some points four), an easy uphill walk. The upper part of town climbs more steeply into the hills for another four or five blocks. The town itself is about one mile long from end to end.

The majority of full-time foreign residents live in town and have polite and friendly relationships with their Mexican neighbors. Some foreigners feel that living in town increases their sense of security, as neighbors look after their houses when they are not home. Others buy in gated communities, feeling more secure with other retirees close by. Often, newcomers want to live within walking distance of the Ajijic plaza. This desire is understandable because of the quaint atmosphere of downtown. But keep in mind that this part of town is also the noisiest, with frequent festivals, church bells, rooster calls, and the clop of horses' hooves along the narrow streets (not to mention cars and trucks).

Houses in Ajijic tend to be more expensive than those in other towns along the lake, with an average of $250,000–350,000 for a three-bedroom house with a nice big garden. It is still possible to find small houses in town selling for $125,000, or even less. Large estates, houses with views, and homes directly on the lake can cost more than a million dollars.

Chapala

The town of Chapala is home to a large number of foreigners, many of them retired military people. Chapala is an energetic town. Within a few steps of one downtown street corner there are five banks. Nearby, the market always has a busy crowd. In Chapala you get the sense of business being done. Yet, at the same time, Chapala has the feeling of a small, quiet village and old-fashioned, seaside resort. As the closest town on the lake to Guadalajara, Chapala receives more weekend visitors and offers more diverse activities than the other lakeside villages.

Chapala house prices are generally quite a lot less than those in Ajijic, ranging from $40,000 for a small two-bedroom to half a million for an elegant home with a view of the lake. The average price seems to be in the $130,000–150,000 range.

Other Lakeside Villages

San Antonio, San Juan Cosala, Jocotepec, and other lakeside villages each have a unique look and feel. While some people may consider Ajijic the most picturesque, each of the other villages has appealing characteristics of its own. La Floresta, for instance, has wide tree-lined streets, with large houses set back behind lawns or old stone walls. Parts of it feel like some residential areas of Houston, Texas, or Pasadena, California. San Antonio has narrow, cobbled streets, with houses packed close together. It has a small, very pretty plaza. Jocotepec, at the end of the lake, is a busy crossroads with a large, active downtown. The lower part of Jocotepec is not as pretty as some of the other towns on the lake, but views of the lake and mountains from the hills above town are spectacular. Several

Until recently, only a few hardy foreigners had purchased land on the South Shore, but with more people moving to the area, it is inevitable that the far side of the lake will be discovered and developed.

well-known local artists have settled in those hills. Parts of Buena Vista, in the hills above a golf course, look and feel like parts of Beverly Hills, California. El Chanté, on the lake to the east of Jocotepec, is an old Mexican village. Quiet and a little funky, it has grand, Italianate villas built on large lots among ancient trees along the lake. Property in these villages can cost anywhere from $75,000 to $500,000.

The South Shore

The road that heads to the south side of the lake is just to the west of Jocotepec. This road passes through rolling farmland that climbs gently from the lake up into the hills. From Ajijic, it is a 45-minute drive to San Pedro Tesistan, one of a number of small villages along the south shore.

The villages themselves are rural, run-down, simple, and pretty. So far, they have been more or less undisturbed by development. Until recently, only a few hardy foreigners had purchased land on the south shore, but with more people moving to the area, it is inevitable that the far side of the lake will be discovered and developed.

RENTING
Home rental prices in the area are still quite reasonable, with prices in Ajijic being the highest. All rental prices increase during the winter season. Rentals range from $550 per month for a two-bedroom, two-bathroom house in the Ajijic village to $1500 per month for a large, luxurious house with a view in upper Ajijic. Fancier estates will cost more. Expect to pay 20 percent to 40 percent less for an equivalent house in the other lakeside villages.

GETTING AROUND
Perhaps Lake Chapala's greatest convenience is its proximity to an international airport. The Miguel Hidalgo International Airport is only 30 minutes away on a good-quality four-lane highway. Most major U.S. and Mexican airlines offer direct flights into the airport, as do several European airlines. Because the airport serves one of the largest Mexican cities, ticket prices are often very reasonable. The taxi ride from the airport to Lake Chapala costs about 250–300 pesos ($24–28).

The drive into Guadalajara from the lake takes about one hour.

Not far from the lakeside villages are the two principal *autopistas* (toll highways) to Mexico's Pacific coast. The more southern highway hits the coast at Manzanillo. The trip takes about three hours. The other highway touches the coast about 150 miles (241 km) to the north above Puerto Vallarta. This trip takes about one and a half hours longer because the highway begins on the other side of Guadalajara. Both roads wind through the spectacular Sierra Occidental (Western Sierra) Mountains. (For driving information from the States, see the Guadalajara section.)

Guadalajara

LAY OF THE LAND
Guadalajara, Mexico's second largest city, has more than five million people, collectively known as *tapatios*. The city is located in the state of Jalisco on a high plateau at about 5000 feet (1,520 meters) in elevation.

Guadalajara, which comes from the Arabic word "Wad-al-jidara" (meaning river of stones), is a modern, sophisticated city that has an almost-perfect climate. The year-round average temperature is 66°F (18.8°C), with a normal maximum high of 87°F (30.5°C) and a low of 41°F (5°C). Average annual rainfall is 34 inches (86 cm).

Guadalajara is home to one of the largest, oldest, and most well-established foreign communities in Mexico. The exact number of members is not known, but estimates put it at between 20,000 and 30,000, mostly from the United States and Canada. The foreign population is made up of all ages and types, including young couples with kids, working people, and older retirees. A large and growing number are working in Guadalajara's expanding electronics industry or at one of the U.S. companies that now make Guadalajara their home base. There is also a large number of students attending Guadalajara's many colleges, universities, and language schools.

In Guadalajara, you will find many modern amenities found in any large city in the United States. Costco, Sam's Club, Wal-Mart, Office Depot, Sirloin Stockade, McDonald's, KFC, and Burger King are a few familiar names. There are English-language bookstores, libraries, and movie theaters. A counterbalance to all these modern U.S. franchises is one of the largest and most interesting, old-fashioned Mexican markets in the Western Hemisphere. El Mercado Libertad is a huge market with thousands of stalls selling everything from food to leather goods, live birds to iron candelabras. A trip to this huge and exciting Mercado Libertad is as much a cultural experience as it is a shopping bonanza. The market is located in Guadalajara's colonial downtown, near the cathedral, museums, and many grand colonial buildings. Here and in many parts of the city you can still easily get a feeling for Guadalajara's romantic past. Maybe it's the flowers, the parks, the many statues, and the quiet residential areas where houses have lush, colorful gardens hidden behind thick walls, often on handsome tree-shaded streets. All evoke images of gallant *caballeros* on horseback and beautiful dark-haired *señoritas* being serenaded by mariachi music.

Guadalajara has first-class universities as well as first-rate hospitals and medical care. Two university medical schools have modern equipment and high-quality medical personnel. The American Hospital, Hospital San Javier, and Hospital Carmen are considered some of the best in the city. Guadalajara also has about every type of alternative health practitioner known. In every case, the cost of care is half, or less, what it is in the United States.

The city is rich with arts, culture, and recreation. Guadalajara boasts a number of golf courses, sports and recreational facilities, great restaurants, and plenty of nightlife. And it's relatively inexpensive, with easy availability of goods and services.

During the past 30 years or so, modern buildings and skyscrapers have changed Guadalajara's skyline. The city has become a major business, electronics, and industrial giant. In the process, many historical and colonial buildings were destroyed and replaced with ugly, utilitarian buildings. Along with these changes have come heavier traffic, urban sprawl, and occasional serious air pollution. Population increases have created poor, overcrowded, and unattractive new *colonias* (neighborhoods), especially on the outskirts, where the city has spread into the surrounding countryside. In spite of all the changes in Guadalajara, though, many visitors still think that it is much prettier than most U.S. cities of its size.

Guadalajara's urban growth has engulfed nearby towns, like the still-picturesque towns of Tlaquepaque and Tonola, two of Mexico's main arts and crafts centers. Tlaquepaque, five miles from Guadalajara's center, still retains its colonial character. It has cobblestone streets, quaint plazas, outdoor cafés, and hundreds of shops selling beautiful handmade pottery, glass, jewelry, leather goods, wrought-iron and wooden furniture, and artwork. Tonala, not quite as grand as its neighbor Tlaquepaque, has similar items at lower prices.

A good source of information about life in the city, the American Society (San Francisco 3332, Colonia Chapalita, 333/121-2395) functions as a nonprofit clubhouse for American, Canadian, and European residents. Or contact the American Legion (San Antonio 143, Las Fuentes, 333/631-1208). Both organizations sponsor activities, such as dinner-dances, Spanish classes, free blood-pressure checkups, and lunches. Each will gladly offer information to newcomers and will send brochures upon request.

WHERE TO LIVE

Guadalajara has many new, upscale developments, which offer golf and mountain-view homes. In some neighborhoods on the surrounding hills, homes have views of the city and the Valley of Atemajac below. There are also quiet upper- and middle-class neighborhoods in the city that offer a very comfortable lifestyle as well as a good value. Neighborhoods with large numbers of Americans include Chapalita, Providencia, and Seattle. But you will find foreign residents living in many other parts of the city: some in stately homes in the beautiful downtown area, some in humble houses or apartments in various *colonias* just outside downtown, and many in the suburbs in both rural settings and gated retirement communities, many of these on golf courses. Housing prices run the gamut from the low hundred thousands up into the millions. A typical three-bedroom home near the Plaza de Sol, on a nice private street, sells for about $195,000.

Rentals in general are much less expensive than in Mexico City. For example, a furnished one-bedroom apartment with living room, kitchen, and bath goes for $275–300 per month. A beautiful, furnished six-room apartment (two bedrooms) in a nice neighborhood rents for $450 per month. An unfurnished garden-style condominium with pool (two bedrooms, two baths) in Guadalajara's best neighborhood costs $550 per month. A nice, modern two-bedroom home in Rancho Contento, a gated golf community, rents for $1,060 per month.

GETTING AROUND

Guadalajara is easy to reach, with an international airport a half hour away. Many flights from the States are direct and nonstop. By car, Guadalajara is only a little more than four hours from Mexico City and three hours to the beach resorts of Puerto Vallarta and Manzanillo. Even Laredo, Texas, is only twelve hours away, and the 1,000-mile (1,609 km) trip to El Paso can be accomplished in less than 18 hours, the great majority of which by four-lane highways. This long drive is most beautiful in the late summer or fall, near the end of the rainy season. That time of year, the countryside is at its greenest (even in the desert) and is covered by a wonderful variety of wildflowers.

San Miguel de Allende

It takes energy and a strong heart to walk the narrow, cobbled, and hilly streets of San Miguel, but it's worth every breathless moment. A colonial town, more than 400 years old, San Miguel has the feel of an old European town transported to Mexico. In fact, with its antique doors set in 16th-century buildings, colorfully painted bougainvillea-draped walls,

© Ken Luboff

San Miguel de Allende alley

ornate churches, clear skies, and steep surrounding hillsides, it could easily be mistaken for an Italian hill town. Six thousand feet (1,824 meters) above sea level, in Mexico's central mountain plain, San Miguel is home to about 100,000 Mexicans and 4,000–6,000 foreigners. At the center of town, on one side of its main square, stands a majestic, fantastical, pink-stone gothic cathedral (the Parroquia), which looks like the castle in Disney's Magic Kingdom. The builder reputedly designed and built it after seeing a postcard of an Italian church.

As you can imagine, San Miguel's beauty attracts a continual flow of tourists throughout the year. During winter, when snowbirds and large numbers of students are in residence, it can seem like San Miguel has been completely invaded by foreigners. The truth is, the large majority of tourists visiting San Miguel are Mexicans. Certainly, foreigners are conspicuous, but San Miguel remains a solidly Mexican town.

The streets of *centro* (downtown) are always bustling and lively. Only during the two hottest and driest months, April and May, does the tempo seem to slow. Boutiques and restaurants are numerous and do a vigorous business, especially on weekends, when large crowds of visitors from Mexico City, three hours south, overrun the town. Shopping in San Miguel is sheer delight for all who appreciate handmade crafts.

The best way to see and discover the hidden alleyways and surprise passageways of San Miguel is to walk. A friend calls San Miguel "one of the most sensual towns I know." Strolling around town is a pleasure—as long as you look where you are stepping and avoid falling off a high curb or into one of San Miguel's ubiquitous street holes, which another friend lovingly calls "gringo traps!" The town is densely packed, so everything is nearby and within easy reach. Usually, a five- to 10-minute walk will get you to an art opening or theater.

For those who live here, walking downtown to pick up the mail or meet someone for lunch or a cappuccino can be slow going. It is almost impossible to walk anywhere in *centro* without bumping into a friend on every other street corner. Steep and hilly parts of town outside of *centro* are easiest to reach by car or cab, unless you are in great shape and love to walk.

June–September is the rainy season. Rains can be spectacular, preceded by lightning and thunder and then a heavy semitropical downpour, which usually lasts for an hour or two. At times, rains and cloudy skies can extend for a week or more. After a rain, the town and countryside have a fresh scent of ozone and flowers. Outside of the rainy season, humidity is low.

Winters can be surprisingly cold—far colder than tourists expect—with occasional light frosts (the first heavy freeze in memory occurred in 1997). Homes have fireplaces and electric or gas space heaters. There is neither air-conditioning nor central heating, and, except for a few really hot and cold nights, they are not needed. But warm sweaters, socks, and jackets are definitely required in winter. Still, winter in San Miguel is a great deal warmer than in most parts of the United States, and the sky is rarely gray or overcast. Many days in mid-winter, you can wear shorts and light cotton shirts, but by evening it is time to bundle up a bit.

San Miguel is a town of celebrations. They happen so often that it can begin to feel like a holiday or saint's birthday is being celebrated almost daily. During these fiestas, incredibly loud, heart-stopping fireworks explode unexpectedly, day and night. People new to town think they are witnessing the beginning of a revolution. But most old-timers get used to the booms in the night. The family dog, on the other hand, lies quaking under the bed, head between paws. At certain times of year, including almost all of September and about two weeks around Easter, the celebrations are continuous and awesome.

San Miguel's Biblioteca

One of the central focuses of life in San Miguel de Allende is the *biblioteca publica* (public library), which is located in a beautiful colonial building that used to be a slaughterhouse. On its large patio, tables are set up around a colonial fountain, where foreigners and Mexicans get together to practice Spanish and English with each other. The library has one of the largest collections of English-language books in Mexico and an entire room devoted to books about Mexico. It operates a computer center, with classes for foreigners as well as Mexican kids and adults. Both its weekly house-and-garden tour and weekly flea market attract large crowds. Located in the library is a quiet café, with an ideal atmosphere for a relaxed lunch or a cappuccino and a read. The library also provides space for poetry readings and group meetings and has a small theater used for local productions and an ongoing film club.

The *biblioteca publica* produces and distributes San Miguel's popular English-language weekly newspaper, *Atención San Miguel*. With a large number of volunteers and income from sales of *Atención*, its house-and-garden tours, the flea market, café, and rental of theater space, the San Miguel library is a profitable enterprise. It has enough funds to be completely self-sustaining, while continually improving its collection and facilities.

The only problem the library seems to have are occasional turf wars between different factions in the community. These erupt every ten years or so. Then things quiet down and life goes on with typical San Miguel tranquility.

San Miguel has a large—and quirky—retirement community, which lives in harmony with a tolerant and accepting Mexican population. The town has a long history of attracting writers, artists, and black sheep. For decades, it remained hidden to the outside world, except for a few pioneers. But like so many other such gems, San Miguel has finally been discovered in a big way.

The effects are both positive and negative. As more foreigners have moved in, services have improved, new restaurants and bars have opened (some very good), and more cultural events are taking place. At the same time, real estate prices have become high, making San Miguel among the most expensive small cities in Mexico. The boom has attracted developers and others looking to make a fast buck—driving prices even higher.

Rental prices are still reasonable, but if you think you can move to San Miguel, live very cheaply, and find low-priced real estate, you may be disappointed. Still, even San Miguel is less expensive than most of the United States.

Besides the 4,000–6,000 foreign residents living in San Miguel year-round, another 3,000–4,000 snowbirds move to town for three or four months each winter. Add to these the foreign tourists who pass through town and those who come to study at one of the local art and language schools and you have a crowded, vibrant foreign social scene.

Mexicans in San Miguel are accepting of foreigners. The town has one of the oldest expatriate communities in Mexico; locals have had foreigners living in their midst for generations. The long interaction has helped create some lasting and very warm friendships. Nevertheless, most relationships between foreigners and Mexicans tend to be polite and good-natured, but somewhat formal.

Culturally, San Miguel is like a mini San Francisco (without the bay). A person could go nuts trying to keep up with the music festivals (classical and jazz), art openings, poetry readings, theater offerings, films, volunteer activities, and social gatherings. People even have to hide out at times to get some rest from the social whirl.

San Miguel has been an art colony for decades, and it still attracts artists and art students from all over the world. The art scene is vibrant. Established schools like the Instituto Allende, Bellas Artes, and Academia Hispano Americana have been offering fine art, music, and language classes since the late '50s. These days, at least 10 additional language and art schools operate in San Miguel. Add to this, classes given by individual instructors in disciplines as varied as aerobics, art for kids, flamenco, Holotropic Breathwork, horseback riding, jazz dance, meditation, Mexican cooking, tai chi, yoga, and a few others you can't even pronounce.

San Miguel has a selection of European and Mexican restaurants, a vegetarian restaurant, a restaurant that serves ribs, one that serves seafood, and an old-fashioned American place that serves burgers and fries. Happily, there is only one U.S. fast-food joint—so far.

After eating, a walk around the dimly lit, romantic streets may be enough for you. If it's not, bars and restaurants offer after-dinner music and dancing, including salsa, jazz, blues, rock and roll, and disco. And a good cup of coffee, espresso, or cappuccino is easy to find any time of day or evening in small cafés and restaurants. Check out the Italian café in the Bellas Artes for an afternoon coffee.

San Miguel is known for its thermal hot springs. There are at least 10 such springs within 10 minutes of San Miguel. The most popular are La Gruta, Escondido, and Taboada.

A Single Woman in San Miguel de Allende

"Why do you want to leave California?" my Uncle Arthur asked. "Why do you want to abandon your friends and family and go to some godforsaken Mexican hill town where you don't have a job and nobody knows your name?"

"That's why, Arthur," I said.

What I should perhaps have explained is that San Miguel de Allende is not exactly your average godforsaken Mexican hill town. San Miguel isn't even really Mexico, the gringo old-timers will tell you ruefully, acknowledging the fact that this famous artists' colony is hardly representative of the whole.

What it is for me and the many gringas like me—widowed, divorced, gay, or whatever, but unequivocally single and happy about it—is a place to reinvent ourselves, to wade shallowly or plunge deeply into the arts, to have massages or facelifts or affairs, or maybe just to watch the bananas ripen and ponder the curious courses of our own lives.

Like Mexico itself, San Miguel is a mixed-up juxtaposition of cultures, peoples, incomes, religions, lifestyles, and philosophical outlooks. And what's nicest about San Miguel is that these outlandish life forms live peaceably side by side. Burros and RVs, Indians and yuppies, mariachis and Mormon missionaries, painters and peasants and priests hang out companionably in the *jardín*. We get to know each other, smile, murmur *buenas tardes*, and go about our business.

And there are certainly a lot of businesses to go about in San Miguel. Restaurants for every taste and pocketbook, handsome *artesanías* and upscale art galleries, cheap *pensiones* and luxury bed-and-breakfasts, discos and devil dancers, *horchata* and *tamarindo* and tamales for a few pesos on the corner and bourbon and filet mignon in the ritzy joints.

And everywhere are the fiestas for which San Miguel is famous.

History

The village of San Miguel de los Chichimecas was founded by Fray Juan de San Miguel in 1542 as a Spanish outpost in hazardous countryside occupied by the Chichimeca. Before that, it was called Itzuinpan. By 1555, San Miguel was a safe stop along the road between Mexico City and the rich silver mines of Zacatecas. Later, the name became San Miguel El Grande, in deference to its growing weaving and leather trade. The College of San Francisco de Sales was founded in San Miguel in 1734.

On September 8, 1810, the little town of San Miguel was catapulted into Mexican history. A small group of men from San Miguel, led by Ignacio de Allende, Juan Aldama, and Colonel Narciso Maria Loreto

There's Saint Michael's Day, of course. There's Cinco de Mayo and 16 de Septiembre. There's Corpus Christi and Semana Santa and the Day of the Dead. There are the transvestite *locos* who take over the town on the feast of San Antonio. There's the *pamplonada,* when the bulls are let loose in the streets to pursue the thousands of young *mexicanos* and occasional intrepid *turistas* who get loaded and prove their manhood the old-fashioned way by tempting death.

It's possible, of course, to insulate yourself from all this messy, pullulating life if you wish. In the golden gringo ghettoes on the hills above the old town, you can hide at your leisure from all things Mexican except the cheap labor and the glorious view, trekking occasionally into Querétaro to pick up supplies direct from *los Estados Unidos* at Sam's or WalMart.

For many of us, though—and I'm thinking particularly of the single women—San Miguel offers the chance to explore corners of our psyches left unvisited during lives devoted to careers, children, and husbands. It's our turn now. Women marry younger and live longer, and so are more often left alone in life. We bear widowhood better, I have read, find greater consolation in solitude, learn to live on our own and like it. Well, we'd damn well better, hadn't we?

And San Miguel gives us ample opportunity to explore ourselves. For the artistic, there are the Instituto Allende and Bellas Artes. For the linguistic, there are Spanish schools on every corner. For the hedonistic, there are wine, song, and—I am told—fantastically cheap drugs. For the altruistic, there are unlimited opportunities to heal and to help. And for the fatalistic, there is that unmatchably practical philosophy that is the Mexican outlook on death. So that's what I should have told my uncle. I get to be myself here, Arthur.

by Kendal Dodge Butler

de Canal, had been plotting to overthrow the Spanish government of Mexico. Conspiring with them was Father Miguel Hidalgo from the nearby town of Dolores. When he learned that the Spanish viceroy had discovered the plot, Father Hidalgo made his famous speech, the Grito de Dolores—the Mexican Declaration of Independence—and inspired a poorly armed ragtag band of rebels to march to San Miguel. Along the way, others joined in, and the revolution was under way. Within a year, Hidalgo, Aldama, and Allende were all betrayed and beheaded. It took 10 more years to end the Spanish rule of Mexico.

After the War of Independence, San Miguel became San Miguel de Allende. The first outsider known to move to San Miguel was Sterling Dickinson, who arrived in 1937. Dickinson, who died in San Miguel in 1998, was a pioneer who helped found the Instituto Allende. After World War II, American soldiers on the GI Bill began coming to the Instituto Allende to study Spanish. Around that time, artists and writers also began arriving to join the small but growing expatriate community.

WHERE TO LIVE

The heart of San Miguel is its historic downtown or *centro*. In *centro*, most homes are restored colonial-style structures, some 350 years old or more. *Centro* is where the action is, and, as such, is one of the most sought-after living areas. With the exception of a few other coveted parts of town, the closer you are to Juárez Park in *centro*, the more expensive the real estate. Views of the Parroquia (main cathedral) and other downtown churches, as well as the sunset, can greatly increase the price of property. You'll usually find a wide assortment of homes on the market, but anyone wishing to build downtown will find that good lots are few and far between.

The neighborhoods surrounding *centro* are called *colonias*. The majority of foreign residents live in *centro* and the *colonias* of Balcones, Atascadero, San Antonio, and Guadiana, which all have a mix of Mexicans and foreigners. Most other *colonias*, which are poorer, are predominantly Mexican, although some foreigners live in every part of town.

Centro

If you can still find one, a two-bedroom, one-bathroom fixer-upper on a small lot in *centro* might sell for $150,000. From there, houses and estates range upward into the millions. The average may be about $300,000.

Atascadero & Los Balcones

Both *colonias* are on hills overlooking town. Both have a mix of large and small houses, though Balcones is newer and more exclusive. Prices range from $250,000 up into the millions.

Other *Colonias*

Guadiana, Guadalupe, Olimpo, Valle de Maiz, and Independencia are in various stages of gentrification. Of these, Guadiana is probably the high-end, with bargains still to be found in the others. Prices range the gamut from $150,000 up.

Los Frailes

Just 10 minutes from downtown by car or bus, this *fraccionamiento* (subdivision) of mostly wealthy and middle-class Mexicans and foreigners has great deals. Large homes with views of the lake start at $225,000.

RENTING

During high season, December–April, the price of rentals increases. More expensive properties always include servants. Long-term rentals cost less. A house renting long-term for $1,000 per month could rent for $1,500 per week during the high season. Long-term rentals in *centro* might be as low as $800 a month or as high as $4,500 or more, depending on size, location, views, and condition.

GETTING AROUND

It takes more than a little effort to get to San Miguel. The closest airport is in León, Guanajuato, about one and a half hours away by car. Aeromexico, Air California, American, Continental, and other airlines offer regular daily flights into León. Taxis run to and from the airport and San Miguel for about $50 each way. Those living in San Miguel usually drive to the airport and leave their cars if they are making a short trip out of Mexico.

Another option is to fly into Mexico City and then take a bus to San Miguel. Flights into Mexico City's airport are more frequent and generally less expensive. Just outside the airport is a plush Aeroplus bus, which travels nonstop to Querétaro in three hours for about $15. From Querétaro, it is easiest to take a taxi to San Miguel, a 40-minute trip, for $15–20. You can take a bus as well.

Taxis in town are ubiquitous and inexpensive, as are buses.

Guanajuato

Guanajuato is the jewel in the crown of Mexico's colonial cities. It is shaped like a huge fruit bowl, with brightly painted houses climbing up its sides. The houses are not located along conventional streets, but are reachable by way of steep, narrow stairs and alleyways that snake up the sides of the bowl.

On the floor of the bowl, downtown Guanajuato has a series of wonderful Italianate plazas, with colonial hotels, outdoor cafés, and cobblestone streets. Located here are the greatest influences in the life of the city: the University of Guanajuato, government offices (this is the capital of the state of Guanajuato), and a unique atmosphere that attracts thousands of tourists.

What really sets Guanajuato apart is its youthful, cultural, and festive atmosphere. On typical nights during the school year, students crowd cafés and narrow streets around the university. On weekend nights, with thousands of tourists in town, it is not unusual for mimes and other street performers to draw crowds in front of the Teatro Juarez, a copy of the Paris Opera house built in 1903.

> *What really sets Guanajuato apart is its youthful, cultural, and festive atmosphere.*

In the fall, Guanajuato hosts the Festival Cervantino, one of Mexico's biggest cultural events. First-rate performers from all over the world come to the city. Ballet, theater, and music occupy all the stages in town and overflow onto the stages of nearby towns like San Miguel and Dolores Hidalgo.

Services in and around Guanajuato are good. The León International Airport is only about a half hour away. From there, you can fly on American directly to Dallas, on Aero Mexico to Los Angeles, or on Continental to Houston. The town has an Internet service provider and a large and colorful downtown market. In the city of León, about 45 minutes away, you'll find a Price Club and a few very fancy, decidedly uptown shopping malls.

Real estate and rental prices are lower in Guanajuato than in nearby San Miguel de Allende, although rentals in *centro* are difficult to find. Surprisingly, there are very few foreigners living here, and you will rarely hear English spoken. The expats who do live in Guanajuato are mostly artists or those who love the culture of the city. Most live in either Valenciana or Marfil, both just outside the city center. If you go for a visit, stay at the Casa de los Espiritus Alegres (House of the Happy Spirits), a bed-and-breakfast in Marfil started by an American woman and now run by her husband.

Pátzcuaro, Michoacán

The quiet colonial town of Pátzcuaro is located just a few kilometers above Lake Pátzcuaro, at an altitude of about 7,200 feet (2,189 meters), in the heart of Purepecha country. The lake itself is located in a beautiful picture-postcard setting in the state of Michoacán, known for its pine-covered mountain landscape of rivers, lakes, and high volcanoes. Here you will find the Plaza Vasco de Quiroga, another of Mexico's magnificent colonial plazas. Adding to the picture-postcard setting are white-painted homes with red-tiled roofs. Fanning out around the center are newer, less picturesque areas of town.

Until recently, only a few foreigners had ever lived in and around Pátzcuaro. The number of adventurous outsiders living in the area (mostly from the States) has grown to about 200. The local population is about 75,000. Foreigners living here are attracted by the low cost of living, the still-low real estate prices, and Pátzcuaro's beauty and relaxed atmosphere.

A very good friend bought 20 acres near the lake a few years ago and operates an organic and permaculture farm on the property. She says the soil is rich and the culture in the area even richer. We have seen her occasionally since her move to Pátzcuaro, and each time she seems ecstatically happy with her new life.

As quiet as it is, Pátzcuaro still has some amenities and activities for foreign residents. There is the *biblioteca* (library), with its good selection of English books; the local Teatro Emperador Caltzontzin, with its cultural events; the Center for Language and Ecotours of Pátzcuaro, a Spanish language and culture school; and a museum of popular arts. Aside from these facilities, the town's main activities revolve around shopping, sitting in one of the two town plazas people-watching, and eating at restaurants. Friday market, where locals display a variety of handmade crafts, including blankets, pottery, serapes, copper, and grotesque masks, is a wonderful experience. Pátzcuaro is also a place to buy carved wooden doors and wooden furniture.

Throughout the year, a steady stream of Mexican and some foreign tourists visit Pátzcuaro. But tourism explodes during Christmas, Easter, and Día de los Muertos—Day of the Dead—when thousands of mostly Mexican visitors come to watch ceremonial graveside activities of Pátzcuaro and Janitzios Purepechas (descendants of the former Tarascan culture).

In the surrounding mountains are a number of very picturesque towns. Tourist favorites include Paracho, about 70 miles (113 km) west, where hundreds of shops manufacture and sell guitars and other stringed instruments lining the streets. Other favorites include Tocuaro, 10 km (6 miles) outside of Pátzcuaro, where some of Mexico's best mask makers live, and Santa Clara del Cobre (also called Villa Escalante), 20 km (12 miles) south of Pátzcuaro, where the manufacture of copper articles has been taken to a new artistic level. Another must see, Tingambata houses ruins dating to A.D. 450–900. The ruins include a ball court, temple pyramids, and an underground tomb.

The fact that Pátzcuaro is only about 45 minutes away from the large and culturally active colonial city of Morelia goes a long way to offset its small size and feeling of remoteness. Morelia, with about 500,000 residents, is the capital of the state of Michoacán. It has one of the most impressive and largest colonial central plazas in Mexico. A university town, Morelia boasts a good variety of restaurants, several language schools, bookstores, and movie theaters.

Pátzcuaro is small and laid back, with accessible cultural activities, but winters are cold because of the altitude and relatively high humidity. This may discourage some foreigners looking to relocate.

PACIFIC COAST

Mazatlán 15D 40 ↑ To Durango

SINALOA

Río Las Cañas 15

DURANGO

Huejuquilla ✈

Laguna Agua Grande

Acaponeta

Novillero

NAYARIT

Laguna Agua Brava

Jesús María ✈

Laguna El Valle

Ruiz

Laguna Los Pericos

Mexcaltitán

Santiago Ixcuintla

Playa Los Corchos

74 15

Huajimic ✈

Río Grande de Santiago

San Blas

Tepic ✈

Bahía de Matanchén

Santa Cruz 76

200

▲ Volcán Sanganguey

Chapalilla

68D

15D

Bahía de Jaltemba

Las Varas

Rincón de Guayabitos

15

Sayulita

San Sebastián ✈

Río Ameca

Punta Mita

Bahía de Banderas

Puerto Vallarta

Mascota ✈

Ameca

200

70

Cabo Corrientes

El Tuito

Talpa ✈

Los Volcanes

Acatlán de Juárez

Aquiles Serdán

Punta Tehualmixtle

Punta Peñitas

Río María García

Cuatla

Juchitlán

San Clemente

54

La Cruz de Loreto

La Gloria

Tomatlán

JALISCO

80

Autlán

200

Sierra de Manantlán Eco-Zone

Nevado de Colima ▲

Volcán de Colima ▲

Minatitlán

54D

Bahía Chamela

Chamela (El Super)

Melaque

Colima ✈

Tenacatita

Bahía Tenacatita

Barra de Navidad

Manzanillo

110

Bahía Manzanillo

0   25 mi

0   25 km

Cuyutlán

200

To Ixtapa-Zihuatanejo and Acapulco

PACIFIC OCEAN

© AVALON TRAVEL PUBLISHING, INC.

© Ken Lutoff

Pacific Coast

The Pacific Coast region does not have the historical or cultural importance of Mexico's Central Highlands. Both big cities and small towns along the coast cater to tourists and have a more transient feeling than inland towns and cities. Yet, large numbers of foreigners of all ages have relocated to this region to enjoy the easy pace of life and the great climate for most of the year. During the hottest months of summer, many visit family in the States or travel to the cooler mountains nearby.

Mazatlán

LAY OF THE LAND

Mazatlán remains one of the prime locations for city living at the beach. This city of 600,000 residents offers an alternative to the more sophisticated, glitzy, and expensive Puerto Vallarta. Foreigners living in Mazatlán seem to be down to earth and fairly laid back. Most

Expatriate Perspective

Bob and Lee Story tell us what attracted them to Mazatlán:

We know that we wanted to be close to water, as we had been living aboard our 41-foot Gibson houseboat, *Revelry,* on the Mississippi River just north of St. Louis for almost 10 years. We were tired of the cold winters, and we liked the idea of retiring on the Gulf Coast of Alabama and northern Florida.

For many years, friends recommended that we check out Mazatlán, but we preferred to stay in the States. In February 1996, we had reservations to vacation in the Destin, Florida, area, but those were canceled due to hurricane damage. The only warm, sunny location that our time-share club had available on short notice was in Mexico.

We went and immediately fell in love with this country. The people are so friendly, the architecture is creative, the land is awesome, and the prices were so low that there was a chance we could retire early. We decided that this was the country for us. All we had to do was find our corner.

We began exploring Guadalajara, Lake Chapala, Manzanillo, Playa del Carmen, Cancún, and the coast

moved here for the low prices, great weather, fishing, golf, and the relaxed atmosphere. The majority are in their 60s and up, but some are working Americans and Canadians in their 40s and 50s.

This is not a town where you will find much New Age thought, a powerful group of writers or artists, or much in the way of intellectual pretentiousness. In fact, the foreign community has a small-town, Midwest feel. The people are conservative and friendly. Most residential areas have a congenial mix of foreigners and Mexicans.

Mazatlán is really three cities in one, stretched out along a beautiful beach on the Pacific Ocean. At the southern end is the port of Mazatlán, north of the port is *centro,* and farther north, stretching along the coast, is where tourist hotels, restaurants, and shopping centers crowd the landscape.

Mazatlán's *centro* is where there is the sense of a city that has seen better days. Here are tattered and worn-out formerly regal colonial buildings sitting alongside newer, more humble dwellings. Some of these run-down mansions have been, or are in the process of being, restored. Many are still in ruins, just waiting to be bought and resurrected. *Centro* has the feel of many other mid-sized Mexican towns, with very clean, residential streets and pockets of high energy around the shopping areas, main market, and grand cathedral in the center of the Yucatán Peninsula. In January 1997, we gave Mazatlán "the acid test" and loved it. In June 1998, we left St. Louis with all our gear and arrived at our new hometown two weeks later.

We chose Mazatlán because it is not totally dependent upon tourism. Mazatlán has a mix of industries: shrimp and tuna fishing, freezing and canning, light manufacturing, commerce and port activities, plus tourism—which accounts for about half of the area's economic wealth. We wanted a medium-sized city, and Mazatlán fit that bill. We wanted to be able to easily merge with the locals, something Mazatlán also offered.

We are in the process of buying a new *casa* on a charming cul-de-sac of about 15 *casas*, with a mix of about half Mexicans and half Americans. We are happy and can tell pleasant stories of our life here. We have made friends with Mexicans, as well as Canadian and American expatriates.

It wasn't easy leaving family and friends in the States, but they look at it this way: We've moved to a great vacation spot for them. And they're coming to see us!

of town. "Old Town," the name some local expats have given centro, has some pretty good restaurants and an archaeological museum.

Mazatlán's only hills tower over and have breathtaking views of centro, Mexico's largest Pacific port, and the city's sprawling commercial and residential districts. The highest of the hills is called Ice Box Hill; in the early 20th century, ships unloaded ice into a cave, called El Diablo, cut into the hillside. The cave is still there, on the ocean side of the hill. Nearby is Cerro del Creston, where the El Faro lighthouse sits on a hill 500 feet above the sea.

About four miles (6.5 km) north of downtown, along a four-lane beachfront avenue called the Malecón, is the main tourist area of Mazatlán—the Zona Dorado, or Golden Zone. This is where the majority of Mazatlán's large hotels, restaurants, bars, fast-food joints, galleries, and real estate offices are located. Crowds invade this part of town during the main tourist season (fall and winter) and especially during the famous Mazatlán Carnaval, one of the largest Mardi Gras celebrations in Latin America.

Mazatlán is a port of call for the "Love Boat." Well, not *the* Love Boat—but almost the same thing. Four cruise lines stop here regularly, on what they call Mexico's Riviera. These are big babies, with one ship bringing as many as 2,200 passengers! And when they hit the Golden Zone they engulf it in a spree of spending and partying.

To the east and north of the Golden Zone are the residential areas, where the majority of Mazatlán's 3,500 full-time and 7,000 part-time (winter-season) foreign residents live. This number includes people living in RVs and the few who live on boats in the marina.

Foreigners choose Mazatlán for its proximity to the States, its great climate (with an average temperature of 82°F (27.7°C) year-round), its low cost of living, and its relatively low crime rate (the city has robberies, but little violent crime). They also choose it for its physical beauty, with long, wide beaches running from one end of town to the other. To the north and south of the city are many miles of deserted beach, some of which are now being developed. Mountains frame the horizon to the east.

Living is easy in Mazatlán. Because it is near the U.S. border, stores carry most anything shoppers could want and at generally lower prices than other Mexican cities. Shoppers can choose between many large—or mega—markets, the main *mercado* in centro, or the many small groceries and fruit stores throughout town. There is also an excellent local English newspaper, the *Pacific Pearl*, which regularly publishes charts comparing the prices of selected items at local stores. There is no English bookstore, but the second floor of the library downtown has a stock of English books, and so do all major hotel gift shops.

> *Living is easy in Mazatlán. Because it is near the U.S. border, stores carry most anything shoppers could want and at generally lower prices than other Mexican cities.*

Mazatlán has a sufficiently large number of doctors, dentists, plastic surgeons, pharmacies, and medical clinics for its population. There is even a branch of the Betty Ford Clinic here—called the Oceanica Clinic. The hospital of choice among expats is the Sharp Hospital, a sister of the Sharp Hospital in San Diego. The staff speaks English, and the hospital has an intensive-care unit, modern lab and radiology equipment, and provides emergency air service to a U.S. hospital if necessary. The hospital also honors most U.S. and Canadian insurance policies (but check your policy to be sure). Ambulance services are provided by the Mexican Red Cross.

Each year in November and December, Mazatlán hosts the Fall Festival of the Arts at the Angela Peralta Theater. Performances include regional dance groups, orchestras from various parts of Mexico, local performers, and chamber groups from the United States.

The biggest show in town is the Mazatlán Carnaval, said to be the third largest in the world after Río de Janeiro and New Orleans. It goes on day and night for five days and completely takes over the town with parades, music, dancing, fireworks, and many thousands of tipsy and happy tourists.

Mazatlán has seven movie theaters, some showing first-run U.S. films in English with Spanish subtitles. Local cable TV offers only four or five channels in English. People who like to watch TV install satellite dishes. There is a large Blockbuster video store in the Zona Dorado and several smaller video rental stores.

In November each year, the El Cid Golf and Country Club hosts its annual Tournament for Amateurs, which draws more than 300 amateur golfers. El Cid inaugurated the annual Team Tennis Challenge Tournament in November 1998. Also in November, anglers compete in the annual Marina El Cid Billfish Classic. Open to all anglers with boats, it is Mazatlán's largest fishing tournament.

The Estrella Del Mar development (800/967-1889 in U.S., 800/PAR-GOLF in Mexico) was built more than 20 years ago by Art Linkletter and friends (we are told that Art is no longer involved). The development itself hasn't grown much over the years, but its 18-hole golf course, right on the beach, is spectacular and of championship level.

The 18-hole course at the El Cid resort was designed by Larry Hughes. In December 1998, El Cid opened a nine-hole course designed by Lee Trevino—his first architectural project in Mexico. Club Campestre has a smaller nine-hole course. El Cid, Costa de Oro, Hotel Hacienda, Club Reforma, and Gaviotas Tennis Club all have excellent tennis courts.

Commercially, Mazatlán is primarily a shrimp and tuna port, but sport fishermen ecstatically haul in a wide variety of fish, including marlin, swordfish, mahi mahi, wahoo, and sailfish. Many residents have fishing boats docked at one of the three marinas in town. Locals also go to El Salto lakes, about 40 miles (64 km) inland to the northeast, for bass fishing.

To the east of Mazatlán is the Sierra Occidental range. Gold was first discovered in these mountains in the 16th century. In the mid-1800s, the mining towns of Concordia and Copala were founded. A drive to these towns makes for a pleasant day trip. This is also a great area for hiking and exploring.

Unlike San Miguel, Cuernavaca, and Puerto Vallarta, Mazatlán has no well-known language or art schools. This eliminates the youthful intellectual energy that you find in those cities. Nevertheless, you can study Spanish at the Centro de Idiomas (669/981-1483), reputed to be a very good school, or join the Friday night Spanish Conversation Club (669/916-7223) held in the reception area of the school.

You won't find anything very spiritually offbeat here. Churches include Lutheran, Apostolic, Seventh Day Adventist, Mormon, Christian Fellowship (offering bilingual services), and, of course, Catholic.

History

Even though Mazatlán had been known to Spanish sailors since 1531, when Spanish explorer Nuno de Guzman founded the town, it took the Germans to really get the place going. Until a group of German immigrants moved here in the 1830s, Mazatlán was fairly uncivilized. The Germans developed the port in order to import agricultural equipment. Then they left their mark on the town in the form of Pacifico beer, which is manufactured in Mazatlán.

Long before the arrival of the Spanish or the Germans, Mazatlán was called Mazatl (Place of the Deer) by the Nahuatl who lived here. Indeed, it is not hard to imagine huge herds of deer roaming the plain between the ocean and the mountains to the east.

In the early 1600s, almost 100 years after the town was officially inaugurated by Spain, gold and silver were mined in nearby mountain towns, transported to the bay, and loaded into Spanish galleons for the trip back to Spain. Stories abound of famous pirates attacking these ships, stealing the treasure, and burying it along the coast.

During the short reign of French Emperor Maximilian in the 1860s, Mexican troops fighting French troops in Mazatlán seized a large quantity of gold from the mines, helping to bring about Maximilian's defeat.

By the beginning of the 20th century, Mazatlán's port was thriving, and its tourist industry was beginning to develop. Early visitors were especially attracted to the weather and the good hunting and fishing in the region. Throughout the 20th century, Mazatlán continued to attract sportsmen and vacationers, as it does today, looking for warm water, a great climate, and an enjoyable place to relax. Although the hunting isn't what it used to be, the fishing here is still first rate.

WHERE TO LIVE

The majority of Mazatlán's foreign residents live in the relatively new developments on the southern end of the Golden Zone. These areas are quiet, clean, and safe. Neighborhoods like Las Gaviotas and Sabalo Country Club (not really a country club) are popular because real estate prices are low, the areas are tranquil, and the beach and marinas are nearby. Even in gated communities on golf courses, marinas, or the beach, prices are reasonable. A small number of foreigners prefer the more Mexican feel of the old part of town. Some of the most expensive real estate is found on Ice Box and Lomas Hills, where the views of the city and harbor are spectacular. We were surprised by the amount of prime, undeveloped land we saw in Mazatlán. Just north of town, along the beach, there are large stretches of undeveloped property without a house in sight. Even in town, on the north side, we saw large undeveloped tracts. Such land provided a contrast to the densely packed centro and the more developed coastal cities like Puerto Vallarta.

Here is an idea of some of the real estate prices in Mazatlán. El Cid Resort is the largest residential and commercial development in town. It includes a large hotel on the beach and, through a gated entrance to the rear, a residential area on a beautiful, 18-hole, par-72 golf course. Set around the course are both modest and opulent homes, including a $2 million home being built by a Mexican rock star. Among the private homes are groups of tennis villas built around several shared courts. These sell for $125,000 and up. A two-bedroom, three-bath home in El Cid sells for about $260,000.

Condos in Marina Del Rey go from $199,000 to $320,000, many with great views. A private home in Sabalo Country Club or Las Gaviotas, both non-gated, middle-class neighborhoods two or three blocks from the beach, can sell for about $112,000.

Ice Box and Lomas Hills are in the uptown part of central Mazatlán. The views from the hills—both up and down the coast—can be breathtaking. Here you'll find a mix of large and small homes, older and new homes, and several with ultra-modern architecture.

Most homes on the hills are owned by Mexican families, with a few foreigners scattered around. Finding houses to buy or land for sale on the hills is difficult and expensive. Homes here sell for $300,000 and up.

North Side

Several small new gated beachside developments have sprung up north of town on the beach road. Prices in these developments vary, with beachfront homes starting at $150,000.

Finding something to rent at a low price is fairly easy here. An average two-bedroom house rents for around $500 per month. In El Cid,

© Ken Luboff

Mazatlán Beach in front of RV park

without much effort, we found a three-bedroom, two-bathroom house for $700 per month. Check the bulletin board outside the *Pacific Pearl* newspaper office for home sales and rentals.

RV Parks
Mazatlán attracts quite a few RVers and sailors, especially during winter. RVers usually hang out with other RVers (staying at the same park), sailors with other sailors. We counted eight RV parks with approximately 950 sites. They include Las Canoas (2800 Avenida Sabalo, Cerritos, 669/914-1616, www.mexonline.com/lascanoas.htm), Holiday Trailer Park (Cerritos, 669/913-2578), Maravillas (on the beach, Alfredo Tirado #1470, Playa de Sabalo, Cerritos, 669/914-0400), Mar Rosa Trailer Park (Avenida Camaron Sabalo #702, beachfront next to Hotel Fiesta Americana, 669/913-6187, www.pacificpearl.com/marrosa/index.htm), Las Palmas Trailer Camp (Avenida Cameron Sabalo #333, 669/913-5311), La Posta Trailer Park (Calzada R. Buelna #7, Centro, 669/983-5310), Playa Escondida (North Side of Playa Cerritos, 669/988-0077), and San Bartolo (Avendia Camaron Sabalo opposite Playa Sabalo, 669/913-5765 or 669/983-5755).

Marinas
Marinas include Marina El Cid Mazatlán (Avenida Camaron Sabalo, 669/916-3468, www.elcid.com/mazatlan_marinas.html), Marina

Mazatlán (Blvd. Marina Mazatlán, Esq. Sabalo Cerritos s/n, 669/916-7799), Isla Mazatlán (669/916-0833), Club Nautico (669/981-5185).

GETTING AROUND

Most foreign residents own cars, which they drove down from the States. Many make the relatively short trip back to the States once or twice a year. Most also use their cars to get around town. Those who don't drive recommend taking buses, which are inexpensive and run often. Taxis include both convertibles and hardtops (convertibles cost more). With either, agree on the fare before you get in for the ride.

Mazatlán is easily accessible by car from the States, only 735 miles (1,183 km) south of the U.S. border at Nogales (just south of Tucson)—the first large beach resort/port city you come to heading down Mexico's west coast. The drive from Nogales takes a day and a half (a day if you push hard) on good-quality, four-lane Highway 15.

It would be an even easier trip if it weren't for the harassment that some drivers receive from Mexican officials on this stretch of road. Immigration at Nogales usually goes pretty smoothly, but about 21 miles (34 km) into Mexico, you come to an *aduana* (customs) inspection point. The officers have been known to harass travelers occasionally with a threat to search cars until a *mordida* is paid, although the government is trying to put a stop to this practice.

You may be stopped again at the Sonora/Sinaloa state line by the PGR, a bunch of thuggish-looking federal police searching for guns and drugs. (Drugs *entering* Mexico? Say what?) They often carry automatic weapons and .45s. Just the threat of having your car searched in high desert temperatures is enough to raise your blood pressure a few degrees. If you are stopped, just be polite and do as the officers say. Nobody has been hurt by these guys—except in the pocketbook. It is smooth sailing once you enter the state of Sinaloa, where Mazatlán is located.

South of Mazatlán, the road continues on to Tepic and Guadalajara and connects with the highway heading south to Puerto Vallarta. Heading north on this road, from Tepic to Mazatlán, you'll reach a checkpoint at which drivers must stop at an old-fashioned auto mechanic's pit for an inspection of the undersides of their cars. The inspection is done quickly with no aggravation, though the slow-moving line of traffic before you reach the checkpoint can drive you crazy. Have a book ready.

Nayarit

When you make the drive down the west coast of Mexico from Nogales, across the border from Arizona, most of the trip takes you through coastal flatlands. In the distance to your left is the Sierra Madre Occidental mountain range, and beyond that to the east lies Mexico's highland plateau. This is mainly farm country, with fishing villages and tourist towns dotting the coastline. Finally, about 300 miles (483 km) south of Mazatlán, the terrain changes and you find yourself in another world. You have reached the Mexican state of Nayarit, where the mountain range touches the sea, and the terrain turns to tropical jungle.

Nayarit is one of Mexico's smallest, least known, and least populated states, with an area of only 10,664 square miles (27,620 square km) and a population of less than one million people. It has also has been one of the last coastal states to be driven by the development craze. This is especially true in the northern part of the state, which is home to both the Huichol and Cora people.

The Huichol and the Cora live in scattered settlements in virtually inhospitable and inaccessible areas of the Sierra Madre mountains. Not much has been written about the quiet Cora, but the Huichol have drawn attention to themselves over the last forty years through their distinctive art, which is sold in galleries in the large cities of Mexico and the United States.

Through their elaborate yarn paintings, beaded bowls, and beaded animal heads, Huichol artists, inspired by visions seen while using peyote, depict with complex images the spiritual mythology of their culture. To the Huichols, peyote cactus is a much revered gift from the gods, with hallucinogenic effects that help them to achieve enlightenment and shamanic powers. Every symbol in a piece of Huichol art reveals ancient beliefs and ritual ceremonies.

It is worth taking the curvy and mountainous coastal highway through the jungles in the northern part of the state. Soon enough, the road flattens out for the trip south toward Nuevo Vallarta, Nayarit's largest tourist development, and the city of Puerto Vallarta, just over the southern border of Nayarit in the state of Jalisco.

By bus, it is a pleasant and inexpensive trip from the States to Mazatlán. Several major Mexican bus lines run from Mexicali, Nogales, and other large border towns to Mazatlán and points south. We recommend top-of-the-line buses for long trips; check out prices for *lujo* and *executivo* buses, which are the most comfortable. Buses traveling both north and south of Mazatlán are pulled over and inspected.

The Pacifico and Sinaloaense trains head south from Mexicali on the U.S. border and arrive in Mazatlán about 20 hours later. Each stops along the way at Nogales, Hermosillo, Culiacán, Obregon, and a few other places. We prefer the more comfortable Pacifico. As with buses, we recommend that you take first-class trains.

If you prefer to fly, many inexpensive flights arrive in Mazatlán daily from Los Angeles, San Francisco, Phoenix, Seattle, Vancouver, and points east.

Puerto Vallarta

LAY OF THE LAND

Though Mexico has many thousands of miles of spectacular coastline, the region around Puerto Vallarta offers a mix of characteristics that make it one of my top coastal choices. It has great natural beauty, a wonderful climate, diversity of housing and lifestyle, availability of consumer goods and services, and easy access to the States. The local people are friendly, and the foreign community is varied enough to make it interesting.

Puerto Vallarta is located on one of the most beautiful bays in the world. The Bahía de Banderas is horseshoe shaped, with almost 100 miles (161 km) of magnificent coastline rimmed with rugged mountains, jungles, farmland, small picturesque villages, almost-virgin beaches, and several major tourist developments.

Over the past 45 years, Puerto Vallarta (or Vallarta, as it is known locally) has grown from a small fishing village into a city with an official population of 250,000. This intense growth becomes obvious as you drive north of downtown past several miles of huge hotels and resorts strung out along the beach almost to the Puerto Vallarta International Airport.

Still, Puerto Vallarta is much more than just beachfront hotels and condos. When you enter downtown (called Viejo Vallarta, or Old Town), you get a sense of the quaint village that Vallarta once was. The cobblestone streets and tile-roofed houses give downtown an old-world, romantic charm, especially if you are able to look beyond the large crowds of tourists and traffic jams.

Most of the year, the Vallarta climate is wonderful. From November to June, there is virtually no rain, and the sun shines almost every day. During that time, temperatures average 85–90°F during the day and 75–85°F at night. The rainy season starts in mid-June and lasts until mid-October. During this time, many locals and foreign residents escape to the mountains or cooler inland towns or head to the States to see family and friends.

During the rainy season, the heat and humidity can be oppressive, although many year-round residents say that summer is their favorite time of year. Torrential rainstorms accompanied by spectacular lightning and thunder make summer the most dramatic season. Locals stay off the streets mid-afternoon and spend more time in the pool. But being in Puerto Vallarta in August, in a *casita* on the beach without air conditioning, beats any summer day in Washington, D.C. or New York City.

Downtown Puerto Vallarta is more or less at the mid-point of the bay. The city stretches along the bay to the north and south of downtown. To the south, in the exclusive Conchas Chinas area, condos, homes, and Italianate villas—some extremely grand—perch on rocky cliffs and hills overlooking the bay. Farther south are the outlying beaches of Mismaloya (sight of the film, *Night of the Iguana*) and Boca de Tomatlán.

To the north of downtown is the Hotel Zone and the Marina Vallarta, which has more than 500 boat slips, hundreds of condos, and an 18-hole private golf course. A few miles north of the international airport is the Ameca River, the dividing line between the states of Jalisco to the south and Nayarit to the north. The river also divides the Central and Mountain time zones, a circumstance new residents and even old-timers occasionally find very confusing. North of the river is Nuevo Vallarta, Mexico's largest seaside residential development. Farther around the bay are the villages of Cruz de Huanacaxtle and Punta de Mita, site of another large development (including a Four Seasons Hotel, wildlife sanctuary, and 18-hole golf course).

It is obvious that Puerto Vallarta's economy depends on tourism, which may be a turnoff to some. During winter, the town is swamped by plane-, boat-, and busloads of short-term fun-seekers from the north. During the summer, Mexicans, whose kids are out of school, come in droves, and this is when traffic is at its worst. The effect on the city is profound. Tourists crowd the hotels, bars, and restaurants. They create traffic jams, noise, and rowdiness and swarm downtown sidewalks and beaches.

Those living away from downtown are affected less. But anyone who lives in a seasonal tourist town has to learn how to deal with the onslaught. There are certain times when locals venture out to shop, and others when they stay home and batten down the hatches. Some long-term residents, feeling that Puerto Vallarta has lost much of its charm, have moved to smaller outlying towns like Bucerías and Cruz de Huancaxtle, Sayulita, and San Pancho, claiming that they are what Vallarta was 25 years ago. If your dream is a quiet little beachfront pueblo away from it all, Puerto Vallarta is not for you. Yet in spite of its problems, it is one of the best all-around living areas on the Pacific coast.

No one knows exactly how many permanent and part-time foreign residents live in the Vallarta area, but numbers run as high as 15,000–20,000. This estimate includes snowbirds, who come for the winter. The majority of expats are from the United States and Canada, but there is also a small European community. Expatriates and local Mexicans get along well in a polite way but don't really spend much time socializing together. For those interested, the social scene can be intense during the "season," with parties every night. These festivities are driven to a large extent by snowbirds who are in residence for a month or two and have nothing more to do than live it up.

Old time residents are just as likely to stay home in the evening or have a few friends to dinner. Nevertheless, Puerto Vallarta is a tourist's town, with a large selection of restaurants available for those who wish a night out. They run the gamut from dumps and fast food joints to bistros with expensive and elegant cuisine. A variety of food styles are represented: American, Argentine, California, Chinese, European, French, German, Indian, Indonesian, Italian, Japanese, natural, Swiss, Szechuan, and Thai cuisine.

Apart from sitting on the beach and eating and drinking, the number one Vallarta tourist preoccupation is shopping for trinkets to bring home. Boutiques sell everything imaginable, from cheap "Mexican" trinkets made in China to fashionable resort clothing and expensive jewelry. Vallarta residents, on the other hand, are more likely to shop in Sam's, Wal-Mart, one of the large Mexican supermarket/mega-stores, or at a mall. The outdoor market down by the river is purely a tourist attraction.

Along with traditional Mexican foods and spices, like fresh cilantro, chiles, and fresh tortillas, all the markets and delis in town also have a wide assortment of U.S. and international goods. Rizo's Supermarket, located near the Río Cuale in Old Town, carries our favorite bread and a type of yogurt we enjoy. (The store also has one of the best bulletin boards in town—a good place to find a house or apartment for rent or a car for sale.)

Communications have improved and Puerto Vallarta residents now have high-speed Internet service available in their homes as well as Vonage, direct telephone service to the States. Even Barbara and I, who live in the boonies about 75 miles north of Vallarta, where there are no telephone lines, have installed a high-speed satellite Internet system. What a pleasure! For the large numbers of Mexicans who still do not own a personal computer, there are Internet cafés within a few blocks of any point in town.

Below the surface of what may appear to be a shallow culture of tourist shops, bars, restaurants, and hotels lives a small artistic, intellectual, and cultural scene made up primarily of Mexican artists and musicians.

Below the surface of what may appear to be a shallow culture of tourist shops, bars, restaurants, and hotels lives a small artistic, intellectual, and cultural scene made up primarily of Mexican artists and musicians. Except for a few artistic types, most foreigners living in Vallarta are unaware and uninterested in this world. They touch it only through their connection to the active art gallery scene, which energetically promotes art openings and parties. Wednesday night art walks organized by groups of galleries in different parts of the city try to stimulate local interest in art. The music scene is even smaller, confined mainly to a few upscale clubs and restaurants. Several local musicians, like Willy & Lobo, are worth making the effort to see. One of the bright artistic moments during the year is the May Arts and Music Festival; another is the Puerto Vallarta Film Festival in November.

Puerto Vallarta is well covered on the healthcare front by an unusually large number of doctors and alternative health care specialists, many drawn by the fine climate and a growing population of well-employed and wealthier individuals. The Puerto Vallarta phonebook contains more than 20 pages listing healthcare providers, including everything from cardiologists, gynecologists, and dentists to homeopaths and naturopaths. Also listed are Vallarta's six hospitals and major medical clinics. I have personally been well treated at both the Hospital San Javier Marina and the Amerimed clinic.

History

Legend has it that farmer Guadalupe Sanchez first settled the valley around Puerto Vallarta in 1851, on land near the Río Cuale, which runs through present-day Old Town. Other farmers soon began migrating to the fertile river valley, and by the late 1800s more than two thousand people lived in the town, then called Las Penas. Corn and other crops were shipped out on boats that regularly used the bay as a safe harbor. The name of the town was changed in 1918 to honor a popular former governor of Jalisco, Ignacio Luis Vallarta.

Nothing much happened in the area for the next 35 years until Mexicana Airlines, prohibited from landing in Acapulco, decided that Puerto Vallarta could be the beach resort for Guadalajaras residents that Acapulco was for residents of Mexico City. Mexicana Airlines began regularly scheduled flights onto a dirt runway in Puerto Vallarta in 1954.

Once Puerto Vallarta was relatively easy to reach, outsiders began filtering in, and some stuck around. A few pioneering foreigners began living along the Río Cuale, in an area that later became known as Gringo Gulch. Even then, Puerto Vallarta remained quiet and relatively unknown until John Huston filmed *Night of the Iguana* there in 1963. It wasn't the film but the hot romance between Richard Burton and Elizabeth Taylor that drew Hollywood reporters and paparazzi to Vallarta like flies on banana peels. The reporters and everyone connected with the film fell in love with the village. It was suddenly on the map. Soon, every Mexicana Airlines flight was booked by fans flocking to see the town where Taylor and Burton had their famous tryst.

WHERE TO LIVE

The majority of foreigners are concentrated in and around the four most expensive areas of town: Gringo Gulch, Conchas Chinas, Marina Vallarta, and Olas Altas, also know as La Romantica. Others live downtown and in the Amapas area, which is close to Conchas Chinas. A smattering also live in Versailles, a mixed residential and commercial area just to the north of downtown.

A few villages on the coast to both the north and south of Puerto Vallarta have had small colonies of permanent foreigner residents for decades. These include Boca de Tomatlán and Yalapa (reachable only by boat, which makes regularly scheduled daily trips from Puerto Vallarta). Because no more space exists for development south of the city, new arrivals wishing to live on or near the beach and away from the city have followed development northward to Cruz de Huanacaxtle, Punta de Mita, Sayulita, and San Fransisco (San Pancho). Until about ten years ago, these were mostly sleepy little fishing villages. In the last few years, they have exploded. Several of these villages now appear regularly in upscale travel magazines touting ideal places to retire in Mexico.

Gringo Gulch

Downtown Puerto Vallarta (Centro) reaches from the ocean up into the hills along the Río Cuale. Gringo Gulch is on El Cerro (The Hill), which overlooks the river. The first foreigners settled here to take advantage of the cool breezes in summer. The area has some of the fancy homes of early foreign residents, including Elizabeth Taylor. The hills offer wonderful views of the Church of Guadalupe, the red-tiled roofs and whitewashed walls of Old Town, and Banderas Bay in the distance. This area is fairly expensive, but it is still possible to find an occasional deal. Homes here are $250,000 and up.

Conchas Chinas and South

South of the Río Cuale, past the restaurants and nightlife of Los Muertos Beach and Colonia Emiliano Zapata, are the hills of Conchas Chinas. Here you will find grand homes and condos overlooking the bay. Homes here start at $500,000. Nice condos sell for about $350,000 and up.

Marina Vallarta

Marina Vallarta is a huge, first-class development on 550 acres (220 hectares) of land. It includes an 18-hole golf course, a 353-berth marina, private boat slips, and a wide variety of real estate choices. Homes here start at about $300,000 and run up into the millions. Condos start at $125,000.

Versalles

Versalles is an area north of downtown and several blocks in from the beach. This is a conveniently located, quiet, and pretty area with a mix of residences and businesses. A friend of ours lives here and loves it. She can walk to the store for groceries, to her bank, her doctor's office, or out to a nice restaurant in the evening. Homes here are much less expensive than those closer to the beach.

North of Puerto Vallarta

Apart from Nuevo Vallarta, the other towns along the bay to the north used to remind old-timers of Puerto Vallarta years ago. That era is quickly coming to an end. Nuevo Vallarta, a mega-resort just north of Vallarta, is the largest development outside of Puerto Vallarta on Banderas Bay. All-inclusive resort hotels take up most of the beachfront property, but there are pretty residential areas with tree-lined streets near the beach. This is a new and decidedly upscale neighborhood. Farther from the beach, newer homes surround a large lagoon. Most of these homes have boat docks and start at $250,000.

North of Nuevo Vallarta, the beach town of Bucerías has some fancy homes, but it still has the funky feel of an old Mexican village. From Bucerías, you can walk for miles along a mostly deserted beach in either direction. Next past Bucerías is Cruz de Huanacaxtle. "Cruz" is fairly small, built on hills, but has recently swelled due to quite a lot of new development. Finally, at the northern point of the bay, is the village of Punta de Mita. This small village has been discovered in a big way. The old village itself is still tranquil, but close by is a huge Four Season Hotel resort, complete with condos, town houses, and two golf courses. A Rosewood Hotel has opened, and rumor has it that a St. Regis is in future plans. Developments and lots along the bay offer wonderful views, and high prices.

North of Punta de Mita are the towns Sayulita and San Francisco (San Pancho). Real estate prices are already high in these small beach towns, and they're going up every day.

RENTING

If you are lucky, a real estate agent in Vallarta will help you find a nice two- or three-bedroom apartment or condo in a good location, possibly with a view, for as little as $800 per month. You may find an even better deal through ads in the paper, local bulletin boards, or word of mouth. People have complained about the difficulty of finding good long-term rentals. Many property owners hold properties off the long-term rental market in order to get higher rents from short-term tourists.

Many potential renters look in Olas Altas, an area also known as La Romantica. This is the closest thing that Puerto Vallarta has to an old-fashioned village in south France. Starting on the south side of the Río Cuale, La Romantica is bordered on the west by the ocean and Los Muertos beach. It then runs east from the sea for five or six long blocks. This is a neighborhood of outdoor cafés, Indian and Chinese restaurants, art galleries, craft shops, and small hotels and apartment houses. Home burglaries are reportedly higher in this area.

GETTING AROUND

From Guadalajara it is a four-and-a-half-hour drive to Puerto Vallarta, over a low coastal mountain range and through valleys of sugar cane that are every shade of green imaginable. From Tepic, the last city north of Puerto Vallarta along the west coast highway, it is a 98-mile (158 km) drive through jungle. Although beautiful, it can be frustratingly slow going on this heavily traveled two-lane highway. (For information on driving to Guadalajara from the U.S. border, see the Lake Chapala area subsection in the Central Highlands section.)

First-class buses depart every half hour each day from Guadalajara for the six-hour trip to Puerto Vallarta.

Alaska, American, America West, Continental, and other airlines offer direct flights to the Puerto Vallarta International Airport from Dallas, Houston, Los Angeles, Phoenix, and other U.S. cities. Longer, less expensive flights are routed through Mexico City. The best deals are on charter airlines, such as Sun Trips.

Getting around Vallarta itself is easy. Local buses stop at corners marked with bus-stop signs and run from daybreak until midnight. They charge only four pesos a ride and are fast and convenient. Taxis charge 25–35 pesos but can cost more if you fail to work out the price beforehand.

Manzanillo, Colima

From one side of the *zócalo,* you might see steel-gray ships docked at the local naval base or large cargo vessels at a loading dock. On the other three sides of the *zócalo,* you'll find restaurants, shops, and a few of central Manzanillo's better tourist hotels. For the most part, few of the shops are really touristy. Walk a few blocks farther into town and you will be caught up in the bustle of Manzanillo's business day. There is a certain funkiness about the town that may not be for everyone. For instance, one downtown street has railroad tracks running down its center—easy to trip over.

It is not possible to get a reliable count of the Manzanillo area's permanent foreign community. There seem to be no more than a few hundred expats, although the number of part-time residents swells during winter, when snowbirds arrive from the north.

Most foreigners live north of town along the beaches, from Las Brisas on Manzanillo Bay to Playa Santiago on Santiago Bay. This stretch is also the main tourist area, with some enormous resorts like the famous Las Hadas. In some areas north of town, like Las Brisas, residential homes are scattered among small hotels and motels. Santiago Bay is cleaner than Manzanillo Bay. The hills at the northern end are dotted with private homes, condominiums, restaurants, and hotels, most with fabulous views of the bay. Foreign residents live in this area and in gated communities, like Club Santiago, located on the beach at the north end of the bay. Foreigners also live in small towns north of Manzanillo, including Barra de Navidad, nearby San Patricio and Melaque, 30 miles (48 km) north, and La Manzanilla, just 13 miles (21 km) north of that. These towns are worth visiting.

The honky-tonk nature of Manzanillo probably draws some foreigners to the town. But more likely, the semitropical climate, relatively low prices, and amenities, goods, and services are the greatest attractions. The area has some very good restaurants, good fishing, plentiful golf and tennis facilities, and fairly easy accessibility. A new four-lane highway from Guadalajara has cut driving time to Manzanillo to about three and a half hours. The Playa de Oro International Airport, about 20 miles north of town, has direct flights to Los Angeles via Aero California. Other airlines will have you change planes in Guadalajara or Mexico City.

For more information about Manzanillo, click on to www.mexico-help.com. The Manzanillo Foreign Community Association, called HELP!, is available 24 hours a day with assistance, translation services, and information for regular and emergency situations. They say they can guide you down from the border and into Mexico with ease and comfort even if you do not speak the language.

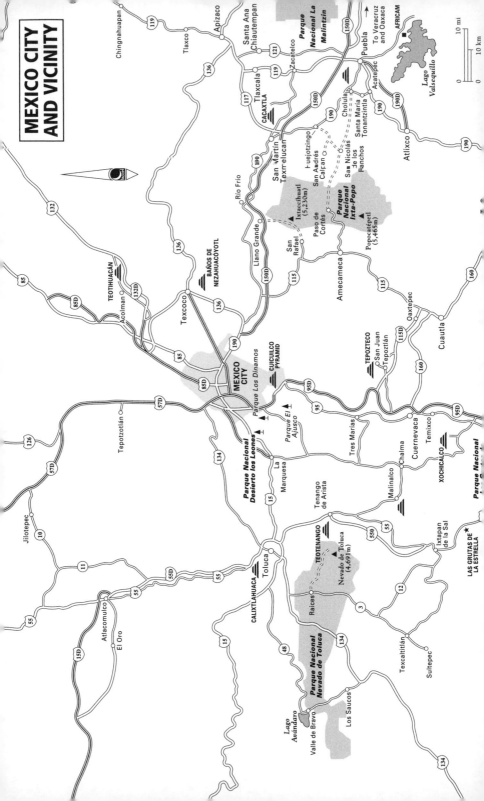

Mexico City and Vicinity

Mexico City (known to Mexicans simply as Mexico or el DF, el Distrito Federal) is a total delight for those who love big, bustling urban centers with high energy and rich culture, but can be a real nightmare for anyone not used to life in a big city. It is a city of extremes—wealth and poverty, beauty and ugliness, chaos and tranquility, all existing side by side. In spite of its reputation for crime, pollution, and overwhelming traffic, the city can be a great pleasure and surprisingly relaxed for those living there.

LAY OF THE LAND
Mexico City's estimated population of more than 20 million is spread out over hundreds of square miles. The complex network of fast-moving highways that weave through the city can make it seem confusing.

But with some patience and a good map, the city can be understood as a conglomeration of smaller villages, and that is what can make Mexico City such a wonderful place to live.

Mexicans seem to have developed a very positive way of being together in such great numbers. Anger and frustration are rarely expressed in public; strangers will smile at you as you walk down the street; shopkeepers are courteous and friendly; people are not pushy or loud. Social etiquette is a high art in Mexico and the language is full of phrases that reflect it. "*Que le vaya bien*" (literally, may it go well to you), "*con permiso*" (with permission, used when passing someone or taking leave after a conversation), "*a sus ordenes*" (at your service, heard in many stores) are just a few of the polite phrases one will hear daily. These social forms help the mass of humanity to live and work together with dignity and grace.

Whenever Americans hear of Mexico City, the first response is usually something about the crime or pollution. Both are serious problems, but exaggeration by the media has created many distortions about the city. Kidnappings make great news stories, but foreigners are rarely the targets for this type of crime. By following some basic rules that apply to cities in any country, you can feel safe in Mexico City. Use registered taxis, and do not walk the streets wearing obviously expensive jewelry or watches, or carrying cameras or video equipment. While the city can be very smoggy on certain days, levels of pollution have declined in recent years. The mile-high altitude can affect many newcomers to the city, but most people adjust within a short time. The climate is a generally agreeable 50–70°F.

> *Mexicans seem to have developed a very positive way of being together in such great numbers. Anger and frustration are rarely expressed in public; strangers will smile at you as you walk down the street; shopkeepers are courteous and friendly; people are not pushy or loud.*

What makes Mexico City such an exciting place to live is the culture. Although just next door to the United States, it has a far more exotic feel than many European cities. The Aztecs arrived in the area in the 1300s and founded their capital, known as Tenochtítlan, in the midst of the swampy lakes. When the Spanish arrived in 1519, the Valley of Mexico had an estimated population of 1.5 million, larger than any European city. Early descriptions of their city make it sound like Venice, with its network of canals. Temples and palaces of great splendor stunned the first Europeans, who promptly reduced most of it to rubble, which they used to rebuild the city in their own style. But vestiges of the Aztec past are found all over Mexico City. Just a few steps from the 16th century Spanish Cathedral, one can visit the ruins of the great Templo Mayor (discovered only in 1978 by accident) and see dancers in Aztec-inspired costumes. Many streets and neighborhoods have tongue-twisting Aztec names, like Nezahuacoyatl and Popocatépatl. There are many Moctezumas listed in the Mexico City phone book. Many of the staple foods—tortillas, tamales, beans—were eaten by Aztecs. You can visit the famed Museum of Anthropology and see sculptures with faces of ancient ancestors, then walk outside and see the same faces in the street. A diorama of an Aztec market in this museum has the same feel as contemporary markets. The ancient and the modern coexist in Mexico City. The Spanish may have conquered the Aztecs in a military and political sense, but the culture still lives.

Street life in Mexico City has a vibrancy found in few places. Elegant shopping malls and modern supermarkets have appeared in more upscale areas, but street vendors and traditional markets still thrive. For instance, the Mercado San Juan, located not far from the Bellas Artes, is a fabulous traditional market made up of many hundreds of stalls containing veggies, fruits, grains, any food imaginable for that matter, and a colorful and seductive array of prepared foods and desserts. The streets of the city are bustling with activity. Almost everything you need to buy can be found without ever entering a building. Musicians are seen on almost every block in the historic center, and jugglers, clowns, and even fire-eaters entertain motorists at busy intersections. The number of people on the street, especially in the *centro,* can sometimes be overwhelming, but a walk through any part of Mexico City is never dull.

The city is home to a myriad of museums, art galleries, concert halls, and theaters offering more than enough cultural opportunities. With frequent film festivals, it is a great city for movie lovers. Unlike those in many European countries, movies in Mexico are not dubbed (children's movies being an exception), and the Spanish subtitles can be a great help in learning the language. For listings of movies, theater, music, and dance events, look for the magazine *Tiempo Libre* (Free Time) at most newsstands (it comes out every Thursday), or on-line at www.tiempolibre.com.mx. The magazine called *DF* also has good listings and culture articles.

Mexico City Statistics

Here are some statistics to give you an idea of just how unwieldy and complex a city of more than 20 million people can be. First, a few geographical facts: Mexico City is in *el Estado de México* (the State of Mexico), Mexico. The metropolitan area is surrounded by mountains, two of which are more than 16,250 feet (5,000 meters) high, and is at 7,280 feet (2,240 meters) above sea level. That's about 23 percent less oxygen than at sea level.

The city is divided into 16 *delegaciones* or counties. The surrounding 58 municipalities in the state of Mexico, and one in the state of Hidalgo, together represent a metropolitan area totaling 1,862,500 acres. Mexico City alone has about 10 million inhabitants, and the surrounding metropolitan area has another 10–12 million people. More than one fifth of all Mexicans live in the metropolitan area of Mexico City. Sixty percent were born in the city; 40 percent migrated there. This flow continues at a rate of 2,000 people arriving in the city each day. An estimated 50 percent live as squatters in illegal dwellings. The average age of a resident is 14.2 years, with 62 percent of the pop-

The Newcomers Club in Mexico City, founded in 1977, is a group of interested volunteers offering an English-speaking support group for those people living in Mexico who want to network and volunteer for the benefit of the community. Their website is www.newcomers.org.mx.

WHERE TO LIVE

Deciding where to live in Mexico City will depend on your lifestyle. The city is made up of many *colonias* (neighborhoods)—each with its own feel. A quality, small-town life can be found in many of the nicest *colonias*, making life in a city of more than 20 million much more pleasant. Most real estate is listed by neighborhood, so it helps to know which are the more desirable ones. Prices for real estate vary greatly even within the same neighborhood, depending on the quality and condition of the apartment, and if it includes parking space or not. One thing to remember is that when you see the word *ámueblado* (furnished), it usually means that the place includes a hot-water heater, stove, and refrigerator—not furniture as used in its American sense. These items are not always included in a rental apartment in Mexico, so be sure to check.

To start hunting for real estate, go to your local newsstand or Sanborn's magazine department and pick up one of the following: *Segundamano*

ulation being 19 years old and younger. It is estimated that 98 percent are Roman Catholic and that together, the unemployment and underemployment rates are about 60 percent in the city.

Mexico City has 25,000 streets, making up 6,324 miles (10,200 km) of the so-called traffic net used by some 4.2 millions inhabitants daily. The electricity is 110 volts, using U.S.-style, two-pin plug outlets. The annual rainfall is 15.7 inches (660 mm), with the heaviest rains in July and August. The average January temperature is 68°F (20°C), and in July the average temperature is 77°F (25°C).

Drainage and artesian wells have lowered the water table so that the surface crust, formerly supported by subsoil water, can no longer sustain the city's heavier buildings, which are sinking some 4–12 inches (10.2–30 cm) a year. Some of Mexico's finest buildings have been damaged, among them the old cathedral (begun in 1553 on the site of an Aztec temple) and the Palace of Fine Arts. Modern office buildings have been shored up with pilings.

The time zone is GMT-6 (Central Standard Time). Daylight Saving Time is observed in Mexico City.

(Secondhand), which also has cars and just about everything else for sale, and *Trato Directo* (Direct Deal, or for sale by owner). Each of these has listings of real estate for sale or rent as well as advertisements for some of the major real estate agencies. Listings are generally by *colonia.*

Recent real estate listings show sale prices for apartments and condos in various *colonias* in Mexico City, all in U.S. dollars, ranging from $45,000 up to several million. For example, $695,000 will buy an elegant condo in Las Lomas (renting for $4,500 per month), and $120,000 will buy a small, two-bedroom condo in Coyoacan.

The Centro Historico

Most familiar to visiting tourists, this neighborhood in not a top choice for most new arrivals to live. The residential areas of *centro* are largely run down and services, such as grocery stores and dry cleaners, are scarce. A new incentive to renew the *centro historico* includes a new high-rise apartment building on the Alameda that could start changing things.

Polanco

This *colonia,* on the north side of Chapultapec Park, is an upscale area of private homes, apartments, hotels, foreign embassies, expensive shops and restaurants, and galleries and museums. It has a large Jewish population and has a more American feel—like part of Los Angeles. Adjacent to Polanco, the neighborhoods of Anzures and Cuatehemoc are also popular, with a bit more of a distinctive Mexican flavor.

Las Lomas

West beyond Polanco, this area of exclusive, walled houses is home to many of Mexico City's most wealthy people. Many foreigners, especially those with children, live in the Lomas area, several miles to the west of the *centro*. Its slightly higher elevation provides a better quality of air much of the time, houses tend to be walled compounds, and the lifestyle tends to be more like suburban America, where cars are needed for all activities outside the home.

Condesa

Tree-lined streets and lush green parks make this one of the city's more desirable neighborhoods. With its beautiful art deco buildings, two lovely parks, hip restaurants, and cafés, it is popular with artists, actors, and foreign journalists.

Roma

Just next to Condesa, Roma shares a similarly hip/bohemian ambience, but is a bit more scruffy in appearance. Both Condesa and Roma have become popular with artists, writers, and young, well-to-do Mexicans.

Del Valle and Navarte

These are clean, safe, and attractive middle-class neighborhoods, where you can find better value than in the more desirable *colonias*. Navarte and Del Valle are a bit south of *centro*.

Coyoacán

Several miles further south are the desirable areas of Coyoacan (Frida Kahlo, Diego Rivera, and Leon Trotsky all lived there) and San Angel. This popular area close to the University (UNAM) still retains the feel of a Mexican pueblo with its delightful central plaza and lively market.

San Angel

Just next to Coyoacan, San Angel also has a village feel, but with more encroachment by the modern city. Large private homes on beautiful

No-Driving Days

Mexico City is one of the most beautiful and sophisticated cities in the world. It is blessed with fantastic museums, restaurants, musical events, architecture, and areas of natural beauty. Unfortunately, it is also plagued by poverty, crime, traffic jams, and very poor air quality. To improve air quality, Mexico City has instituted a program to reduce auto emissions called *"Hoy No Circula"* (Don't Drive Today). This program restricts cars from driving in the city one day per week.

The no-drive day is determined by the last number on your license plate. If your plate ends with the number 1 or 2, no driving on Thursday; if it ends with 3 or 4, no driving on Wednesday; if it ends with 5 or 6, no driving on Monday; if it ends with 7 or 8, no driving on Tuesday; if it ends with 9 or 0, no driving on Friday. All cars may drive on Saturday and Sunday and during the week between the hours of 11 P.M. and 5 A.M. If your plate ends in a letter, call 800/250-0123 or 01/555-250-0151, or go to www.sima.com.mx/sima/df/hoyno/indice.html.

Driving on the wrong day can result in a large fine. Even on the correct day you may be pulled over and accused of an infraction. Mexico City traffic police have a well-deserved reputation for corruption. Unscrupulous Mexican traffic police (known as sharks) lie in wait to pounce on drivers, both Mexican and foreign, and hit them up for *mordidas* (bribes). Some friends were pulled over twice in a 10-minute period! We have often added hours to our driving trips just to make a broad sweep around Mexico City.

When you live in Mexico, you learn a few tricks from old hands, which can help you enjoy a visit to the city. For instance, during Christmas and Easter, when many Mexicans are on vacation at the beaches, Mexico City is quieter and less polluted. Conversely, these are times to avoid crowded coastal tourist towns.

streets are hidden behind the main plaza. Both Coyoacan and San Angel were villages swallowed up into the urban matrix of Mexico City, but both still retain certain aspects of small-town life. Many people connected with the nearby university, UNAM, live here.

GETTING AROUND

A word about driving in Mexico City. Don't do it if you don't have to! But if you must, be aware that the city has instituted a "no-drive-day" plan to reduce air pollution. For more information, go to www.sima.com.mx/sima/df/hoyno/indice.html.

It is best to park your car in a safe parking garage and walk, take a taxi, or use public transportation to get around the city. Only take a taxi from a *sitio*. These official taxi stands can be found on street corners throughout the city. If you are in a hotel, ask the desk to call a cab for you. This is also true of fancy restaurants after dark. Do not flag down random taxis as this can be dangerous.

Mexico City has an extensive public transportation network, which includes buses or *peseras* (normally VW vans), street cars, and the Bullet Train in the south Tlalpan area. Depending on the distance you cover, most bus rides cost about 3 pesos ($.30)!! Millions of Mexicans, as well as foreign residents on fixed incomes, students enrolled in the university, and tourists regularly use this inexpensive way of commuting. If you decide to use public transportation, please take the following precautions. Many of these same common-sense precautions apply to walking in the city and sightseeing.

Pickpockets and petty thieves love to operate crowds and tight spaces so, if possible, carry nothing in your pockets. Instead, carry cash and identification in a pouch with a strap that hangs around your neck and under your shirt, or in a shoulder-strap bag that can be tucked close to your body and under your arm. Take only enough cash for a day or two, and leave your credit cards and other valuables at home or in the hotel safe. As mentioned previously, do not carry a laptop or an obvious camera. Dress down and do not wear flashy jewelry. If you are going to use public transportation, become familiar with the routes you plan to take before you leave, and have exact change in your hand when you board. You may or may not receive a ticket from the driver. Bus drivers often take off suddenly, so be cautious when entering and leaving the bus. Locate the bell so you can announce your stop in advance to the driver. If you are not predisposed to taking all these precautions and have the money, I recommend hiring a car and driver to transport you around the city.

Cuernavaca

LAY OF THE LAND

Cuernavaca has long been among the most desirable cities for foreign residents. It is renowned internationally for its beauty and perfect climate. The city drapes over miles of a steep, broad valley, surrounded by layers of high mountain peaks. The highest and most imposing is the magnificent, 15,000-foot (4,560 meters) Mount Popocatépetl volcano, which dominates the horizon (when it is not shrouded in clouds).

Adding to the drama of the setting is a change in altitude from the upper end of town (6,000 feet or 1,824 meters) to the lower (5,000 feet or 1,520 meters), which doesn't sound like much but creates pronounced differences in climate. At the upper end of town are mountain pine forests, where residents experience chilly nights and clear, dry days. Descending into the valley, the climate becomes warmer and more humid. At the lower end of town, the climate is semitropical. Homes here have lush tropical gardens and swimming pools. Though the upper and lower ends of town are each only about 10 minutes away from the center, the change from one to the other is radical. It is said that some Cuernavaca residents live in the warmer, lower part of town and have second homes (weekend getaways) just 20 minutes away in the drier forests of the upper end.

Because of its near-perfect climate, Cuernavaca has been called the City of Eternal Spring.

Because of its near-perfect climate, Cuernavaca has been called the City of Eternal Spring. Average year-round temperatures are between 70 and 90°F (21 and 32°C), with relatively low humidity, even at the lower end of town. The rainy season, in summer and early fall, brings sunny mornings and, usually, late-afternoon or evening showers. Winter days are sunny and dry.

From the valley, the city radiates out onto hills, with *barrancas* (canyons) separating them. It is often impossible to cross from one *barranca* to another without first going back toward the center of town to connect with the road that goes up the *barranca* you want. Recently, a new and convenient bridge was built connecting two of the main *barrancas*. With so many hills overlooking the valley below, residents have spectacular views from most parts of town.

Cuernavaca has definitely grown into a city of contradictions. The colonial downtown is bustling, noisy, and traffic-clogged, like any big city. It is a commercial and tourist hub of museums, markets, outdoor cafés, sidewalk balloon sellers, shops of all kinds, government office buildings, and streets bursting with people scurrying in every direction. Magnificent colonial buildings on quaint streets huddle next to ugly modern monsters. *Centro* is the place to play tourist, visit museums, eat in great restaurants, and people-watch in the park.

To improve the air quality and slow the pace of life in *centro,* the present mayor is planning on closing it to vehicular traffic, which will change it profoundly and pleasantly. Traffic-free downtown areas have been created in several other Mexican cities, producing a more relaxed and "user-friendly" atmosphere.

Outside *centro* are sections of the city that look like they haven't changed much in 400 years (except for overhead electric wires, TV antennas, satellite dishes, and cars). Here you can discover old-fashioned winding streets, made narrow by beautifully hand built stone walls. Small houses sit next to grand mansions with swimming pools and lush gardens. These streets are in direct contrast to the newer, less attractive, and humbler areas, where the majority of Cuernavaca's citizens live.

Since the time of the Aztecs, Cuernavaca has been a home and weekend getaway for Mexico's (and the world's) rich and famous. The Italian royal family chose Cuernavaca as its new home when it was forced out of Italy before World War II; many family members still live there. Many of Mexico's wealthiest families have homes in Cuernavaca, as do the executives of multi-national corporations with offices an hour away in Mexico City.

The cost of living here is higher than the other prime locations (except for parts of Mexico City). Some goods and services cost even more than in the United States, but for those who want elegance, the amenities of a large city, and perfect weather, Cuernavaca may be ideal.

Cuernavaca's Newcomers Club lists about 150 families as members, but the total number of foreign residents is more on the order of 2,000—about 70 percent American. The other 30 percent include Canadian, British, Australian, Irish, Dutch, German (there is even a Swiss German school in town), French (a French school as well), Japanese, Korean, and Israeli residents. Mexicans and foreigners meet each other through school (especially if they have young kids), work, and activities, such as the gym, charitable work, and sports.

Though Cuernavaca is relatively near the culture and amenities of Mexico City, it has plenty of culture of its own: universities, research institutions, movie houses, concerts, art galleries, spas, theaters, discotheques, sidewalk cafés, and modern shopping malls. It also has fine schools, first-rate medical facilities, and though the best hospitals in the country are reputedly in Mexico City, Cuernavaca has four public hospitals that provide high-quality care. Hospital Cuernavaca is recommended, as is Hospital de Niño Morelence for children. One of the largest medical clinics is the Grupo Médico Río Mayo, which has a large staff of specialists and excellent lab facilities. The Dental Specialty Clinic has on-staff specialists in pediatric dentistry, reconstructive surgery, general dentistry,

© Bruce Brigham

Cuernavaca has shops and restaurants of all kinds set among colonial buildings on quaint streets.

and orthodontics. The local phone directory lists pages of dentists and doctors, who represent most medical and psychiatric specialties.

Mexico City, just an hour away, is also a shoppers' paradise, where you can find just about everything available in any of the world's major cities. Still, Cuernavaca has its share of shops, galleries, and shopping malls, the largest of which is Plaza Cuernavaca. Mexican as well as U.S. companies, like Woolworths, Kmart, Sears, Sam's Club, and Costco, are represented. Most locals agree that the lowest food prices in town are at the Adolfo Lopez Mateos Market in *centro*. This is where most people shop when they don't mind fighting the crowds and the traffic.

The city's social life revolves around dinners and parties among friends, nights out at one of Cuernavaca's famous restaurants, or activities at local clubs, galleries, and museums. One, the Robert Brady Museum, also known as the Casa de la Torre, offers a classic film club, a lecture series, conferences, and events like the annual Day of the Dead celebration. The museum, in the former home of Robert Brady (1928–1986), houses his collection of more than 1,300 objects of art, including Mexican colonial furniture, pre-Hispanic figures, native art of Africa, Asia, the Americas, and India, and paintings by Diego Rivera,

Oaxaca

In Oaxaca City, as in the entire state of Oaxaca, ethnic arts and crafts and indigenous culture still flourish. The state, with a varied topography of high mountains, deep caverns, and virgin beaches, is scattered with dozens of small villages dedicated to producing a particular type of art or craft. Mexico's indigenous heritage is very powerful in this southern state, where there are said to be 16 different indigenous languages and more than 200 dialects spoken. Nothing brings this ancient heritage into clearer focus than a trip to the beautifully preserved and restored archeological sights of Monte Alban and Mitla.

Mexico's colonial past is represented in Oaxaca City by the grand, 16th-century colonial architecture in and around the city's *zócalo*. It is here that both locals and tourists sit in outdoor cafés under shaded *portales* and watch the constant flow of tourists, vendors, musicians, and locals. The area's atmosphere has been improved by the closing to traffic of many streets leading into the plaza, a move that has turned it into a colorful pedestrian bazaar. Outside the center of town, Oaxaca looks like many other sprawling, fairly attractive Mexican cities.

Out of a population of about 250,000, there are probably fewer than 300 foreigners living full-time in Oaxaca. This is a surprisingly small number, given the beauty of Oaxaca's setting, its warm, dry climate, and its creative environment. It is also much less expensive than most other mid-sized, sophisticated Mexican cities. Perhaps there are so few foreigners because of the city's remoteness. Oaxaca is 340

Frida Kahlo, and Rufino Tamayo among others. Other museums in town are the Xochicalco Museum, exhibiting indigenous baskets, and the Ethnobotanical Museum, with a collection of traditional herbal medicines and native Mexican plants.

The Guild Library, a lending library with a selection of used books for sale, is part of the Guild House, which raises money for charity through monthly thrift and bake sales. The library at the University of Morelos has a reading room, and the Cemanahuac Educational Community also runs a library. The only bookstores in town selling new books in English are Sanborns (two locations) and the American Book Store.

Unfortunately, Cuernavaca's proximity to Mexico City has caused problems. Along with more people comes more crime. But when asked, many residents merely shrug and say that crime is no greater a problem here than it is in any other medium-sized city. Crime may be even less of a problem here because, as in other colonial cities, many residents of Cuernavaca live behind walls. The growth in population has also miles (547 km) southeast of Mexico City and a long drive from the States. Getting there can be a real nuisance because it is difficult to avoid driving through Mexico City. Once past Mexico City, a new toll road makes driving the curvy roads through the mountains easier and cuts the driving time from 10 hours to six.

Oaxaca's remoteness, beauty, and relatively low cost of living are probably the major attractions for the artistically inclined expatriates who do live there. Oaxaca has libraries and bookstores with English-language books. It has respected language schools and museums, and numerous restaurants, coffee shops, and bars. There are even a couple of golf courses: Brenamiel Golf Club and Oaxaca Country Club.

The air of Oaxaca is filled with music, free on the *zócalo* and for a small cover charge at restaurants and cafés. Atmosphere is everywhere, from the European feel of the *zócalo* to the huge open markets near downtown, breathtaking in the sheer quantity of handmade rugs, jewelry, leather goods, hand-loomed cottons, pottery, wooden animals, and crafts on display. Oaxaca is a place for artists and other expatriates who really want to immerse themselves in a unique blend of Zapotec, Mixtec, and Spanish cultures.

Communication services are good, with many cyber cafés. The *Oaxaca Times* (www.oaxacatimes.com), a small newspaper, is published in English and Spanish. Local Stan Gotlieb publishes a monthly electronic newletter, www.realoaxaca.com, as well.

brought polluting industries, and a greater number of cars and buses have taken up residence in the city. Though not as bad as Mexico City, Cuernavaca's air pollution can be noticeable at times. The city's normal population of about one million has been known to explode by half again on holiday weekends, with an invasion from Mexico City.

History

The valley around Cuernavaca is so beautiful that it is easy to see why it attracted the Chichimecans in the 13th century and then the Aztecs. Before cars, when it was a small town, the area must have been a perfect paradise. At 7,000 feet (2,128 meters), Mexico City can get pretty chilly in the winter, and the Aztec emperors were no fools. They would escape the cold by moving to the year-round, spring-like climate of the town they called Cuauhnahuac (place of great trees).

After the conquest of Mexico in 1521, it didn't take long for Hernán Cortés and his buddies to discover the climate and beauty of the town whose name they mispronounced as *cuerno de vaca* (horn of the cow). Cuernavaca was one of 30 Mexican cities awarded to Cortés by the Spanish crown, and it was his favorite. Cortés began building his palace in the city in 1530. "Palace" is not quite the right word to describe Cortés's home. The building in downtown Cuernavaca looks more like a small castle or fortress.

In 1529, Cortés founded the St. Francis Cathedral, one of the oldest churches in Mexico and known for its mariachi masses. Eventually, Cortés retired to Cuernavaca, splitting his time between his fortress in town and his sugar plantation on the outskirts of town.

Cuernavaca remained a haven for the rich of Mexico City and the surrounding areas. Jose de la Bordo, Taxco's silver baron, built a palace here, as did Emperor Maximilian and Empress Carlota. Maximilian even had a home in Cuernavaca for his mistress, La India Bonita.

In nearby Cualtla, in 1911, Emiliano Zapata signed his famous Plan de Ayala, calling for land reform. A large statue of Zapata on horseback at the top of a major boulevard pays tribute to him.

Americans first became aware of Cuernavaca in the 1930s, when Dwight Morrow was the U.S. ambassador to Mexico. Morrow and his family loved the city and spent as much time there as possible. After Dwight's daughter, Anne Morrow, married Charles Lindbergh, Cuernavaca became widely known to people in the States.

Still, Cuernavaca remained a relatively small, quiet city until the Mexico City earthquake of 1985. The quake caused so much destruction and fear in the city that, to escape future quakes, people who could afford to began buying land and building in Cuernavaca. The population has continued to grow rapidly ever since.

WHERE TO LIVE

In Cuernavaca, you have a choice of *colonias* (neighborhoods) with diverse geological features, ethnic makeups, and climate zones. People seem to choose their neighborhoods according to their preference in weather, schools for the kids, and accessibility to Mexico City and/or their job.

Many people like to live on a golf course. Tabachines, the largest golf course in town, also features a large, very safe condominium. Residents there can take long walks. There are few walls around the houses so it feels a lot like the States. The clubhouse includes a gym, tennis court, and pool. All this of course is very expensive, and many executives like living here.

Vista Hermosa, Reforma, and Delicias are some of the nicer *colonias* in town. They are fairly central and have some nice *privadas* (private, secure streets) to choose from. Palmira, which is on the south side of town, is a *colonia* that also has many beautiful *privadas*. It used to be one of the most sought-after areas in town, but these days, it is less popular because of its distance from the center of action (restaurants, supermarkets, etc). Still, many people settle here for the warm weather. Sumiya, near the Camino Real Sumiya Hotel, is another desirable area. Those who like the heat and don't mind the commute can find some wonderful homes in this part of town. People with budget considerations can find one- or two-bedroom bungalows or guesthouses that are part of larger estates that often have a garden and pool that they can enjoy. Some people like living in the center of town, where there are some beautiful old colonial homes. Another favorite neighborhood is Acapatzingo, near the center, with quaint little streets, and a pueblo-like atmosphere.

Real estate prices in Cuernavaca vary greatly. Here are two ads posted in 2004:

> *If you like rustic, this could be the property for you. It's located just 1 km on the Carretera Federal a Mexico in Sta. Maria de Ahuacatitlan. As you enter the property, there is a guesthouse with a bedroom, kitchenette, and living room. In the main house is a large living-dining area plus an open terrace with views of the surrounding forest. There are 4 bedrooms and 4 bathrooms, US$80,000.*

> *A cozy one-floor colonial Cuernavaca-style house available in a secure gated street in Palmira with only 8 other houses. Only 5 minutes to the Centro. The house has Mexican tile floors and "boveda catalan" ceilings. There is a family room apart from the 3 bedrooms and a servant's room on one side of the kitchen. The garden is small but nice, no pool, perfect for a small family that prefers the convenience, $1,750,000 pesos (US$152,834).*

Lush and beautiful communities near Cuernavaca, many with colonial buildings, are also attracting foreigners. In most of these places, prices are far less than those for similar properties in Cuernavaca. Towns like Jiutepec, just south of Cuernavaca; Tepoztlán, about 20 minutes away; Xochitepec, to the south; and Cualtla, 45 minutes to the east, are very peaceful and crime free.

Each of these outlying towns is uniquely attractive. Tepoztlán, for instance, is located in one of the most spectacular mountain settings in all of Mexico. The town itself, built in a gently sloping valley, has interesting shops and restaurants that attract a tourist crowd from Mexico City on weekends. Views in every direction are breathtaking. If you can live without the action of the city, these towns are an excellent choice. Here is an ad from 2004 for a fancy home for sale in Tepoztlán:

> The property is in a quiet, tranquil area in Tepoztlán overlooking the majestic Tepozteco mountains. It has two cisterns receiving municipal water plus a private well, so there is always plenty of water. This is a lovely Mexican colonial with a large garden, a swimming pool with both gas and solar heating systems, and a paddle tennis court. It has 4 bedrooms, 3 bathrooms, a TV room conveniently beside the kitchen, a terrace with a fireplace for its sitting and dining area. The garage is for 3 cars—above it is a study with full bath and a view, a staff room with bathroom, and the laundry room, $4,000,000 pesos (US$349,344).

RENTING

In 2004, nice furnished houses and one-bedroom apartments rented for $400 to $600 per month in town. A two-bedroom, one-and-a-half bathroom furnished house, only one block from Plaza Cuernavaca, rented for $500 per month. A two-bedroom house with a pool and garden in a nice area rented for about $1000 per month. Here are a couple of ads for rentals that were posted in 2004:

> Large contemporary-style house on 2 floors with 2 terraces, 4 bedrooms, 3.5 bathrooms, and a private Jacuzzi room adjacent to the master bedroom. There is also a loft (study) above the kitchen. The property is in a gated privada in Palmira with 24 hours security, $1,500 pesos/month [US$131— this price is not a typo!].

> Brand new modern construction patterned like one of the villas in Carreyes [a luxury seaside Mediterranean-style hotel/condo on the west coast of Mexico] with spacious rooms that can be either receiving rooms or living rooms or bedrooms; each have their own complete bathrooms. One enters the property and sees the inviting pool with a soft and calming waterfall on the wall. Two large rooms are on either side and an equipped kitchen nearby. Upstairs is the largest room (bedroom or study) with a covered patio that can be used for entertaining or even for working. The rest of the patio outside has a view of Maximilian's gardens. This can be a functional residence for a young couple who can combine both home and work in one place, US$2500.

GETTING AROUND

You can fly directly into the Cuernavaca airport from the larger cities in Mexico. From most points in the States, you'll fly into Mexico City's Benito Juárez International Airport and then take the direct bus to Cuernavaca (ask a porter in the airport to show you to the bus). Buses leave frequently, but on an erratic schedule. Shared vans depart for Cuernavaca every two hours or so.

Buses also head to Cuernavaca on a regular basis from the Terminal de Autobuses de Sur in Mexico City. A taxi from the airport to the bus station costs just a few dollars, but a taxi directly to Cuernavaca costs about $80.

If you are driving from the north or west and have time for a detour, avoid driving through Mexico City. Instead, head toward Toluca on *autopista* 55D, which originates in Guadalajara, where it is called 15D. You can also connect with it driving south from Querétaro. From Toluca, you will head south to Cuernavaca on a wonderfully picturesque road that eventually goes on to Taxco. A good map will help you get through Toluca.

Driving down from Texas, it is easier to bite the bullet and drive through Mexico City. Be sure not to drive in Mexico City on the wrong license-plate number day (see the *No-Driving Days* sidebar). Go to AAA for a map and detailed instructions for traversing Mexico City.

Cuernavaca, like every Mexican city, has an extensive and very inexpensive bus system. Look for blue-and-white signs with a picture of a bus and the word *parada* (stop). Buses are slow and crowded, but at least they are cheap.

Taxis cost more (but are still reasonable), are plentiful in good weather, and are convenient. Ask what the fare will be before you get in.

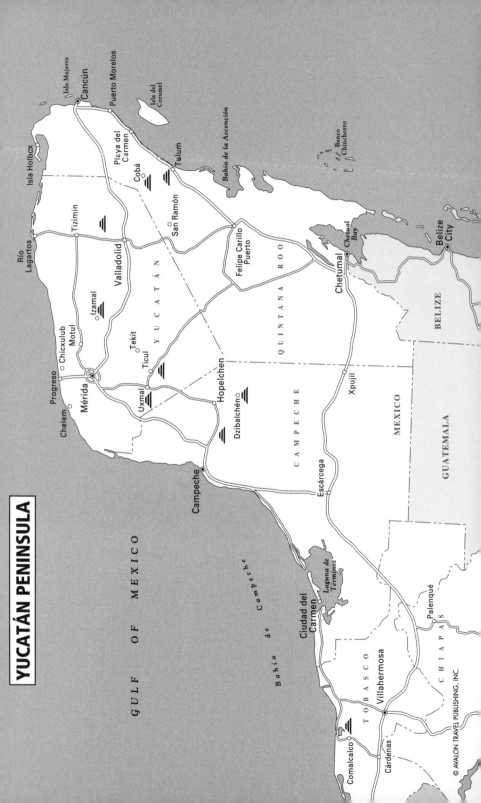

YUCATÁN PENINSULA

GULF OF MEXICO

Isla Mujeres
Cancún
Puerto Morelos
Isla del Cozumel
Isla Holbox
Río Lagartos
Playa del Carmen
Cobá
Tulum
Bahía de la Ascención
Banco Chinchorro
Tizimín
San Ramón
Belize City
Valladolid
Felipe Carillo Puerto
Chetumal Bay
Chetumal
BELIZE
Izamal
YUCATÁN
QUINTANA ROO
Chicxulub
Motul
Tekit
Ticul
Hopelchén
Progreso
Chelem
Mérida
Uxmal
Dzibalchén
CAMPECHE
Xpujil
MEXICO
GUATEMALA
Campeche
Escárcega
Bahía de Campeche
Laguna de Términos
Ciudad del Carmen
Palenqué
CHIAPAS
Comalcalco
Villahermosa
TOBASCO
Cárdenas

© AVALON TRAVEL PUBLISHING, INC.

Yucatán Peninsula

The eastern, Caribbean side of the Yucatán Peninsula around Cancún is as different from the western side—where Mérida and Campeche are located—as a huge "Love Boat" is to a fine, old-fashioned motor yacht. Cancún, after all, is Mexico's number-one tourist destination, visited by more than three million tourists each year.

Cancún and the Mayan Riviera

Cancún is really two cities. One is the *Zona Hotelera* (Tourist Zone)—a narrow, 14-mile-long (22.5 km) island of beaches, along which sit massive hotels, resorts, condominiums, and time-share units. The "Party Zone," on the inland side of the island, consists of a lagoon, several marinas, shopping malls, and waterfront restaurants, all catering to the huge tourist trade.

While the tourist zone is where to find the more expensive hotels, shops, and restaurants, the downtown area, known as *centro,* is a slightly

© James and Ellen Fields

flower shopping in Mérida

more tranquil and business-like city, where most of Cancún's 450,000 residents live and where the business of Cancún takes place. *Centro* is an energetic city of outdoor flea markets, modern malls, and U.S. stores like Sam's Club, Office Depot, Ace Hardware, and Staples.

Many foreigners own time-share condos in Cancún, or come for short vacations. This is not a place where expats live, though, unless they are planning to work in Cancún or open a business.

Even if working is your goal, you may want to consider going a short way down the coast to Puerto Morelos or Playa del Carmen. There you will find many foreigners who have started small businesses. These people were initially drawn to the area not by the business atmosphere, but by its fine, white-sand beaches, warm, clear blue-green sea, beautiful weather, fishing, extraordinary Mayan Ruins, and incredible biodiversity. In fact, in front of the Isle of Cozumel is the largest coral reef on this continent, second in the world only to the Great Barrier Reef in Australia. The Palancar Reef is renowned for its beautiful marine fauna found in extremely transparent water. Divers consider it an undersea paradise.

Puerto Morelos has a small square, a grocery store, a church, a bookstore run by a Canadian couple, and a couple of restaurants. Everything here is new, including new condos built along the beach to the north of the town. There is a moderately large snowbird community, but life in Puerto Morelos is fairly quiet, especially in summer. Puerto Morelos is not especially charming or filled with Mexican culture. A little farther down the coast are Playa del Carmen and the island of Cozumel, 12 miles (19.3 km) off the coast. Cozumel is 28 miles (45 km) long and 10 miles (16 km) wide and is world renowned for its white-sand beaches and coral reefs, with abundant varieties of tropical fish and clear water. With 90,000 inhabitants, Playa del Carmen is the largest town on the coast south of Cancún. Many foreign residents, European and American, live in both Playa del Carmen and Cozumel year-round. While many of these people are retired, some fell in love with the area during a vacation, identified a need, and eventually moved back and set up a business to fill it. These businesses appear to be quite successful. Foreigners have opened sushi bars, gelato ice-cream parlors, diving shops, retreat centers featuring yoga and meditation, restaurants (some are quite good), bars, hotels, and a wide variety of other enterprises. Many of the owners are young and are raising families. It is not unusual here to find full-time foreign residents who speak Spanish and have an interest in learning about and fitting into the local culture. Some have married locals.

More typical foreign residents are snowbirds who return to the area every winter, often with a group of friends, to stay at their time-share or condo and enjoy the weather, the fabulous beaches, and the food and drink.

Add to the snowbirds the thousands of European, Canadian, and American tourists flying in each week, as well as people coming daily off the cruise ships, and you get a robust, busy, tourist scene—one that has a very European feel. Playa del Carmen's and Cozumel's bars and many international restaurants are packed during the season.

There is a down side to all this activity for some old-time expats, who are now talking about moving to Mérida for tranquility and culture. Also, the cost of living on the Mayan Riviera is going up. Land is expensive and good housing at reasonable prices is more difficult to find than it used to be. The population is growing quickly and some expats complain that construction is out of control. There is fear that overdevelopment will destroy the beauty that has brought people here, and that soon only the rich will be able to afford the real estate prices. This is a concern that we have all heard expressed about other parts of Mexico, and the entire world, for that matter.

New development is also taking place farther south in the area of the Tulum ruins. Here, lots are being sold not far from the sea in what will eventually be a large development of single homes. As yet, this area is not nearly as developed as Playa del Carmen and points north.

Living in Cancún and along the Maya Riviera presents a variety of choices of lifestyles. To find the right place to live, it is important to make an exploratory trip to the area to see the cities and to connect with a community that shares your interests and your budget.

WHERE TO LIVE

In Cancún and vicinity, foreigners tend to buy low-priced time-shares starting around $12,000 or condos in high-end luxury residential mega-developments. A 3,000–3,500 square-foot beachfront condo with views of the ocean and lagoon and three to four bedrooms starts at $692,000. Private beachfront villas cost one million or more.

Further down the coast, around Puerto Morelos and Playa del Carmen, condos cost much less, often in the $150,000–200,000 range. Further south toward Tulum, a greater number of private homes and lots are available as development moves south. An "elegant jungle home" was recently advertised for sale near Tulum. The ad read, "Own your own beautiful piece of the jungle just 12 miles from the white sands and turquoise blue waters of Tulum beach. This 2 br/2 bath home is a wonderful getaway from the hustle and bustle of the city. Price: $235,000 US."

GETTING AROUND

Most U.S. airlines, including American, Continental, Delta, and Northwest, have regular flights into Cancún's airport.

Taxi fares are set, and most drivers charge set rates. It is best to check with the desk at your hotel. They should be able to tell you appropriate fares. Then, check again with the taxi driver before you get into the cab. Taxis can also be hired for day trips to other parts of the Yucatán.

Buses run up and down the hotel zone at all hours, and every few minutes. For just a few pesos, you can go almost anywhere.

Public buses take tourists south along the Mayan Riviera. These buses run frequently, as do the buses headed for Mérida and points west. Many tour companies run vans along the coast, to other Yucatán cities, and to archeological sites.

To really get a feel for the lay of the land, it may be best to rent a car for a day or two. For a complete and well-planned itinerary, contact Trudy Woodcock of Iluminado Tours Ltd. at woodcocktrudy1@prodigy.net.mx.

Mérida

Mérida is a city of more than one million people. While it is difficult to get a take on the exact number of foreign residents living here full time, it is clear that Mérida has a large, thriving, and very social foreign community. The heart of that community is the Mérida English Library. A natural meeting place, it often holds community events, like the annual Chili Cook-Off. Cultural events include readings from works in progress by some of the many expat writers living and working in Mérida.

In Mérida and the surrounding area, the social scene is active, with numerous house gatherings throughout the year. The Mérida English Library hosts a party on the first Friday of every other month for the expat community and their local Yucatecan friends. The other months, Denis Lafoy of the Yucatán Trails Travel Agency organizes the get-to-gethers. These provide a great way to meet the community and make some friends, and everyone is welcome. You can check with the Mérida English Library to find out where the next one is being held.

Mérida has a symphony orchestra in which many international musicians play. Add to this theater, dance, film, and a constant stream of concerts presented by guest artists, and there is some cultural event to attend every week. Many are free or else very inexpensive. They are well attended by both the expat and local communities.

The city of Mérida sponsors a series of entertainment events all week. There is the *serenata,* with regional music, poetry, and dance, on Thursday evenings at Santa Lucia Park. It has been going on for many years and is well attended by the local population. On Tuesdays, a crowd always gathers in Santiago Park for dancing to big band music. Every Sunday, *Mérida en domingo* (Mérida Sunday) hosts a flea market, craft fair, food fair, and free street entertainment. Saturday nights you have to choose between *noche mexicana* (Mexican night)—with its craft fair, food fair, and stage for music and dance from various parts of

Living in Mérida

Years ago, on one of my travels through Mexico, I decided to stay in Merida for four days. When I left four weeks later, I knew I would some-day return. I had been drawn to the Mexican culture since my first visit to the Yucatán 25 years ago. To me, it has always felt like coming home.

A little over three years ago, I made the decision, sold every-thing, and moved to Mérida. I didn't know a soul and didn't speak much Spanish, but I was amazed at how everything just fell into place. I rented a beautiful colonial house in the historic center and spent the first year settling in. What I remember most about that time is how really happy I was. Every day, I would go to the market and buy what I was going to cook for dinner. Local women would smile and say, *"Buenas días."* I felt wel-come. Sometimes, I was so happy it almost made me cry.

The locals do find it strange that a woman over 50 would move to a foreign place and live alone. They asked me the most personal ques-tions about my life. They didn't hesitate to ask how old I was, was I married, where my husband was, my family, my children, and on and on. It was hard to make them understand that I was very happy on my own in a strange place.

Another thing that surprised me was how visible I became. In our society back home, nobody pays much attention to a woman over 50. Here, they do. Young people are polite and attentive. Once they meet you, they remember you, and when they see you again, they are really pleased and make a point to speak to you. I like that.

Mexico—or the entertainment on the main square and along Calle 60. This is all free and great fun. Expats often go over to *noche mexicana* and meet friends, eat ice cream, and watch the dancing. Mexicans, with their entire families, go out to enjoy the festivities as well.

A new gallery, which opened in the fall of 2004, is one indication of a thriving art community in town. Established galleries have tended to show work of the same artists but this new gallery, made up of many young and exciting working artists, is expected to bring more vigor to the art scene. The favorite artist of the local foreign community is Alberto Castillo, an 84-year-old local artist who studied with Diego Rivera in Mexico City when he was young. He knew Frida Kahlo and Diego well.

Many of the foreign residents speak excellent Spanish. Some don't speak any. Others see it as a lifelong challenge and are working away at it as they can. You can live in Mérida without speaking the language but you miss so much. There are many language schools, and the Library

I found it physically harder on a day-to-day basis to live here. I did more walking. I washed clothes by hand and hung them on the line. I did my shopping daily and carried things home. I lost weight and became stronger. It feels good at this age to be able to use my body for simple things without feeling tired and sore.

One of my smartest moves that first year was to volunteer at the Mérida English Library. It is the center for the expat community and I met everyone. I did a four-hour shift every Thursday evening and loved it. The expat community is great. Mérida is a city of one million people, so we will not take it over. It will always be Mexican, and we are constantly reminding each other when we are dealing with the frustrations of living in a different culture that this is a good thing.

Now I am in my fourth year here and can't imagine another way of living. I accept that learning Spanish will be a lifelong challenge, and I will just continue to work at it when I can. I am studying the ancient wisdom of the Maya with a wonderful Maya master teacher. I have created my retirement career, Iluminado Tours, and now give people authentic experiences of the Yucatán. I bought a ruin of a house last year and am having it restored. I have lived through three summers without air-conditioning, survived the worst hurricane in memory, made many good friends both from the expat community and the local Mexican population, and feel more a part of the city every day. All of this has happened in just over three years. I can't wait to see what the next few years will bring!

by Trudy Woodcock

has a conversation group every Monday where you can help Mexicans with their English while they help you with your Spanish. These days, people are moving to Mérida in greater numbers. Old-timers claim to meet new people at every party they go to who are buying homes in Mérida. They describe some of the newcomers as retired, while others are looking for a retirement career. Some are young people who just want to live in a foreign country, and many are saying they are leaving the United States because they don't like what is happening in their country.

Generally speaking, the "gringo" community is liberal. There is a large gay community that is a big part of the party scene and mixes well with the rest of the community. There are many writers, artists, and musicians moving to Mérida. Some spend their time visiting ruins and studying the ancient Maya culture. One expat opened a cooking school and is very busy teaching the secrets of the Yucatán cuisine. It is a very interesting and eclectic group. Relationships with the Mexicans are excellent;

although sometimes it seems like the Mexicans don't quite know what to make of the foreigners, they are generally friendly, and many friendships have developed. This is where learning Spanish can really help.

There are a few favorite watering holes for the expat community in Mérida. One is Pancho's bar and restaurant. During happy hour—from six to eight—you'll often find some of the local gringo community sitting at the bar.

Mérida has one golf club just north of town. More golf can be found on the Cancún side of the Yucatán Peninsula. Baseball fans follow the local Mexican league team, called Los Leones. A number of expats go to the games and cheer them on. Ocean sports, like diving, snorkeling, and fishing, can be found on the Cancún coast. People here sail, kayak, and ride bikes.

Mérida is a city of more than one million people. While it is difficult to get a take on the exact number of foreign residents living here full time, it is clear that Mérida has a large, thriving, and very social foreign community.

For those thinking about a long-term move to the Yucatán Peninsula, don't forget to consider the weather. Though fine during the winter months, overall the weather can take a little getting used to. In April, May, and the beginning of June, it is very hot and dry—often over 100°F (37.7°C), without any rain. The nights cool down and might drop into the mid–high 70s F (high 20s C). Spring is when locals have to slow down and take it easy. People don't try to do as much and everybody relaxes a little.

Sometime in June, the rain starts, often with big, dramatic thunderstorms two or three times a week. By July, the storms come almost every day. Then you may get a week without rain, but with very high humidity.

August and September often bring very short thunderstorms. A local expat describes this time of year: "It is very hot and humid and it feels like the rain is either coming down or the steam is rising up and you are living in a sauna. We will get a five-minute rain shower and it cools off for two minutes and then you can see the steam rising up again and rain getting ready to come down a little further down the road. You give up on the idea of ever being dry or cool again."

During this time of year, residents go to the movies whether they like the movie or not, just to cool off in the air-conditioned theater. Or they spend time on the beach, either the Gulf or the Caribbean, where temperatures are about 10 degrees cooler. This is especially true of Mexicans, who go to the beach as often as possible. Many expats stay through the summer and seem to enjoy it, although others who can't take the heat use this time for a trip to cooler climes.

August and September (and a little of October) are the hurricane months. The coast near Cancún is vulnerable, but Mérida and Campeche do not often get hit. From about mid-October to Christmas, there is perfect weather. The days are hot and sunny (mid–80s to low 90s) (high 20s to low 30s Celsius) and the nights are cool and comfortable (mid 70s) (low 20s Celsius). There is very little rain, but occasionally the odd shower.

Sometime around Christmas, a cold spell arrives in the form of *nortes*, which are cold winds from the north that lower the temperature. If it is freezing in Chicago and New York, the cold weather will often work its way down and arrive in the Yucatán as cool weather: days in the 70°F (21–27°C) range and nights in the 50–65°F (10–18°C) range. This may not seem cool, but because heated homes are virtually nonexistent, and many homes do not even have glass in the windows, the chilly temperatures are felt to a greater degree. After a week or two of the cold, people are ready for a change.

January and February are a mix of hot and cold weeks. It may be 84°F (29°C) at midday but it can be cool at night. By March and April, it starts getting hotter and there are fewer *nortes*. By the end of April, it is hot again.

WHERE TO LIVE

Because Mérida is inland, many local residents own summer homes on nearby beaches, where temperatures are at least 10 degrees cooler during the hottest months. These homes are also a good investment as many of them are rented during the winter season. For those looking for a beach rental, prices here are very reasonable. In the most popular beach towns of Chelem, Yucatecpeten (near Progreso), and Chicxulub, rental prices run from $400 to $1,200. The most expensive town, Chicxulub, is also the liveliest, as it is popular with snowbirds.

In Mérida itself, the real estate market is booming, though there are still some great deals to be found. A small two-bedroom, two-bathroom house with a big *sala* (living room), dining room, kitchen, and small garden area, in the heart of the historic center, sold in 2004 for $12,500. The new owners will more than likely spend another $15,000 to renovate it. Still a deal! In and around *centro*, there are many abandoned ruins of old houses that are just waiting for imaginative people to purchase and renovate. At the other end of the spectrum are large homes in excellent condition, with a pool and garden, for around $250,000. Generally, houses cost between $50,000 and $300,000.

You can rent a nice house in the historic center for between $300 and $550 per month. For example, a two-bedroom, two-bathroom house with a small garden will rent for about $350 a month.

There are many smaller neighborhoods within the city. Each one has a square, a market, a church, and a park. They include Santa Ana, Santa Lucia, Santiago, San Sebastian, San Juan, and a few others. These are all within walking distance from the main square and are considered to be downtown. Rents in these sections are slightly lower than in the historic center.

In the north end of the city are gated communities, new developments, and a golf club. Sometimes locals move to these developments after they sell their old places in the city.

GETTING AROUND

If you are flying from the United States, Continental has daily flights to Mérida from Houston. Other airlines fly through Mexico City and there are daily flights from there to Mérida as well.

The buses in Mérida all start from downtown. Although old, ugly, and spewing fumes, they are dependable and cost only a few pesos. Locals take buses to get around.

Taxis are easily available for trips both in and out of town.

Campeche

In some ways, Campeche may be the most interesting city in the Yucatán Peninsula. The capital of the state of Campeche, it's located on the western (gulf) side of the peninsula and has a population of 250,000. It is only a two-hour drive south of Mérida.

Campeche is a city with a long and exotic history dating back to the third century, when it was a principal city of the Mayan province of Ah Kin Pech. The first of the battles between the indigenous people and Spanish conquistadores began in 1517 when Francisco Hernandez de Córdoba landed 40 miles (64 km) south of the city. Córdoba died from wounds he received, and it wasn't until 1540 that Francisco de Montejo was able to return victorious. He founded the city of San Francisco de Campeche in 1541.

For the next century, pirates and marauders harassed Campeche, which had become one of the main ports of New Spain. They even managed to capture it at one point. Eventually, fortifications were built, including a thick stone wall shaped like a hexagon and stretching some one and a half miles (2.5 km) around the city. Eight strategically placed fortresses made the city impregnable. The wall is now gone, but the eight original bastions still stand, as do two hilltop fortresses. Most of the bastions and both forts now house museums.

In a way, old town Campeche itself is a museum of the colonial period. The facades of all the houses have been repaired and painted, electrical and telephone cables have been routed underground, and the streets have been cobbled. As in other colonial cities, like San Miguel de Allende, Mexican movie companies have used the colonial streets of Campeche as background for period films and *telenovelas* (soap operas).

Considering its location, beauty, and tranquility, it is surprising that so few expats have made Campeche their home.

Still, most tourists seem to pass through Campeche on their way to ruins at Palenque, 250 miles (402 km) southwest, the Edzna archaeological site 40 miles (64 km) east, or the Calakmul Biosphere Reserve, 150 miles (240 km), which occupies the state's eastern border with Quintana Roo. This enormous reserve safeguards Mexico's largest track of tropical jungle, covering 1.5 million acres. Because the city of Campeche has no beaches, people travel 20 miles south for a beautiful beach at Seybaplaya, complete with white sand and small fishing huts.

Those visitors who do stop not only enjoy the city's beauty, but its colorful markets, which sell some of Mexico's best Panama hats and world-famous Yucatán hammocks.

Considering its location, beauty, and tranquility, it is surprising that so few expats have made Campeche their home. Though a small expat group does live there, they are not very visible. Campeche undoubtedly draws foreigners with a more pioneering spirit. It would be necessary to speak Spanish and not be put off by the fact that, unlike Mérida, there is fairly little in the way of tourist infrastructure in the city. Campeche is a sleepy town with little nightlife. It is a place that may not change quickly, although the city has an aggressive marketing team selling tourism to Campeche. As more and more people visit this very pretty city, the expat community may grow. A place in Campeche could be a very good investment for those willing to wait.

WHERE TO LIVE
Real estate prices in the historic center vary from fixer-upper deals in the $15,000–20,000 range to finished homes for $150,000 and more. Homes and building lots are available on nearby beaches.

GETTING AROUND
Aeromexico (981/816-6656 at the airport) flies once daily to and from Mexico City. The airport is several miles northeast of the town center, and you'll have to take a taxi into town (about $4).

Most sights, restaurants, and hotels are within walking distance of the old city, except for the two fort-museums. Campeche isn't easy to negotiate by bus. Take a taxi for anything beyond walking distance, or rent a car for a trip down the coast.

Bus Travel Warning: Although none have occurred recently, in the past there have been some bus holdups on highways in the state of Campeche. All occurred at night. The U.S. State Department therefore recommends that you avoid traveling at night.

© Ken Luboff

Daily Life

Making the Move

Having all your paperwork in order is a prerequisite for a smooth trip. If you are a non-Mexican entering Mexico either to travel or to live, you will need one of the following visas: FMT, FM3, or FM2. An FMT is the tourist visa most people receive when entering Mexico. You can get one at any Mexican consulate, at the immigration booth after you cross the border, or on any flight into the country. When you fly in, your visa will be good for 90 or 180 days and the visa entry fee is automatically added to the cost of your airline ticket. You can get a 90-day visa extended for an additional 90 days.

If you drive in, you'll usually receive a 180-day visa at the border. If border officials give you less, ask for the full 180 days if you think you will need them. If you drive your car into Mexico, it will be noted on your visa, and you must leave with the same car. To get an FMT when driving into Mexico, you need only fill out a simple form, have a credit card, and show your passport and car registration. An FMT visa costs $20 at the border, paid by credit card. When you leave the country, you must turn in your visa.

Red Tape

An FMT visa is typically given to tourists on short trips into the country, but we know people from the States who have been living in Mexico for more than 20 years on tourist visas. For one reason or another, they never got around to switching and just keep renewing their visas every six months. A tourist visa does not permit you to work in Mexico.

With a tourist visa, the number of personal and household items that you can bring into the country is limited—although the limit isn't really specified. It is common for people living in Mexico to ask friends driving down from the States to fill their cars with goodies that are unavailable in Mexico or less expensive in the States. Although customs inspectors occasionally search cars, travelers are rarely questioned about items unless they are high-priced electronic equipment, like computers or TVs. I recommend unpacking these and most everything else so it all appears to be used. Carry the receipt along just in case an inspector insists on duty being paid.

> *Although customs inspectors occasionally search cars, travelers are rarely questioned about items unless they are high-priced electronic equipment, like computers or TVs.*

If you are going to be living in Mexico for six months, one year, or more, in my opinion an FM3 visa is the way to go. An FM3 is a non-immigrant residency visa that is renewed only once a year. With a valid FM3, you can leave and reenter the country as often as you like and by any means of transportation that you like. If you drove your car into Mexico with an FM3, and you want to fly back to the States for your high school reunion, no sweat! Just leave the car in Mexico and go.

With all types of FM3s (there are 10 types in all), you can work in Mexico. If you know in advance that you want to work, go to an immigration office (or consulate) and find out what documents you will need in order to apply for working papers (see the Employment section).

Getting an FM3 is more complicated than getting a tourist visa. You will not be able to get an FM3 at a consulate in the States unless you have a Mexico address. In other words, you must already have a home or rental in Mexico.

In either country, you will need certain documents to apply for an FM3. These include proof, in the form of bank or investment-company statements, that you have an income equal to at least 250 times the minimum wage in Mexico City, which means about $1,000 per month if you are single, plus half that for each dependent. This amount is reduced by 50 percent if you own real estate (in which you claim to live) in Mexico. Along with proof of income, you will be asked to write a letter to the immigration office giving your name, address, and reason for wanting an FM3—something like, "I want an FM3 because I am planning to spend two years living and studying Spanish in Mexico." You will also need your passport and your tourist visa if you have one. If you are married and your spouse wants an FM3, you will need your marriage certificate as well as a letter stating that you will be responsible for your spouse. You will then fill out a form, provide photos of yourself and your spouse, make copies of all the documents, and pay a fee of about $150.

Sound easy? Could be, but we know people who have had to return to an immigration office in Mexico five times to complete some detail before getting their FM3s. Because of the frustrations some foreigners feel in dealing with *migración,* private immigration services have opened to guide people through the process. Using such a service, you may have to pay up to $200 for each FM3 but it can be well worth it. By the way, if you obtain your FM3 in the States, you must register at the nearest immigration office to your home in Mexico within 30 days of entering the country.

Several FM3 business-visa designations have been created since the passage of NAFTA. These do not affect most people moving to Mexico or long-term visitors. These special designations include a 30-day business visitor visa, a one-year professional visa (in certain fields), and visas for intra-company transferees in managerial or executive capacities or investor/traders.

The U.S. State Department suggests that all U.S. citizens register with the nearest U.S. embassy or consulate after arriving at their permanent residence in Mexico. They say that registration will make your presence and whereabouts known in case of an emergency.

FM2 immigration status is for those who know they want to reside permanently in Mexico and eventually apply for Mexican citizenship. (By the way, you can now apply for citizenship after a minimum of five years with an FM3.) Years ago, FM2s were the only visas available to foreigners who wanted to work in the country. These days, the FM3 replaces the FM2 as a working visa.

The FM2 must be renewed every year for five years, after which you can apply for immigrant status and need not renew again. During those first five years, you cannot leave the country for more than 18 months or you will lose your status and need to start over again. Once you achieve *imigrante* status, you will have a Mexican passport and all of the rights of a Mexican citizen, except you cannot join the Mexican army, vote, or run for office.

The application process for an FM2 is about the same as that for an FM3, but you have to show a higher monthly income—about $1,500 if you are single and half that for each dependent. Applying also costs a bit more—about $100. As with an FM3, the monthly income requirement is reduced by 50 percent if you own Mexican real estate. Neither an FM3 nor an FM2 changes your U.S. citizenship, only your country of residence.

Moving with Children

Parents entering Mexico with their child (or children) must have a passport for the child or the child's birth certificate. A child entering (or leaving) Mexico with only one parent must have notarized consent from the absent parent. Similar consent is required if the child is traveling alone or with a non-parent. A notarized letter written by the absent parent is sufficient for Mexican immigration officials. A U.S. court order authorizing the travel will work if one parent refuses consent or cannot be located. A custody document will work in the event a minor is in the custody of one parent. Show a death certificate if one parent is deceased.

Mexico is a wonderful place for kids. Mexicans have a much more traditional take on families than we do in the States. It is not unusual for three, and even four, generations of a family to be living together in a single-family home or compound. Children are ubiquitous, with older children looking after their younger siblings. Mexican kids are curious about and accepting of foreigners.

Children from the United States living in Mexico have the opportunity to learn another language, and more importantly, to broaden their understanding of the world by experiencing a different culture firsthand. Parents of younger children will find a plethora of very well-trained and affordable baby-sitters and nannies. Older kids can be enrolled in Mexican public school anywhere in the country, or in a private bilingual school in certain cities (see the Language and Education section).

Moving with Pets

CATS AND DOGS

There is no quarantine and absolutely no problem crossing the border in either direction with a cat or a dog. Whether driving into Mexico or the States, cats and dogs are required to have a veterinary health certificate, dated within five days of crossing the border, that shows a current rabies vaccination. These are the rules, but the reality is that when you cross the border, you will most likely be waved through. At most, you will be asked to show a rabies vaccination certificate. Nevertheless, it would be prudent to have the required documents if possible.

In the case of young animals under four months of age, the veterinary certificate should note that the animal is "age exempt" from the rabies requirement. If someone is flying their pet into Mexico, the airlines also will require the veterinary certificate at check-in. The paperwork will be requested when you arrive at the Mexican airport with your pet.

Good-quality veterinary care for dogs and cats is available in many parts of Mexico, but it is advisable to get recommendations from people who have used a particular vet. In San Miguel de Allende, the Lake Chapala area, and most of the other cities mentioned in this book, there are a large number of veterinarians and clinics with modern facilities and lab equipment. All vaccines, heartworm medication, flea and tick treatments, and medicines are available. Spaying and neutering, as well as other surgeries, are routinely performed.

Several U.S. pet food brands are available in Mexico depending on location. These include Eukanuba, Diamond, Science Diet, and Nutro. Pedigree, Purina, and other less expensive brands also are available.

Barbara and I have found that when we are touring around Mexico in our car, it is easier to travel with our dog than without her. Jane, our Rhodesian Ridgeback, is big and expressionless, so when we pass through checkpoints in Mexico, officials usually take one look at her and ask if she bites. We kind of shrug noncommittally, and they wave

Birding in Mexico

Mexico is home to more than 1,000 species of birds, or about 11 percent of the world's species. This is more than the United States and Canada combined. Ten percent of these species are found nowhere else in the world. Mexico's bird diversity reflects the country's great diversity in habitat. A list of Mexico's birding paradises would fill an entire book, but here are a few:

El Cielo Biosphere Reserve (www.si.edu/botany/projects/cpd/ma/ma.htm) is a tropical cloud forest in the state of Tamaulipas near the town of Gomez Farias, about 75 miles (121 km) south of Ciudad Victoria.

Sierra Gorda Biosphere Reserve (www.geocities.com/RainForest/2240/Queretar.htm) is a huge, relatively unexplored area of the Sierra Madre Oriental, known as the emerald jewel of Mexico. It is within the three states of Querétaro, Vera Cruz, and San Luis Potosí.

The Copper Canyon (www.canyontravel.com/birding.htm) starts west of the city of Chiuhahua and as one of the largest and most complex canyon systems in the world, the area contains a vast array of habitats.

us on. If our car is loaded down with valuables, which it usually is, especially coming back from the States, we know we don't have to worry about break-ins while Jane is in the car. At the hotels or motels where she isn't welcome, she simply sleeps in the car all night after we take her for a walk. The only time Jane presents a problem is when we want to explore a city on foot. Because we can't take her into cathedrals and markets, we must leave her in the car with the windows open. In this case, we find a parking lot with an attendant who we pay to watch the car. We have never been ripped off.

BIRDS

Bringing birds to Mexico is not easy, but it's much easier than entering the United States with a bird or two. The United States requires a good deal of paperwork, plus one-month quarantine in either Los Angeles, Miami, or New York (all at the airports). The fee is about $20 per day, so that makes a minimum of $600 per bird just to get through the quarantine. In addition, the birds must be flown in, another expense. Coming from the United States to Mexico requires a CITES (Convention on International Trade in Endangered Species of Wild Fauna and Flora) permit (almost all parrots are endangered species) and a U.S. Fish & Wildlife "Declaration for Importation or Exportation of Fish or Wildlife," plus a vet health certificate.

La Laguna de Santa Maria del Oro (www.geocities.com/TheTropics/Reef/2688/koalabrd.htm) is a volcanic lake in the Sierra Occidental, in the state of Nayarit. There are a large number of birds in different habitats (lakes, streams, fields, roadsides, mountains, and urban settings) in a relatively small area.

The Yucatán Peninsula (www.yucatanbirds.org.mx) offers a wide variety of habitats and locations for birding. These include Ría Celestún Biosphere Reserve, the Dzibilchaltún archeological zone and surrounding area, the Ría Lagartos Biosphere Reserve, and many more.

The Pacific Coast, from Puerto Vallarta north to San Blas (wingsbirds.com/tours/sanblas.htm, www.discoverpacifictours.com/birds.html), offers coastal waters, freshwater lagoons, shrimp ponds and marshes, coffee plantations, thorn and pine/oak forests, mountain slopes, and valleys and is one of the most extraordinary birding areas in all of Mexico.

Opportunities for birding in Mexico are limitless, with every type of terrain and climatic condition represented, and literally thousands of websites to sort through. Good luck on your search!

Birds are more stringently controlled than cats and dogs for two reasons. First, they are wild, not domesticated, species that are endangered in their native habitats. Since 1992 or 1993, the United States and many other countries have banned the importation of wild-caught parrots. Only domestically raised parrots may be sold in the States. And secondly, there is the fear of bird diseases that can decimate the poultry industry. Mexico, which also subscribes to CITES regulations, continues to have a thriving black market in wild-caught and illegally bred parrots.

Some people take their chances that the bird might be seized and drive their pet birds across the border into Mexico. People have crossed successfully without papers, but it is risky.

In Mexico, it is more difficult to find a veterinarian experienced in avian medicine then one used to caring for domestic animals, though in the larger cities, there probably is at least one vet who specializes in exotics including parrots.

HORSES

Horses can be brought from the United States to Mexico and vice versa. Crossing the border with horses requires permits, veterinary health verifications, and brief quarantines. Most horse people advise hiring an import broker who specializes in horses to make the crossing.

Mexico is home to a thriving horse culture. In the Spanish tradition, since the time of the conquistadores, horses have played major roles in the lives of Mexicans at all levels of society. Horses, burros, and mules are essential to the farming communities in rural Mexico. They are beasts of burden and primary modes of transportation. As in Spain and other parts of Europe, national and international competitions in dressage and stadium jumping are of great importance to horse aficionados of the Mexican upper and middle classes. The art of the *rehoneo*, referring to the highly trained horses and riders who participate in bullfights, is a greatly valued, albeit esoteric, practice in Mexico.

The greatest tradition among the common people is the *charreada,* the Mexican version of the American rodeo. Like the American counterpart, the events of the *charreada* are based on the skills and tasks performed by *vaqueros* (cowboys) on the ranchos. Single cattle charge out of a chute at a full run, and the mounted charro's task is to catch him by the tail and make him drop to the ground, a nerve-shattering event for the spectators.

Elaborate events showcasing advanced horsemanship are embellished with mariachi music and fanciful embroidered costumes and sombreros. The most remote areas of Mexico manage to stage *charreadas* with relative frequency. The *charreada* is a team sport, with each town or region having its own team, supported with an enthusiasm equal to that for soccer and other team sports.

Opportunities abound for those interested in riding in Mexico. There are excellent equestrian facilities for boarding and training at all levels outside most major towns and cities. Rental stables exist in most tourist areas. For Western riders, the purchase or rental of horses for trail riding will get you away from the crowds and afford you glimpses of startlingly beautiful country visible only on foot or on horseback.

What to Take

One of the advantages to FM3 status is the one-time opportunity to import up to $5,000 worth of personal household items duty-free. This may seem like too low a value for all your beloved furniture and knick-knacks, but because all of your things are used, you can place a low value on the lot. No one will question your valuation, and you can easily stay under the five-grand limit.

For shipments into Mexico, the Mexican consulate requires that you make a list of everything you are shipping, including the serial numbers of all your electrical appliances. Number each cardboard box, listing the contents of each, and leave three copies of the list with the consulate. Then pay the required $100 fee. You will undoubtedly receive heart-stopping and outrageously high quotes from giant moving companies like Mayflower and United Van Lines. Check around and see if you can get a lower quote from one of the smaller shippers in your area. If not, you may want to look on the Internet or contact one of these shipping companies located in Mexico: Strom Moving (376/766-4049, strom@laguna. com.mx), Transportes Balderas (333/810-4859, marcelabalderas@infosel.net.mx, mbalderasm@terra.com.mx), Gou Shipping (333/666-1404, gougdl@infosel.net.mx). (See the Travel and Transportation section for tips about bringing a car into Mexico.)

For shipments into Mexico, the Mexican consulate requires that you make a list of everything you are shipping, including the serial numbers of all your electrical appliances.

There are some people who, when they move to Mexico, bring everything from their old homes—from the accumulated stuff in the catch-all kitchen drawer (used birthday candles, ballpoint pen tops, twist ties, spice jar lids . . . which they throw into a box) to grand pianos! The decision on what to bring has much to do with how attached you are to your possessions and also where you are relocating. For instance, if you live in a high, dry climate like Arizona and relocate to a *palapa* on the coast near Puerto Vallarta, where the humidity is high, you will not want or need your sink-into down-cushioned sofa, your woolen navajo rugs and the painting of Great Grandfather Jones in the ornate gold-leaf frame. Even if you *are* attached to them, it is better to give or lend them to a friend or relative and have "visitation rights."

These days in Mexico, it is possible to buy and replace just about anything that you leave behind. It is true that some things, like appliances, are more expensive in Mexico, but if you take into account the hassle and cost of moving it all, you may as well replace many items with new ones. In the last few years, Sears, Sam's Club, Costco, Office Depot, and Home Depot have sprung up all over the country, and although not as well stocked, nor as inexpensive, as in the States, they will have most of what you need.

Additionally, if you buy a home in an area with many expatriates, most likely it will be completely furnished! This is the rule rather than the exception.

Although you can buy just about everything you have left behind, you will most likely bring your own computer as well as your books, CDs, DVDs, and video collection. Towns with expat communities usually have very well-stocked libraries and some offer DVD and video rentals, not to mention that there are video rental stores everywhere. CDs of every kind are available throughout Mexico; Mexicans love music and this is reflected in their music stores, except of course, in small towns. Do you like Tom Waits? No problem! Charlie Mingus? Opera? The Tokyo String Quartet? You will be blown away when you go into a music store. They often have a larger choice than in the United States!

Before bringing down your DVD player, make sure it is universal and plays in all regions. DVDs sold in the States are for Region 1; in Mexico, Region 4. If you search, you can find DVDs that will play in all players and occasionally in Sam's Club you will see DVDs that say "for Region 1 and 4 players." Most people stock up when they visit the States or have friends bring them down.

Books in English, unless there is a library or you are in a large city, are harder to come by. Tourist areas usually have a book exchange store but oftentimes all you can get is "vacation" reading, like mysteries and romance novels. Powell's Bookstore in Portland, Oregon, (powels.com) will ship to Mexico *free* with orders of $50 or more. It usually takes about a month.

Clothing and shoes are fun to buy in Mexico but you must be in a tourist area and buy clothing manufactured for the tourist trade. In general, clothing in Mexico is very expensive, unstylish, and poorly made. This is changing with the new Mexican middle class and the brand-new shopping malls (with 21-screen cinema complexes) springing up in middle-size cities. These malls have some European chains that have beautifully made, high-style—but not inexpensive—clothing. Shoes and leather goods are everywhere and many towns have malls that sell shoes only. Can you imagine 230 shoe stores all under the same roof?

It is important to keep in mind that most of what you wear in the States won't be appropriate for your new, more relaxed life in Mexico. Mexicans, though, are considerably more formal. It was not until very recently that Mexican men might be seen in shorts outside of their homes. Even in a store like Wal-Mart, it is always easy to spot the Americans with their flip-flops and extremely casual dress. Most Mexicans, except in rural villages or for a day at the beach, wouldn't be caught dead outside of their homes without being "properly" dressed.

CAMBIARK

FRENTE

LICORES

MIRAMAR

© Ken Luboff

Language and Education

Many foreigners living in Mexico don't speak a word of Spanish other than to name a few dishes on the menu or veggies in the market. The lack of Spanish is one reason most new arrivals start out living in larger expatriate communities where English is commonly spoken.

Almost everyone born in Mexico speaks Spanish as a first language. The exceptions are a few remote indigenous groups who still speak one of 288 remaining indigenous dialects. The language most commonly spoken other than Spanish is Nahuatl, with 2,563,000 speakers. The languages with the smallest number of fluent speakers are Matlatzinca, with 50–100 speakers, Teco, with 50 fluent speakers, and Opata, with only 15. For more information about native languages visit www.ethno logue.com.

Increasing numbers of Mexicans speak English, especially those working in business and tourism. Even in more remote cities, lawyers and doctors usually speak at least a little English. However, even in a town loaded with your countrymen, it is unlikely that the woman behind the counter at the grocery store, your housekeeper or gardener, or even your landlord will speak English. It quickly becomes clear that learning some basic Spanish and, in time, improving to a conversational level will make life in Mexico much easier.

Spanish schools and tutors are plentiful in areas where foreigners live; individual instruction costs about $8–10 an hour. Group lessons are less expensive and often just as effective. A combination of private and group lessons is recommended for faster learning.

Learning the Language

Although learning Spanish can seem daunting at first, it's worth every minute. The ability to speak and understand a second language is immensely empowering.

Aside from the obvious frustrations of not understanding or being understood, to live in Mexico without speaking Spanish is to miss out on a great deal of fun. Spanish is a multifaceted and deeply poetic language, with a great many nuances. Comprehension of the language is key to grasping the psyche of the country and its people. For those who want to understand the complexities of Mexican culture, learning to speak Spanish is an absolute prerequisite, and learning a few simple phrases can immediately create a surprising amount of goodwill.

Spanish is a multifaceted and deeply poetic language, with a great many nuances. Comprehension of the language is key to grasping the psyche of the country and its people.

Most Mexicans have a wonderfully droll sense of humor and a rather delightful—almost whimsical—outlook on life. They deeply appreciate foreigners who make the effort to learn their language, no matter how badly they slaughter it at first. Unlike many other nationalities, most Mexicans are patient and helpful to a foreigner learning Spanish. Occasionally, if a Mexican is trying to learn English, he or she will playfully swap words with you.

At first, a newcomer to Spanish can make some extremely funny mistakes. Our friend Margaret, after her third Spanish lesson, went

Steven's Mexican Road Trip

We had driven no more than 10 minutes from Boca de Iguanas when we hit a military checkpoint. We'd been through a number of them and had always been waved through, with no more than a glance inside by the soldier on duty. This time was different. They were waving most of the cars through, but they signaled for me to pull over to the side. Three men dressed all in black with rifles over their shoulders and pistols on their belts came up to the two front windows. They were all business. No smiles. No warmth. Later, I noticed that they had the words "Delta Grupo" stenciled to the back of their shirts.

The soldier who came to my window said something that I couldn't understand. I asked him to repeat it. Finally, I understood that he wanted to search the van. "Okay," I said. While one soldier started going through the van, the other two stood on either side of me and stared at me with very steady, very black eyes. They started to ask me questions that I couldn't quite understand. Of course, I'm not carrying any illegal drugs, but I do have two bags full of bottles of pills. The guy performing the inspection was doing a rather superficial job. As he went from item to item, I'd say: "That bag has a camera in it. That one has a computer."

The continuing inspection gave birth to a rapid stream of questions from the two guys on either side of me. It seemed clear to me that they wanted to establish their dominance. My mind was not really well focused on Spanish at this point, so I could understand only about a third of what they were saying, and I could hardly come up with a competent sentence in response. Yet, somehow, the whole scene felt reasonably well in hand. I thought of my friend Donna's daily prayer: "I put my future in God's hands." It was more or less the theme of this journey.

One soldier asked something like: "What are you doing driving on this road?" My jumbled response probably sounded something like: "I make for a vacation like the beach." Then he asked something like: "Where are you from and where are you going?" I said something that probably came out like: "I'm made of New Mexico and I'm about to put a big one in Oaxaca." I was having some serious problems finding the words that I needed. They stared at me with very sober impatience while the third guy continued to open cabinets, bags, and drawers.

Finally, the inspector said I could go. I asked him slowly and directly, to avoid any confusion, "Are you saying that I can go now?" "Yes," he said and waved down the road. Across the front seat, through the passenger window, I said to the soldier standing there something that probably sounded like: "I used to hope that you come down with a very next year." He cracked a slight smile and waved me down the road.

—An excerpt from our friend Steven Cary's Mexican road trip, January 2005 home and began boiling a large pot of water. Her young maid, who was used to purifying the water with *gotas* (iodine drops), asked what she was doing. Margaret turned to the maid and, taking great care, said in Spanish, "I am boiling the water because it has germs in it, and I am going to kill you." The maid fled. Only later did Margaret realize that she had used the wrong pronoun, *you,* instead of *them.*

Some words have double meanings, and if used in the wrong way, they can be embarrassing. For instance, *huevos* means eggs, but it can also mean balls (as in testicles). A big *chile* can mean a large penis, and the verb *coger* (pronounced co-hair), which means to grab or grasp, also means to fornicate. The Spanish word for handcuff offers insight into the Mexican gender roles. The word is *esposa*, which also means wife! I'll let you interpret that one.

Spanish can be a formal language, but it is far less brusque or curt than English. For instance, in Spanish one rarely gives a direct order, and for a foreigner to do so is to invite offense. However, it is easy to avoid this practice.

The very psychology of Mexicans is expressed in their language. Little, if indeed anything, is a certainty in Spanish. For instance, the phrase "when I arrive" is expressed in the subjunctive *cuando llegue*, which actually means "I may arrive." If you drop and break something, you don't usually say, "I dropped it." You say, "It dropped itself." If you crash the car: "The car crashed itself." Barbara and I have avoided spats about missing keys because they always lose themselves. And, of course, you are never late—something made you late. This language pattern may have come about from indigenous people's terror at being reprimanded by their Spanish conquerors.

Over the centuries, words from other cultures have insinuated themselves into Spanish, as they have into most languages. Often, you will hear the word *ojalá* (pronounced oh-ha-LA; meaning God willing), which is actually a shortened form of "may Allah hear." The word has Moorish origins. Very few people probably give any thought to what it means; they just use it.

The histories of Mexico and the United States are so intertwined that many U.S. cities have Spanish names, such as Chula Vista (pretty view), Las Vegas (the flat lowlands), and Los Alamos (the aspens). Likewise, hundreds of Spanish words share roots with an English equivalent. For example, *observer* is to observe, *aplaudir* is to applaud, and *adaptar* is to adapt. Many English and Spanish words share the same spelling but are

Expatriate Perspective

Unless you know the country well, speak Spanish, or are an explorer, like Lewis or Clark, you will most likely live in a city with an established foreign population and as many of the comforts of home as you can find. A friend, Maureen Earl, describes the relationship between the local and foreign populations of the Mexican town she lives in:

My town has a large foreign population—and sometimes an uneasy mix between the foreigners and Mexicans. We foreigners have certainly improved the economy of the town, but we have also bought up some of the best real estate and have inflated prices. As a result, lower-income Mexicans find themselves pushed farther and farther out of the center of town.

Still, it remains solidly a Mexican town, and gringos are very much the minority. Most of us moved here for one reason: We love Mexico and its people. While most expatriates make efforts to learn Spanish and fit in with the mores and precepts of the country, others do not. They enjoy the low prices, servants, bridge games, and cocktail parties and continue to live what is essentially an American lifestyle.

Whether we fit in with the locals or not, for the most part, we foreigners are much like passengers on a ship at sea. We are tight-knit and are often obliged to tolerate people with whom we wouldn't be bothered under other circumstances. It's very much like living on an island—and actually makes for an interesting life.

pronounced differently, including *simple* (SEEM-play), *mediocre* (may-dee-OH-kray), *material* (mah-tay-REE-al), and *hospital* (ohs-pee-TAL). Sometimes, if you add an *o, a,* or *e* to a noun and speak with a Spanish accent, you may be pointed in the right direction: *farmacia* for pharmacy, *banco* for bank, *restaurante* for restaurant, and so on. Once in the *farmacia,* you can ask for *aspirina,* the *banco* will cash your *cheque* (pronounced CHECK-ay), and the *restaurante* will serve you a *coca* (coca cola).

You needn't always puzzle over a translation, however. Once, while trying to help a tourist at a pharmacy, Barbara made a long, convoluted request in Spanish for panty liners. She had just about exhausted herself when the pharmacist said, "Oh, Always Panti Liners!" implying, "Why didn't you just say so?"

REGIONAL DIALECTS

Historically, Mexico City played a prominent role in the colonial administration of the Spanish empire north of the equator. As such, the population of the city included relatively large numbers of speakers from

Castile, Spain. This tended to create a standardizing effect within the capital's very broad sphere of linguistic influence, which stretched from the middle of what is now the United States in the north to Panama in the south.

In such a large territory, you can expect to experience regional dialects in the same way you do in the States. For example, the dialects in the Yucatán Peninsula are similar to those of Central America. This is also true of the Spanish spoken in the areas that border Guatemala, as in the state of Chiapas. Also, the Caribbean coastal areas of Veracruz and Tabasco are distinctive, as the Spanish spoken there exhibits more Caribbean phonetic traits than that spoken in the remainder of Mexico.

Of course, unless you speak Spanish quite well, the differences are not apparent. Possibly the clearest differences are between the Spanish spoken in the cities and that spoken in the *campo* (countryside) and along both coasts. Mexico-City Spanish has a clipped sound and is spoken very quickly. Speaking rapidly is common in all the large cities, like Guadalajara, Monterrey, and Ciudad Juarez, but each area has slightly different inflections. In the countryside, the differences are not great, but they are perceptible. People speak more slowly, slur their words just a bit, and are not as grammatically correct. For instance, rather than "*si*," you may just get the sound "eh," and *pos* may be used instead of *pues*.

LANGUAGE SCHOOLS

In each of the prime locations described in the book, there are several Spanish language schools. Along with these schools there are a myriad of individuals who advertise themselves as Spanish teachers. Many of these people are highly skilled, but before choosing one I would ask for a recommendation and be certain that the person has at least a good working knowledge of English. English fluency would be best. Many of the schools offer credit, which can be fully transferred to colleges and universities in the United States. All offer a range of levels from beginner to advanced, and many will arrange lodging with a Mexican family for those interested in a more intensive Spanish experience. This is especially effective for short, intensive courses directed to business travelers. Those of you planning to live in Mexico for some time may want to enroll in classes at a local language school for the basics and then switch to one-on-one instruction from a private instructor for more advanced study and to learn important idioms and slang expressions.

Thousands of language schools throughout the country offer courses through their websites. Before making a decision, you might want to check out www.123teachme.com, which lists and rates many of these schools. In general, the cost of instruction ranges from $10 to $25 per hour for private instruction, and from $100 to $200 per week for classroom instruction, although a few schools charge up to $300. The price varies depending on the number of hours of instruction each week, the class size, and whether or not housing is included. (For a list of some of these schools, see the Language and Education section in the Resources chapter.)

Schools and universities offer programs and accreditation for a wide range of interests and students, such as nurses, teens, medical personnel, mature adults (over 50), younger children, language teachers, public health workers, professionals, diplomats' families, police, social workers, and business people. Other programs focus on literature, music, art, art history, mythology, and cultural studies.

Many schools offer excursions as well as cultural and outdoor activities, like cooking, salsa dancing, hiking, kayaking, biking, rafting, and scuba diving. Sometimes excursions are included in the package, but more often an extra fee is charged.

Education

For the majority of Mexicans, education has historically been of little or no importance. Until this century, education was not available to the masses, and even if it were, there would have been almost nowhere to make use of it. Even today, there are more college-educated Mexicans than there are jobs.

By law, children must attend school from the ages of six to 14. But the government doesn't spend as much money or place as much value on primary education as it does on university programs. President Vicente Fox has attempted to change this by spending more money for earlier grades. Though most children do attend school for at least a few years, it is not unusual to see children working at menial jobs during the day.

In 1989, official government sources put the literacy rate at 87 percent. While it is true that Mexicans read newspapers or watch TV to keep up with the news, relatively few read books for information or pleasure. Recently in Mexico City, kiosks selling books opened in several subway stations and have been very successful—at least commuters are starting to read!

PRIMARY SCHOOLS

Those of you with children who are considering moving to Mexico will be pleased to know that there are a surprising number of excellent educational options. For many of you, the best choice will be a private bilingual school. The advantage to a bilingual private school is that the curriculum is geared toward both the English and Spanish languages and that a relatively large number of students are English speaking. In fact, in the preschool and primary grades of some bilingual schools, English is the only language spoken. Generally, as the classes progress from primary grades upward, more Spanish enters the curriculum.

Tuitions at private schools vary greatly, so it is best to contact the school directly or check out their website (see the Language and Education section in the Resources chapter). Some private schools may require uniforms and have additional fees for books and transportation. The largest number of bilingual private schools are in Mexico City, Guadalajara, and Monterey, but smaller cities like Puerto Vallarta, Cuernavaca, San Miguel, and Ajijic each have at least one excellent school.

The American School Foundation of Mexico City is an example of the high-quality private schools available in Mexico. ASF is the oldest institution of its kind in the world. The school began in 1888 with a kindergarten-level class. Today, it provides a coeducational, bilingual, bicultural education from kindergarten through high school for an international student body. Students who complete their education at the American School Foundation are prepared to attend colleges and universities in the United States and Mexico, as well as in other countries. The ASF is an American school with a diverse enrollment and an international flavor. By nationalities, the student body of 2,400 is approximately 60 percent Mexican, 30 percent American, and 10 percent from some 40 other countries. Its campus facilities and activities (both academic and extracurricular) are comparable to fine private schools in the United States.

Another high-quality private institution, the Greengates School, is a British International school. Founded in 1951 and located in the northern suburbs of Mexico City, it teaches British English. With just over 1,000 students between the ages of three and 18, it mainly serves the foreign diplomatic, commercial, and banking communities. English is the language of instruction and the majority of teachers are British, many of whom are contracted from the United Kingdom. The Infant and Junior School follows a modified British National Curriculum. Though this may not be your cup of tea, it is included here as an example of the diversity of choices that exist in Mexico. In Mexico City, there are also German, French, and Japanese private schools, which teach all grades through and including high school.

Another option would be to consider sending your child to a public school. The advantage here is that your child would be immersed in Spanish and in a welcoming atmosphere. At first your son or daughter may have some difficulty with the language, but, curious about your child's life back home, Mexican classmates will want to make friends quickly. Barbara and I have several friends whose kids have had excellent experiences in Mexican primary schools. Your child would meet ordinary Mexican kids rather than the privileged children of the wealthy. There is no tuition, and any fees are quite low. Public schools also consider accepting a child midway through the school year. This decision is up to the principal of the individual school.

A disadvantage of public schools is that you will not be able to compare facilities and curriculum online or over the telephone as easily as you can with private schools, which have a websites and sales brochures. In addition, facilities will most likely not measure up to those of a private school. You will probably have to wait to compare area public schools after making your move.

In any case, it is critical to ascertain the correct grade for your child to transfer into. To begin the process, you need your child's official transcript from the school or department of education in the district where your child last took classes.

HIGH SCHOOLS

All of the schools mentioned previously offer classes from primary grades through high school. In many cases, however, when children of expats reach high-school or even junior-high-school age, they prefer to return to the United States to finish school. This is especially true of children who have been enrolled in Mexican public schools. But even kids with a private-school background may want to be involved in the "cooler" teen culture in the States. Kids enrolled in Mexican public high schools who are thinking about college may find a more academically oriented curriculum in United States.

COLLEGES AND UNIVERSITIES

The majority of Mexican universities and colleges require a reasonably good working knowledge of Spanish and many require a proficiency test before enrollment. These schools offer remedial Spanish classes for all levels. There are also a few universities in Mexico City that offer a bilingual curriculum. These include the excellent Alliant International University, Endicott College, and Westhill University.

Among the hundreds of other colleges and universities throughout Mexico, the largest university is National Autonomous University of Mexico. Known as UNAM, this institution has an amazingly large enrollment, somewhere around 265,000 students. Including academic staff, research, and support personnel, more than 300,000 people are involved in the university community. The university is located in Mexico City and has campuses in 16 other Mexican states, as well as in the United States and Canada. UNAM also runs two types of preparatory schools. The Escuela Nacional Preparatoria (National Preparatory School) has nine locations, and the Colegio de Ciencias y Humanidades (College of Sciences and Humanities) has five.

To give you a sense of the size of UNAM, consider these stats: It has a library system that includes 143 libraries with more than four million books, and 19 bookshops; 18 buildings of extraordinary historical and architectural value, including the Antiguo Colegio de San Ildefonso, the Palacio de Minería, and the Museo de San Carlos, constitute part of its heritage. It also has an invaluable collection of 152 mural paintings, 800 sculptures, 86,190 masterpieces, and 50 stained-glass pieces. In addition, it has 28 exhibition rooms, two concert halls, seven theaters, nine presses, three aquariums, 13 museums, two oceanographic ships and two oceanographic plateaus, 28 dental clinics, two botanical gardens, 365 acres of ecological reservoir, a CRAY-Y-MP/432 super-computer, more than 15,000 computers and workstations, more than 150 computing centers, 200 local nets connected via TCP/IP, two stadiums, two observatories, three ranches, seven swimming pools and areas in which 39 sports can be practiced, 24 dining rooms, 35 cafeterias, and three supermarkets.

> The majority of Mexican universities and colleges require a reasonably good working knowledge of Spanish and many require a proficiency test before enrollment.

Cuernavaca is also an academic center, with fine universities and research institutions. The Instituto Tecnológico y de Estudios Superiores de Monterrey, for instance, operates 20 or so research institutions in fields such as physics, electrical engineering, traditional medicine, solar energy, biotechnology, genetic engineering, marketing, and anthropology. These and other fine facilities draw a large number of PhDs, MDs, scientists, and researchers to the city.

Founded in 1949, Instituto Allende in San Miguel de Allende is an institution of higher education incorporated with the University of Guanajuato since 1950 and registered with the Departments of Education of the United States and Canada. The Instituto offers a Bachelors Degree in Visual Arts, an Associate of Arts in Visual Arts, a Masters Degree in Fine Arts, and continuing education courses in art and Spanish as a second language.

For program listings and descriptions as well as enrollment information at most Mexican colleges and universities, check the Web: www.mexonline.com/univrsty.htm and www.solutionsabroad.com/a_schoolsmexico.asp are good places to start.

STUDY ABROAD

Study abroad programs are available through the following schools as well as many U.S. universities and private organizations. These programs include academic year/semester, summer, summer law, summer business, volunteering, high school, language, and graduate. For a list of programs, go to www.studyabroad.com. Here are two examples of available programs:

Rutgers Study Abroad at Universidad Autonoma de Yucatan in Mérida offers Full Year, Fall, and Spring programs. Applications for Full Year or Fall must be received by March 1; October 1 for Spring.

The Full Year program (approximately 30–33 credits) runs between late July and mid-May. The Fall program (approximately 15 credits) runs between late July and mid-December. The Spring program (also approximately 15 credits) runs between early January and mid-May.

Tuitions vary, depending on New Jersey residency status. New Jersey residents pay the following: Full Year, $17,253; Fall or Spring, $9,771. Non–New Jersey residents pay: Full Year, $22,553; Fall or Spring, $12,421. Tuition, fees, housing, most meals, and basic medical insurance are included in this fee.

The University of Miami offers a variety of study abroad programs through Universidad Iberoameric Mexico City, D.F., including undergraduate, graduate, semester, and year programs. One of their study abroad options, the Centro de Investigaciones y Docencia Economicas (CIDE), is a university center for advanced research in economics and social sciences. The Centro offers both undergraduate and graduate programs in economics, public administration, international studies, and economics. Its extensive faculty and research staff—foremost in their fields—publish research articles and studies impacting policies and development strategies throughout Mexico.

All coursework is conducted in Spanish, so students must have a high level of fluency in the language. Prerequisites include a minimum 3.0 GPA and fluency or an advanced command of the Spanish language. UM students should have completed at least one 300-level Spanish-language course prior to participation in the exchange. International Studies majors are highly encouraged to apply.

There are no on-campus dormitories or residence halls; however, CIDE's international office will work with Iberoamericana's international office to place you with a host. Students make all room-and-board payments directly upon arrival to the necessary party. A semester, including UM tuition, room and board, and books and supplies, is estimated to cost $25,838; a full year, $32,738. Program dates are from late August to early December, and from early January to mid-May. For more information go to www.cide.edu.

Health

One of the first questions asked by both short- and long-term visitors to Mexico regards the quality of health care. Are doctors and hospitals in Mexico on a par with the States? Expat experiences are varied. In some ways, healthcare in Mexico is superior to that of the United States, but in other ways it falls dismally short.

For instance, sanitation, which has improved greatly over the years, is still not as good in Mexico as it is in the States. Visitors occasionally get what is known as the dreaded *turista*. If you get *turista*, which is really parasites, Mexican doctors and labs can easily diagnose and treat the problem at a cost of about 20 bucks. In the States, after extensive and expensive testing, the diagnosis will often be "inconclusive"!

Doctors throughout Mexico are skilled in other common problems, like broken bones, fevers, and the various conditions that can befall any of us, and they have expertise in performing surgeries of various kinds. Typically, large cities and towns with a sizable number of foreigners and/ or wealthy Mexicans have caring and sharp general practitioners, many of

The Tomato Cure

Food can be a cure for more than hunger or a bad mood. Take, for instance, what happened to us many years ago in a restaurant in Zacatecas. Our daughter, Liza, was about 18 months old and sitting in a high chair at the table. We ordered coffee after our meal, and as was the tradition then, hot water was brought to the table to which you could add your own Nescafé. A jar of Nescafé was a permanent fixture on every restaurant table, along with the salt, pepper, and bottles of varying strengths of salsa.

This time, however, the young waitress tripped over one of the legs of Liza's highchair and, to our horror, spilled almost the entire pot of just-boiled water over Liza's arm. I screamed, Barbara screamed, Liza screamed, and so did the waitress as I tore Liza out of the highchair and ran with her toward the kitchen sink and cold water. The cook, realizing what had happened, frantically began dicing tomatoes like a crazed Benihana chef. As we passed her, she grabbed Liza, cradled her in one arm, and immediately covered Liza's burnt arm completely with them! She followed that with a large dose of salt and then wrapped the arm in paper napkins! To our amazement, Liza immediately stopped howling and we took a deep breath. By the time we returned to our hotel room, Liza appeared to be fine, so we carefully unwrapped the napkins and removed the tomatoes. To our amazement and joy, her skin was absolutely perfect, with only one tiny triangle of very red, angry flesh that the "spaghetti sauce" had missed.

Along these same lines, one effective "cure" for itchy insect bites is to squeeze some fresh lemon juice and then salt on the bites; i.e., make like a margarita!

whom were trained in the United States and speak at least a little English. As you might expect, cities with large numbers of older retirees tend to have higher numbers of heart specialists and plastic surgeons.

Unlike many found in the United States, Mexican doctors and medical staff invariably treat patients with warmth, friendliness, and attention. Even surgeons and specialists treat patients with a respect that is unheard of in the States. A friend who went to the ABC (American-British-Cowdray) Hospital in Mexico City for surgery on her neck raved about the care she received, especially from the nursing staff.

One concern people express relative to healthcare in Mexico regards the diagnosis and treatment of serious and potentially life-threatening illnesses. Modern, high-tech diagnostic equipment and analysts in many Mexican hospitals are said to be inferior to those in the United States, although it is widely agreed that specific hospitals in Mexico

City, Monterrey, and Guadalajara are first class. If you are in a situation where you have a difficult or life-threatening medical problem, it makes sense to go to the States for a second or third opinion.

After your trip to the States, you may make the decision to return to Mexico for treatment. All treatments and therapies, including those for serious illnesses requiring chemotherapy, dialysis, and respiratory problems, are available in Mexico, often for one-third of the U.S. cost. The low cost of health care in Mexico is one of its greatest attractions. On average, an office visit with a doctor—specialist or otherwise—costs 350–500 pesos ($31–44). A visit to the dentist for a cleaning costs about 250 pesos ($22). Most drugs also cost about 30 percent to 50 percent less in Mexico.

Rooms in many private hospitals are more like those in a five-star hotel. Every mid- to large-sized city has at least one first-rate hospital, many of them associated with hospitals in the States. In Mazatlán, for example, the Sharp Hospital is a sister of the Sharp Hospital in San Diego. In Querétaro, the new Hospital San Jose is associated with the Herman Hospital at the University of Texas Medical Center.

The best hospitals in Mexico are said to be in Mexico City and Guadalajara, the two largest cities in the country. The Hospital del Carmen in Guadalajara, for example, has luxurious rooms, which include an additional bed and sitting area for family members to spend the night. Per-night room costs are as follows: Standard, 1,529 pesos ($139); Jr. Suite, 2,081 pesos ($189); Suite, 2,639 pesos ($240); Master Suite, 3,473 pesos ($315). Public hospitals and clinics run by IMSS (Mexican Institute of Social Security) are much less expensive.

A friend who needed a CAT scan went to a local hospital in the morning, had the scan done, and returned after lunch to pick up the films and a written interpretation. The entire experience was hassle-free and inexpensive. It cost about $400—about 30 percent of what it would have cost in the United States.

Types of Insurance

Your U.S. health insurance will most likely not cover you in Mexico. Some companies will provide a rider covering short-term international travel, for which they will reimburse you at a later time. If you plan to live in Mexico, look into buying an insurance policy that provides long-term international coverage. Many companies sell just such policies online, including Sanborn's (800/222-0158, www.sanbornsinsurance.com), Solutions Abroad (www.solutionsabroad.com), and Seguros Insurance (www.seguros-insurance.net).

If you are already in Mexico, inquire at any branch of Lloyd Bank (www.lloyd.com.mx), the American Society in Guadalajara (333/121-2395), or an independent insurance agent like Stephen M. Patton (555/533-1620, 800/001-9200 toll-free in Mexico, stephen@patton.mexis.com). Many other insurance providers run display ads in local English-language newspapers. The larger the number of resident foreigners, the larger the number of independent insurance agents there will be.

Medicare does not cover hospital or medical services outside the United States. The Department of Veterans Affairs will pay for hospital and medical service outside the United States only if you are a veteran with a service-related disability.

IMSS provides the least expensive insurance option in Mexico. Anyone living legally in the country can sign up for IMSS. Its health insurance costs about $250 per year if you are aged 60 or older and about $150 per year if you are younger. It must be paid in one lump sum. The cost covers check-ups, hospitalization, surgeries, lab work, x-rays, prescription medicines, and some dental. It will not cover individuals with preexisting conditions. When you fill out the application, it is important to list every medical condition you have ever had, so that they cannot later deny coverage on the grounds of a preexisting condition.

Once you sign on, undergo a checkup, and pay, it takes about six months for coverage to become effective. Then, for medical care, you must go to an assigned clinic for evaluation. Many foreigners with IMSS insurance use it only for catastrophic medical problems. For minor health problems, they go to private physicians rather than wait in line at an IMSS clinic. If you do go to the clinic and need a specialist or a more complicated procedure than that clinic can handle, you'll be referred to a larger clinic or hospital. The downside is that all this takes time. More importantly, not all the clinics and hospitals are of equal quality. Check out, in advance, the hospitals that you would be referred to in an emergency or for a difficult procedure.

Pharmacies and Prescription Drugs

It is a pleasure to be able to walk up to the counter in a pharmacy in Mexico and buy almost any drug you want without a prescription. The only exceptions are restricted drugs like narcotics and sleeping pills. Many of the drugs sold by prescription in the States sell for half the price or less in Mexico. One thing to keep in mind is that Mexican doctors will sometimes prescribe a drug in a high dosage or one not approved by the FDA. Barbara once took an antibiotic that was strong enough to cure a sinus infection in an elephant. Within 15 minutes of taking it, she felt like she had been hit by a truck. This places the burden on the buyer to be informed and aware. Question your doctor at length if you are not familiar with the prescribed drug.

> *Many of the drugs sold by prescription in the States sell for half the price or less in Mexico.*

Mexican *campesinos* (country folks) have traditionally gone to the local pharmacist for medical advice. This was especially true in small villages, where often the only people in town with any medical information were the *curanderos* (healers) and the druggist. Many Mexicans can barely afford to put food on the table, let alone the luxury of seeing a doctor. So Mexicans would (and still do) get medical advice, diagnoses, and drugs from their trusted pharmacists. The same is true for many foreigners with minor health problems who don't want to go through the hassle of seeing a doctor.

In the year 2000, the average price to fill a prescription was $3.90 in Mexico, compared to $12 in the United States. That same year, Mexicans on average spent $34 per person on medicines annually—that figure in the United States was $334.

Preventative Measures

Living in Mexico may bring immediate relief from one of the greatest and most debilitating health problems of our time: stress. Living in a laid-back culture will improve your mental health. And once you eliminate the commute to work, the high cost of everything, and the crazy, competitive, frightening, fast pace of life in the States, improvement in your physical health will miraculously follow.

When *norteamericanos* think of Mexico and health, they think mostly of Montezuma's revenge. When *la turista's* intense diarrhea and cramps hit, it can really ruin your day, to put it mildly. Fortunately, *la turista* hits residents far less often than it does short-term visitors. Most foreign residents learn to take precautions against stomach problems. Plus, their systems adapt somewhat to the local bacteria, although a bout of amoebas every now and then is not uncommon. Expats joke about getting diarrhea when they return to the States! They call it "tourist."

Before cooking, wash and soak all veggies and fruits in a disinfectant solution (many brands are sold in the supermarket). In a bind, you can use one drop of Clorox to one quart of water. Tourists, who generally eat all their meals out, are at the mercy of the restaurant or food stand. While most are hygienic, some should be avoided. Residents figure out which restaurants and stands to avoid.

Some couples traveling together have observed that, although they eat the same foods in the same places at the same time, the one who handles the money gets sick more often.

The basic rules of thumb for good stomach health are (1) always drink bottled water, (2) wash your hands throughout the day, as though you are possessed, and (3) hope for the best. Even though most tourist restaurants are attentive to good hygiene and serve both purified water and purified ice cubes in drinks, people get sick. One guess is that the principal way *turista* is passed is by handling money. Some couples traveling together have observed that, although they eat the same foods in the same places at the same time, the one who handles the money gets sick more often. Whether you believe this or not, it is an excellent idea to get serious about washing your hands—four, sometimes five, times a day. Antiseptic hand lotions come in small bottles that will fit in a purse or pocket. Keep one in the glove compartment of your car for washing up before quick food stops.

Other than stomach-related illnesses, there are few especially dangerous health problems endemic to Mexico—nothing that will require you to get shots before crossing the border. However, there are occasional outbreaks of hepatitis in one part of the country or another, and rare outbreaks of dengue fever.

It is not uncommon in homes and businesses to find a small trash can next to a toilet for the disposal of toilet paper, which if flushed can clog sensitive septic systems. It is especially important to wash hands after a visit to the WC.

Curanderos

Since long before the Spanish Conquest, every village in Latin America has had its shaman or *curandero*. Even today, *curanderos*, both male and female, probably outnumber licensed medical doctors in Mexico and serve as the first line of defense in medical care for the average person of Mexico. Though a *curandero* has the skill to treat a wide variety of illnesses, he or she is the only healer in the culture who can treat *mal puesto*, illnesses caused by witchcraft. The *curandero* is thought to have been given a *don de Dios* (a gift from God) to heal the sick. Typically, the *curandero* works on three levels—the material, the spiritual, and the mental. They may prescribe an herbal remedy or conduct a religious ritual. Quite often, a *curandero* is called upon to treat the physical symptoms that patients believe come from supernatural causes. Thus, some *curanderos* function as *espiritualistas* (mediums).

The *curandero* often works from the ancient principle that good health is preserved by maintaining a balance in the body, between hot and cold. Thus, a disease that is viewed as being a "cold" can be remedied by adding a "hot" element. This might be accomplished by having the patient eat hot foods, soak in a hot bath, spend time in a sweat lodge, or consume herbs whose basic nature is hot. The *curandero* uses a classification system in which foods, drugs, plants, activities, and the illnesses themselves are recognized as having the essence of hot or cold. Optimum health requires eating a balanced diet of hot and cold foods and a lifestyle that conforms to the same balance.

Often, the *curandero's* cure consists of making contact with the *bruja* (witch) who is responsible for the illness. This is done with the use of potions, incantations, rituals, and powders. Tobacco and sounds are often used as well, as are sacred objects, such as eagle feathers and bones.

If you are looking for a *curandero* in Mexico, you will find one quickly. All you have to do is ask.

As in every country, you should take precautions against AIDS and other sexually transmitted diseases. AIDS is called SIDA in Mexico. A government report has stated that the number of AIDS cases was 150,000 at the end of 2001. The number of people infected with HIV was 300,000, with another 300,000 at high risk because they are sex workers or their clients. Mexico ranks third in the Western Hemisphere in the number of reported HIV/AIDS cases, and women constitute about 17 percent of all cases.

In some parts of the country, especially the more tropical areas, you will see some scary-looking bugs. The stings and bites of scorpions and black widow spiders can be dangerous and painful, but are rarely deadly. If you will be traveling to places where these crawly creatures live, stock an antihistamine. Take one or two tablets if you get bitten to avoid a possible allergic reaction. If you wind up living in the tropics, you will probably assemble a special tropical medicine cabinet containing such items as anti-scorpion venom. You will also learn a few preservation tricks like this one: If you are stung by a stingray or jellyfish (both stings can hurt like hell), the best immediate antidote is for you—or someone close to you—to pee on the sting! If you are not in the mood for such a remedy, don't worry. No matter where you are in Mexico you are not far from a medical clinic—even in the most remote areas.

Medicine men and women *(brujos* or *curanderos)* and other alternative healers hold a place of honor in Mexico, probably because of the country's deep indigenous and spiritual roots. In every Mexican town, healers offer a wide array of treatments, from chiropractic to herbal remedies, homeopathy, Reiki (energy work), and massage. It is not unusual to find an indigenous shaman, well known in the area for his or her healing power, taking on foreign clients.

Mexico is a land of natural hot springs. Throughout the country, a wide variety of beautiful spas and healing clinics offer nutritional, relaxation, and body-cleansing programs, usually including thermal waters, mud baths, and vegetarian cuisine. One, located next to a very hot river, channels the river's water (first filtered) into hot tubs in each guest room. What a treat for about $50 a night for two! Another spa, located in a semitropical area, offers rigorous weeklong packages with special vegetarian meals, daily massages, hot herbal wraps, and high colonics—all for a fraction of the cost of a health spa in the United States.

Abortion is illegal in Mexico, with its regulation falling under the jurisdiction of the states. Women face six months to five years imprisonment for having an abortion, and a doctor or midwife who performs the procedure faces suspension from the medical profession for a period of 2–5 years.

AA meetings are ubiquitous in Mexico. Driving through even the smallest villages, you may notice the AA symbol mounted on even the most rudimentary, bamboo-walled building. Towns with a large number of foreign residents hold meetings in English as well as Spanish. Meetings also come in a variety of styles. In San Miguel for instance, there is a women's meeting, and in Puerto Vallarta, a meeting for gay men. Even if you do not speak Spanish, don't be intimidated by a Spanish meeting.

People will be very welcoming and friendly, and may even encourage you to talk. Just look for the AA symbol inside a triangle and a circle, usually on a blue background, or advertisements in the local paper or phonebook. The people you encounter at the meeting can usually direct you to the local Al-Anon, if there is one.

An agency of the Mexican government, *Instituto National Senectitud* (National Old Age Institute), issues INSEN cards, which can be used by people over the age of 60 to get discounts. Most retirees don't know about the card. To get one, find an INSEN representative, usually in a DIF Office (DIF stands for *Desarrollo Integral de la Familia*, meaning Integrated Family Development). You will need proof of age and residency (an FM3 will do) and two or three photos of yourself. There is no fee, but you may come up against some resistance from officials who are not aware that all residents of Mexico, whether nationals or foreigners, are entitled to the card. Just persist if officials balk, and you should eventually get one. With the card, you'll get free admission to museums and exhibits, discounts on buses and national flights, and discounts at movie theaters and some hotel chains.

Environmental Factors

Mexico is rich in silver, copper, gold, lead, zinc, natural gas, and timber. It is the sixth-largest oil producer in the world. But in exploiting its resources, Mexico has wreaked havoc on its environment. Overgrazing, poor crop choices, and inefficient farm management have led to the deterioration of the topsoil. Forests have been hacked down, lakes and rivers polluted, and air quality in some areas has deteriorated badly.

Both Mexicans and visitors to the country are affected in many ways by environmental degradation. The most obvious example is the poor air quality in Mexico City. Air quality in the city fluctuates according to weather, time of year, day of the week, and the area of town you are in. If you pick a bad air period to visit the city's great museums, you may be forced to cut your visit short after just a few days to avoid a sore throat and watering, burning eyes. Some visitors are not affected by the pollution very much, while others have a higher sensitivity and must escape.

The fires of 1998 were started in the slash-and-burn tradition and whipped by the winds of El Niño. A catastrophic environmental disaster, they burned throughout Mexico, wiped out portions of the rain

Mexico and Greenhouse Gases

In 2004, Mexico launched a new partnership that makes it the first country to adopt internationally accepted standards to measure and report business greenhouse gas (GHG) emissions for establishing a voluntary national program.

The partnership, called the Mexico GHG Pilot Program, was launched with the signing of an agreement between Mexico's Secretariat for the Environment and Natural Resources, the World Resources Institute, and the World Business Council for Sustainable Development.

The two-year partnership will develop a voluntary reporting plat-form for Mexican businesses, while at the same time benefiting corporate bottom lines, reducing local air pollutants, and mitigating global climate change.

"While many industries throughout the world have adopted the GHG Protocol, Mexico is the first country to adopt it," said Jonathan Lash, WRI president. "In the absence of international leadership in tackling climate change, Mexico has taken the lead in showing what can be done to mitigate global warming."

The partners believe that the successful implementation of the program will serve as an inspiring

forest in the state of Chiapas, and affected air quality throughout the country. After 1998, Mexican laws were changed, making it illegal to slash and burn. The practice has slowed down but, due to lack of enforcement, has not been stopped. These burn-offs, which occur during the driest, dustiest months of April and May in central Mexico, can create mild respiratory problems for sensitive individuals.

Before the 1970s, plastic packaging was not yet in use in Mexico. For trips to the market, people had to bring, at the very least, a large shopping bag, a bottle or two for oil and honey, which were sold only in bulk, and a specially designed wire basket for eggs. When something needed to be wrapped, the shopkeeper used old newspaper. Now, plastic and other types of packaging materials are prevalent, often strewn along highways.

Roadside trash and impromptu dumps attest to the fact that many Mexicans don't consider litter to be an eyesore. This can be a real blemish for people touring the country by car. But as you drive around, you will notice that some states have cleaned up highways while others have not. It seems to be a question of awareness and resources. Most Mexican cities have daily trash pickup. Several have even tried recycling, but the infrastructure is really not in place to make that work.

example for other countries in the region—and the world. They hope more countries will consider adopting similar initiatives to lessen climate change.

"Mexico's adoption of the GHG Protocol is a significant step to the further standardization and harmonization of GHG accounting and reporting frameworks worldwide," says Björn Stigson, president of WBCSD. "We hope other countries will also use the GHG Protocol."

The GHG Protocol, first launched in 2001, has become the most widely used global standard for corporate accounting of greenhouse gas emissions. It was developed by more than 500 experts from businesses, non-governmental organizations (NGOs), and governments. It has been adopted by more than 150 companies, including industry associations representing pulp and paper, aluminum, and cement, and enjoys the support of NGOs and governments alike.

Mexico ranks as the 14th-largest emitter of greenhouse gases in the world and is second only to Brazil in Latin America. In 2000, according to WRI's Climate Analyses Indicators Tool, GHG emissions in Mexico equaled 1.4 tons per person, compared to 6.6 tons per U.S. citizen and 1.3 tons per Brazilian.

Runoff from chemical plants and dumping have had catastrophic effects on many of Mexico's rivers and lakes. To make things even worse, water has been steadily pumped from these same bodies of water to meet the needs of nearby, growing cities. Lake Chapala and Lake Pátzcuaro, for example, are now almost dead. Not too many years ago these lakes provided local populations with a fresh catch every day. Fishermen had jobs, tourists an enjoyable fishing and boating experience, locals a place to swim and cool off in the hot season. Very few cities treat their sewage. Raw sewage flows into nearby rivers and lakes, polluting them and sometimes creating foul odors. Keep this in mind before taking a swim. This too is beginning to change, though. San Miguel de Allende is in the process of constructing its first sewage treatment plant.

In response to continuing environmental degradation, grassroots groups, many with foreign volunteers, have sprung up around the country and have begun reforesting, cleaning up rivers and streams, and reeducating people about environmental issues. Some more enlightened state governments have also begun to recognize the problem and have funded local environmental departments or matched funds with independent organizations. This has lead to some major environmental successes. In 2003, for instance, Lake Chapala was included in the list of endangered lakes by the international Living Lakes network.

Still, Mexico's environmental movement is perhaps at least 25 years behind that of the United States. Even with the efforts of dedicated and hardworking people, without economic growth and government backing of environmental education programs, there will not be any significant improvement.

Unlike in the United States, smoking is completely accepted everywhere in Mexico. Restricting smoking in public places is unheard of, though we have recently begun seeing nonsmoking sections in some higher-priced restaurants. When you live in Mexico, you get used to the fact that someone may sit at the table next to you in a restaurant and light up. That is just (cough, cough) the way it is.

Disabled Access

There are no legal requirements anywhere in Mexico to provide accessibility for individuals with disabilities. Nevertheless, if you are disabled, you can travel in Mexico if you make arrangements to stay in newer, high-end hotels, which are more likely to have accessibility. After arriving at the airport, take a taxi to your hotel. Public transportation would be very difficult, if not impossible. If you want to see sites in the area, take a taxi or hire a car and driver. Call ahead to tourist sites and restaurants if you have any doubts about accessibility. Lastly, do not be afraid to ask for help. Mexicans are very kind and resourceful and will come up with a way to help.

Safety

Cruz Roja (the Mexican Red Cross) operates ambulances and medical clinics throughout Mexico. They provide transport in the event of an accident or emergency and are a revered institution in Mexico. In large cities, there are also private ambulance services that can get you to a hospital relatively quickly. If you are in the middle of nowhere and have an accident, you may be forced to ride to a nearby clinic in the back of a pickup or strapped to the back of a burro. If your injuries are severe, you have insurance to cover it, and you're not too far out in the sticks, you may be flown out. Many Mexican and U.S. health insurance companies include emergency helicopter evacuation services in their policies. Some pay to fly patients back to the United States for treatment. If you have allergies, reactions to certain medicines, or other unique medical problems, you should wear a medical alert bracelet or something similar that will alert medical personnel.

Mexico has an undeserved reputation as being crime-ridden and dangerous. This most likely resulted from the years of chaos that Mexico experienced during and after their revolution in the 1910s and '20s. Today, most Mexicans are very honest people. For example, shop attendants will call you back or chase after you to return forgotten change. But take normal precautions against thieves. Leave valuables in a safe place when you go out walking or carry them in a fanny pack or a tightly held handbag.

Be aware that pickpockets love operating in large crowds, at parades, and at other public events. When traveling around Mexico, carry enough pesos in your pocket for just one day. Hide extra cash somewhere else on your body or in your car if it is parked in a lot with a guard, a garage, or behind walls. That way, if you get your pocket picked, it won't hurt too badly. (By the way, in 35 years this has never happened to me).

Many travel writers recommend using money belts to hide cash, traveler's checks, and passports. Undoubtedly, these writers never got a chapped chest or waist from wearing a money belt on a hot day, to say nothing of the hassle of reaching into one without looking like a pervert. Mexico City is the place to break out the money belt. When you stay at hotels, make use of the hotel safe-deposit box.

Don't leave packages or items that might look interesting to a thief in your car on the street overnight, and don't flaunt your wealth by showing off large rolls of cash or fancy jewelry. Theft is possible anywhere, though generally speaking, the smaller the town, the less crime it has. Even mid-sized cities like Mazatlán, San Miguel de Allende, Ajijic, Oaxaca, and Puerto Vallarta are still fairly low in crime.

Foreigners who live in Mexico know that crime is a fact of life but do not allow that fact to overshadow Mexico's wonderfully enriching qualities. They learn to take reasonable precautions against crime, as they would in the United States, then get on with their lives. In most smaller retirement communities when there is criminal activity, it generally takes the form of robbery and burglary. Cuernavaca is reputed to have a larger than normal number of kidnappings. While true, it is also true that the victims are always Mexicans.

To protect against crime, many people live in gated developments or in homes within a walled property. You can take other precautions to be certain that their home is secure during trips out of town. Hire a house-sitter or arrange for someone to check the house each day. Install good sturdy locks on doors and windows, and consider having a secure room in the house where valuables can be kept. Most important, know your neighbors and ask them to keep an eye on the house. Sound familiar? These are more or less the same types of precautions people should take in any mid-size to large city in the world.

In general, crime in Mexican cities is less violent than crime in comparably sized U.S. cities. When homicides do occur, they are usually crimes of passion or drug related. Most violent crimes occur in Mexico City, but that is no surprise given the population of the city. In 2004, Mexico City's mayor hired Rudolf Gullianni and his firm as consultants on lowering the crime rate as he did in New York City when he was mayor. If you travel to Mexico City, become super conscious of your surroundings and try not to be flashy. Also, take only official taxis.

In some parts of the country, especially in northern Mexico, crime is related to drug trafficking—but few tourists or foreign residents are affected. Political violence still occurs occasionally in some remote areas in the states of Guerrero, Oaxaca, and Chiapas. Crime statistics in Mexico, when they are available, are misleading because distrust of the police is so much a part of the Mexican psyche that many crimes go unreported. Domestic and sexual violence perpetrated against Mexican women is widespread and vastly underreported. Guns are illegal, though many Mexicans own them.

Many people feel that Mexico's greatest crime problems are its ineffectual and corrupt justice system, which allows convicted criminals to go free with little or no punishment, and police corruption, which continues to confirm citizens' long-standing distrust of authority. Modernizing the justice system and cleaning up the police were two important planks of President Vicente Fox's unrealized agenda.

© Ken Luboff

Employment

Mexico, like many third world countries, has a problem with unemployment. Thus the government does not encourage foreigners to come and work unless they are experts in a certain field, so as not to take away jobs from locals. The best plan for working in Mexico is to contact a U.S. firm with a presence in Mexico and inquire about employment. In general, foreigners who work in Mexico usually fall into one of three categories. The first category is made up of those who arrive in Mexico with a job. For the most part, people in this category are employees of a U.S. or multi-national corporation with offices in Mexico. The second category is made up of entrepreneurial types who either arrive in Mexico with the intention of starting their own business or live in the country for a while, then recognize a need and fill it. Third are those who attempt to find work once they get settled in Mexico. This may be the most difficult job of all.

People who fall into the first category generally have a smooth transition because their company cuts through the red tape and often provides perks that lead to an extremely luxurious life in Mexico. A case in point is the western director for a large international elevator company based in Mexico City. He is married with three children. His company took care of all the paperwork necessary for him to work in Mexico and assisted with visas for the rest of the family. His wife was not given permission to work in Mexico. His salary is exactly what he was making in the States, and his benefits are quite impressive. He and his family are also provided with housing. They chose to live in Cuernavaca, where they lease a small villa complete with pool and tennis court. The rental cost is $1,800 per month, which would be an excellent price in the States. Other benefits include one family car, another car and driver to take dad to and from work in Mexico City, tuition for the three children in excellent bilingual schools, a maid, a nanny, a cook, a full-time gardener, and a membership in a golf/country club. This sweet deal not only allows him to save a bundle, it also gives him a break on his U.S. income tax.

Another friend works for an international insurance company based in the UK and specializing in catastrophic incidents, such as hurricanes and earthquakes. He came to Mexico with his fiancée after duty in Indonesia. He's now based in Mexico City. Again, the company arranged all the paperwork with the Mexican government, which was particularly difficult since one of the parties is Indonesian. Being unmarried didn't seem to be an issue except that his fiancée was not allowed to work in Mexico. The company pays for their housing in Mexico City, a five-bedroom colonial with a pool, in a nice neighborhood. They also provided the services of a maid, cook, and gardener, as well as a car and driver. It would appear that large international companies treat their employees very well indeed.

If nothing else, almost all companies will take care of obtaining working papers for their employees. They will also help obtain an FM3 if the employee doesn't already have one. But just in case you have a promise of a job and must obtain permits on your own, here is the procedure:

You must have a job offer before you apply for permission to work. The offer must be written on the company's official letterhead and include your full name (correctly spelled), the position you will hold, the date you will begin (you may begin work before you receive the permission as long as you have already started the application process), and the amount of money that you will earn. An official of the institution must sign the letter, and you must include a photocopy of this individual's identification. Start your application process no later than 30 days before your supposed start date of work, as visa applications are not accepted before this time period. The process is more or less the same if you are planning to start a business, with or without employees.

Self-Employment

Entrepreneurs, who fall into the second category and plan to start their own business, will be happy to know that it is relatively easy to get a business off the ground in Mexico. Establishing a business is also the easiest way to gain employment in Mexico other than coming with a job, or the promise of a job. The key to running a legal business as a foreigner is to register to pay taxes. All you do is visit the nearest SAT (Hacienda) office, which is the government office that registers Mexican corporations. SAT also registers a variety of permits, acts as a tax collector, and is where you will receive and complete your tax papers. They will issue an RFC, or tax identification number, which allows you to pay taxes and issue *facturas* (legal receipts for services performed and items purchased, all tax deductible). The next time you renew your FM3, you merely take your RFC and corporation papers with you so that Mexican immigration can put a special working permit in your FM3. The process is really that simple as long as your paperwork is in order. Some people use an attorney to complete this process but it is not necessary, and is, in fact, a waste of money. Better to consult a *notario* (a particular classification of lawyer) if you need clarification and advice.

As a corporation, you are permitted to employ Mexican nationals, but you must either pay their social security health insurance or give them the money to purchase their own insurance. This is also true when you hire a domestic worker for your home. Non-Mexican citizens are not permitted to occupy jobs that can be held by Mexican nationals.

Be aware that as a business person you will almost certainly be required to pay *mordidas* (bribes) on occasion. These payoffs may also come in the form of charitable contributions.

Unless you are a one-person business, like an artist or therapist, for example, operating a business in Mexico can be trying, requiring a enormous amount of patience and a steady temperament. Most Mexicans have not grown up in a capitalistic business environment that prides itself on

Fred's Business

Fred Feibel was a real estate agent prior to his move to San Francisco, Nayarit, in 1997. San Francisco, known locally as San Pancho, is a quiet seaside village, with a pristine and picturesque beach, located about 45 minutes north of Puerto Vallarta.

Though life in San Pancho at the time was fairly lazy, Fred decided to open a small real estate office on the main street, Fred Feibel y Associados. In order to start his business, Fred first got permission, with his FM3 in hand, from immigration to operate a business. He was also certified as a *persona de confianza* (a trustworthy person).

Next, Fred formed a Mexican corporation, naming himself as the *Administrador Unico,* basically its sole manager. He then registered the corporation with both the Mexican Secretary of Commerce and the Secretary of Foreign Relations (because it is considered a foreign investment). Lastly, Fred registered the business with SAT (formerly known as Hacienda), the Mexican equivalent of the IRS. With all the red tape completed, Fred was ready to open his doors for business, but first he hired an independent CPA to make the required monthly reports to the tax people (which, by the way, can be done on the Internet).

After a few dry years, including the dismal post-9/11 2001 and 2002 seasons, things began to turn around in a big way. Droves of U.S. and Canadian citizens decided that beautiful, peaceful, and semi-remote Mexican beach property was the place to invest. An AARP article in 2004 identified San Francisco as one of the best places on the Mexican coast to buy real estate and live.

Fred's business grew, as did his tax bracket. SAT considers Fred's business a "major contributor." As such, he is in the 37-percent bracket. This designation is reserved for businesses grossing more than $150,000 per year. Businesses with this designation are able to write off all their expenses with the use of a *factura,* a tax number used for any business-related purchases. Anything from office rent to utilities to supplies to gas for the car is deductible using a *factura.*

Fred loves living in San Pancho, and his business continues to grow.

efficiency. Subcontractors may not produce on time, and quality control can be a problem. Locating supervisory personnel may be difficult. You will spend a great deal of time and energy finding qualified people, or you will need to train them yourself. This is less of a problem if you are in a business with a pool of experienced people, like restaurant workers, seamstresses, or laborers. On the other hand, if your business can use them, the latest generation of college graduates is intelligent and motivated.

Whether you are an independent operator or working for an employer, you will receive some nice tax breaks from the U.S. government (if you have to pay U.S. taxes at all). One such break comes in the form of a foreign earned income exclusion (for more information, see the Finance chapter).

TYPES OF BUSINESSES

There are no restrictions on the type of business you can operate in Mexico as long as it is legally constituted and you are not blocked by powerful lobbies, as were several phone companies that tried to gain territory from Telmex. Americans operate many successful enterprises in Mexico, including import-export businesses, U.S. tax preparation services, real estate companies, bed-and-breakfasts, restaurants, computer repair businesses, therapists, clothing design and manufacturing companies, retail boutiques, tour guide outfits, and an agave farm (that's the plant used to make tequila) on 100 leased acres. (After four years, a large tequila manufacturer purchases the plants for a handy profit.)

All of the following professions operate with few problems in Mexico (after applying to immigration). If you're involved in journalism or media, you can be issued a Correspondent's Permit, which enables you to carry out journalism work. The permit lasts for a year but can be renewed as many times as required, provided that you continue working as a journalist. Religious ministers or members of religious associations can be issued a permit that allows them to undertake religious duties and services, as well as social services, regardless of which religion it is. People seeking this permit will need to register and show their ministry qualifications. They can receive an immigration permit if they are willing to invest their own capital in Mexico. Such an investment can be directed at industry or services and must equal a minimum of 40,000 times the minimum daily wage in Mexico City. If you are involved in science, or are a qualified technician, whether commercially or for education, you can apply for an immigration permit in Mexico. You may need an invitation from one of the established scientific or technical organizations in Mexico, however. Artists and sports people can apply for an immigration permit. Each case is considered individually, and entry is at the Interior Ministry's discretion.

Another option is to teach English in Mexico. With salaries ranging from $3 to $10 per hour, this is not a high-paying job. The salary is usually commensurate with the local economy you will be working in. On the

The Turtle Camp

Not far from our house is a fabulous 12-mile-long beach lined with groves of palm trees. The only structures on the beach are a few homes in a small residential community and a turtle camp. The camp consists of a funky group of mismatched buildings and tents in varying states of disrepair. The one-room *palapa* where volunteers sleep needs a bit of plastering and a good paint job. The incubation building where the eggs are cared for until they are hatched, as well as the kitchen/dining building are both tattered but extremely serviceable. The mild state of disrepair of the turtle camp is a result of underfunding by the Mexican government and the University of Guadalajara, which owns and operates the camp. The camp sits empty about half the year.

Activity at the camp starts heating up in early June, just before the rainy season, which is the time of year when the giant leatherback sea turtles begin coming ashore to make nests in the sand and lay their eggs. The rains continue into October. It is during these months that volunteers come from all over the world to walk the beach late into the night to help collect eggs. The eggs are then incubated until they are ready to hatch. Volunteers then help release thousands of tiny turtles safely back into the sea. These turtles can live 200 years!

Our turtle camp is just one of hundreds of opportunities that are available for people who want to come to Mexico and help out. Volunteers teach English, build homes, work with orphans, get involved with various types of marine conservation, medical programs, and an almost-infinite variety of other projects. Not every volunteer program in Mexico is listed on the Web, but it is likely that one of those described there will pique your interest. And what better way to enjoy a holiday than to volunteer your time.

Web you can find a large number of sites that help find employment for English teachers and other professions. Here are a few: www.employnow.com/mexico.htm, www.escapeartist.com, and www.jobabroad.com.

To teach English as a foreign language you will need to have a TEFL certificate (as a minimum). The best bet is to apply at one of the many private schools and language centers in Mexico. Spanish fluency is not always required. Learning English is an absolute requirement for Mexicans who want a professional qualification. Most private schools teach at least half of their lessons (including mathematics and sciences) in English.

Several industries are restricted wholly to Mexican nationals. These include oil, electric utilities, and transportation, all of which have powerful unions.

EMPLOYERS

Your most likely employer in Mexico will be another foreigner selling a product or service to the foreign tourist market. These folks need an employee who understands and relates to that culture. Employment opportunities could include anything from writing articles or having an editorial position at an English newspaper—like the *Pacific Pearl* in Mazatlán, the *Guadalajara Reporter,* or *Atención San Miguel*—to working behind the scenes at a resort or selling real estate. Opportunities also exist for business and marketing consultants from the States to work with growing Mexican companies.

Several helpful books are on the market with more detailed information about doing business and working in Mexico, such as *A Guide to Doing Business in Mexico* by Gary Newman and Anna Szterenfed. Also try websites, such as www.amcham.com.mx (the American Chamber of Commerce in Mexico), www.einnews.com/mexico/newsfeed-MexicoBusiness, or www.executiveplanet.com/business-etiquette/Mexico.html. Remember: It is unlikely that a Mexican will hire you if a qualified Mexican citizen can be found.

BUSINESS PRACTICES

The pace of business in Mexico is slower than it is in the United States. Offices open at 9 A.M., and most retail business do not open until 10 A.M., or even later. Offices are closed 2–4 P.M. for *comida* (the main meal), but then stay open until 7 P.M., and often until 8 P.M. Long lunches and breakfasts are where networking and social interaction takes place.

Mexicans often do not show up for appointments and they most likely will not call in advance, a difficult custom for people from the States to get used to. It is best to call them yourself and double-check your appointment beforehand. Even then, it may not start on time. Once the meeting gets under way, a period of small talk is expected before the actual business is conducted.

The businessperson with whom you are meeting should always be referred to by their professional title. Many people without a specific license will be known as *licenciado* (Lic.). Various kinds of engineers are *Ingeniero/a* (Ing.). Same for doctors (*Doctor/a*) and architects (*Arquitecto/a*). Be

> *Offices are closed 2–4 P.M. for* comida *(the main meal), but then stay open until 7 P.M., and often until 8 P.M. Long lunches and breakfasts are where networking and social interaction takes place.*

sure to use the correct name to address the person, as most Mexicans have four names, the last two being the paternal family name followed by the maternal family name. Always use the paternal name. Women in business may use their maiden name.

Foreigners who move to Mexico and set up a small business, like a bar or a restaurant, may have to get used to the fact that some Mexican employees expect more from a boss here than in the States. You may be asked to help out financially if a family member becomes ill or to participate (financially and/or physically) in a wedding, a baptism, or other family celebration. Depending on the type of business you are in, you will likely find yourself making contributions to local organizations, as you would in the States, to maintain or improve your public image.

In Mexico, customer service is spotty. It can be better in restaurants and retail businesses, where sales people seem more attentive and eager to help. On the other hand, try taking something back to Sam's Club in Mexico. After giving you the third degree, they often will not accept the return. Also, some sales people have a tendency to drop everything (including you) and help the next person that shows up with a question. Be patient.

The Job Hunt

Employment opportunities in Mexico are very limited unless you are working for a large multinational corporation or operating your own business. Jobs are primarily available selling real estate, in the tourist industry selling time-shares, or working in customer relations for a hotel or tour company. Some foreigners find work teaching English, although this generally doesn't pay very much. For a small fee, the American Chamber of Commerce (555/141-3800 in Mexico City, 333/634-6606 in Guadalajara, amchammx@amcham.com.mx) offers help finding employment for qualified individuals. There are also a number of employment and headhunter firms in Mexico City. A short list can be found on the Solutions Abroad website: www.solutionsabroad.com.

Mexico Business Magazine (713/266-0861, mailbox@mexicobusiness. com, www.mexicobusiness.com) and its website are an excellent source for up-to-date information about businesses in the country. Included are classified and display ads listing jobs as well as executive search companies.

For those who have the time and money, there are opportunities to volunteer throughout the country. All of the cities listed in this book as Prime Living locations have active community volunteer organizations. These organizations do everything from feeding and clothing the poor to educating people and helping solve reproductive and environmental problems. Some of these organizations are mentioned in this book. Others can be found on the individual city's website. Apart from these local groups, there are organizations serving indigenous and poor people throughout the country. This can be rewarding work.

Employment opportunities in Mexico are very limited unless you are working for a large multinational corporation or operating your own business.

One friend, disgusted with the proliferation of plastic bags (including a few drawers-full in her own kitchen), made a thick mattress cover and started stuffing it with plastic bags. When finished, she gave the mattress to a neighbor, who was very grateful. That was years ago, and now stuffing mattresses is a thriving "business," with friends getting together for stuffing parties. Hundreds of mattresses have been given to the needy. Be creative!

Keep in mind that things in Mexico move a lot more slowly than elsewhere in North America, and things often take twice the time to accomplish than originally planned. Be certain to arrive in Mexico with enough money in the bank to last at least six months without earning any income.

LANDING A JOB

If you are contemplating a move to Mexico with the intent of soliciting work from Mexican companies, the challenge will be great, if not impossible. You can, on the other hand, live in Mexico and work for a company not doing business in Mexico and do so without Mexican government approval and without having to pay any income taxes to Mexico. However, if you are a U.S. resident/citizen, you are required to report the income and pay U.S. income tax on any income earned from the work you do for a U.S. company.

BENEFITS

Businesses are required to pay employees no less than the minimum wage for that area of the country. On average, the minimum wage runs about 45 pesos ($4.50) per day. Workers also receive a two-week paid vacation after one year of work, and at least seven other national holidays. Vacation days increase by a few days with each subsequent year. Employers must pay social security (IMSS) benefits and high severance pay if the worker is fired without cause.

Labor Laws

WORKERS' RIGHTS

Mexico's constitution and laws generally guarantee freedom of association, the right to organize, the right to collective bargaining, and the right to strike. Moreover, the constitution provides for extensive economic and social rights: the eight-hour day, paid maternity leave, profit sharing, minimum wage, overtime pay, housing, vacations, and workplace health and safety. Labor laws are federal, applying throughout the national territory. Worker rights' observers often charge that Mexico has great labor laws but does not enforce them. The problem is not that laws are not enforced at all. More often, the problem is one of selective enforcement.

MINIMUM WAGE

The *sueldo minimo* (minimum wage) in Mexico varies slightly in different regions of the country. The average minimum wage for all of Mexico in early 2005 was 46.80 pesos per day or $4.20 US. This comes to 17,082 pesos ($1,535) per year. Over and above the minimum wage, employers are required to give a *prima vacaciona* (vacation bonus) of 65 pesos ($5.75) and an *aguinaldo* (Christmas bonus) of 655 pesos ($58). They also must pay into the social security system, a retirement fund, and several employment and housing taxes. This all adds up to about 7,514 pesos ($665) per year for each minimum wage employee, or a total annual compensation of 24,167 pesos ($4,271).

To be clear about this, there is almost no conceivable way to imagine a foreigner working a minimum-wage job in Mexico. This work is reserved for Mexicans and includes day laborers, household help, restaurant workers, and other similar jobs.

Finance

When I stopped working I wondered if I would have enough money for the rest of my life. Now that I am older, I wonder if I will have enough life for the rest of my money." While thinking about your move to Mexico, you have most likely spent many hours crunching numbers to determine whether or not you can afford the move. You may even have spoken to experts, who assured you gravely that you will need big bucks to live well without working. The discussions may have been disconcerting, to say the least.

Cost of Living

When you take your fact-finding trip to Mexico and talk to foreigners living there, you will find that many are living well on $1,200–1,800 per month, some even less. What gives, you might ask? What gives is that almost everything in Mexico costs 25–50 percent less than it does in the United States, depending on your U.S. location. A decent lunch in Mexico, for example, might cost around $10, while the same lunch would cost $15 in Houston and $25 in San Francisco. Prices also vary from place to place within Mexico. An elegant meal for two in a restaurant in Mexico City can easily cost more than $120, while the same meal in San Miguel de Allende will cost only $60. And if you move to a city with few or no other foreigners, the most expensive restaurant in town might set you back only $25 for two. And no matter where you are in Mexico, two people can always find a delicious meal for under $10.

House rental costs vary the same way. In the Lake Chapala area, a two-bedroom house in a nice neighborhood costs about $700–900 a month to rent. That same house in San Miguel de Allende might rent for $1,000–1,200 a month, but in Mexico City the rent could be $1,500–2,500 a month. In any out-of-the-way Mexican village, you could rent that same house for almost nothing (if you could find it). It would not be out of the question to rent a house for $500 a month and live well in Mexico for about $1,200 per month total, including the cost of a part-time maid and gardener. Barbara and I own a house and live a more luxurious lifestyle than we did in the States for less than $25,000 a year. In part, this is due to the fact that our food and utility expenses are low.

My guess is that almost anyone reading this book can afford to live in Mexico. Begin by examining your resources. Do you have money flowing in each month from Social Security, a pension, a part-time job, royalties, investments, or inheritance? Would you consider selling your business or home or renting your home to free up enough cash to help fund your new lifestyle?

Estimating what life below the border will cost is tricky. Even if you intend to maintain the same lifestyle you have in the States, your life is likely to change in unconsidered ways. For example, Barbara and I never imagined that after only one month in Mexico we would have a maid, a cook, and a gardener coming in for a few hours each day. In the States, only very wealthy people can afford such luxuries. But in Mexico, where the wage is about $1.50–2.00 per hour, almost anyone can.

Obviously, if your dream is to live in a multi-million-dollar home in Puerto Vallarta with 10 servants and a heated Olympic-size pool, life can get a little pricey (however, it will still cost you less than it would in the States). But the majority of people from the United States, espe-

Many foreigners in Mexico can afford household help. Shown is our wonderful cook, Bertha.

cially those living on pensions or savings, will be amazed at how much further their money goes and how much higher their quality of life can be in Mexico.

It is estimated that you will live an equal, if not more gracious, lifestyle in Mexico for about 50 percent of what it costs in the United States, depending on where you live. But don't forget that even when you live in Mexico full-time, you will still have some ongoing expenses in the States. Add to your estimated Mexican cost of living U.S. mortgage payments, life and auto insurance, car registration, college tuition, loans, and so on. Once you are settled in Mexico, you can reduce many of these expenses. For instance, you may decide to reduce the cost of health insurance by replacing a high-cost U.S. policy with an international policy of equal quality, including coverage in the States, for about half the price. Anyone living in Mexico with an FM3 is eligible for IMSS health insurance, which runs about $300 per year! Whether you're insured or not, medical costs in Mexico can be as much as 75 percent less than they are in the United States (for more on healthcare, see the Health chapter).

And these days, inflation in Mexico is lower than it has been in years. The Bank of Mexico announced that the official rate of inflation between 2002 and 2005 was 3.98 percent, the lowest rate since they began keeping track in 1968. Also, during the last three years the peso has devalued about 15 percent relative to the dollar. This helps to balance the effects of inflation.

Like many expatriates, you may be able to partake of one of the pleasures of life in Mexico, being able to afford household help.

Some foreigners claim that their cost of living in Mexico has actually gone down after living in the country for a while. They say they learn to live in a peso-based economy and begin viewing costs in a more Mexican way. When they first arrived, an item costing 1,000 pesos seemed cheap: "Why it's only $100 U.S., Marge, let's buy it!" But after a few years, the price of the same 1,000-peso item now seems steep: "One thousand pesos, you've got to be kidding!"

A word about lifestyle: Ask yourself how important it is to maintain your current lifestyle. You must be seriously considering changing it or you wouldn't be reading this book. Not being locked into your former lifestyle can allow you the freedom to move to Mexico. It can also increase your options greatly and give you maximum flexibility and liberation. Much about your new lifestyle will depend on your attitude, as well as a realistic assessment of what you can afford each month. Maybe you will live in a cozy, two-bedroom house with a peaceful little garden and a small painting studio instead of your current 5,000-square-foot showplace. You may drive your car for a few extra years or take fewer vacations. But so what? Your entire new life is more relaxed and casual. In many ways, it is a vacation! Alternatively, you may be able to afford a much nicer home in Mexico than you can in the States. If you are working in Mexico, your company may pay your rent or provide you with a car and driver!

Basically, many expatriates in Mexico have come to realize that less is more. For one thing, they have so much more than the average Mexican. For another, they find that things that were important to them in their "past lives" just do not matter as much anymore. Who cares if you're wearing last year's (or even last decade's) fashions? How often will you need a necktie or three-piece suit? Who cares if the place mats don't match or that one of your wine glasses broke and you have to use a glass jar instead? That may be an exaggeration, but you get the idea.

Like many expatriates, you may be able to partake of one of the pleasures of life in Mexico, being able to afford household help. You will easily find a gardener and a housekeeper to help clean, do laundry, babysit, and maybe even cook. Most servants speak only Spanish, so you will also have a great opportunity to practice the language. Our housekeeper, Bertha, is a wonderful cook. She makes breathtaking chicken mole, a spaghetti sauce that would make your Italian grandmother salivate, and her green chicken enchiladas are to die for. Barbara has even taught her to make tofu from scratch and Asian stir-fry, using ingredients Bertha had never known existed!

Bertha's secret ingredient is oil. We have asked her to use less oil many times, and she has cut back a little, but seems constitutionally unable to go any further. Finally, we just switched to olive or grapeseed oil and gave in. Nowadays, she cooks for us only one or two times a week, especially when we are in the mood for a great old-fashioned, stick-to-your-ribs meal. Bertha is also a wonderful housekeeper and has a great sense of humor.

The average pay for a housekeeper/cook is between $1.50 and $2.50 per hour, depending on where you live, how much you expect done, and length of time they have worked for you. We highly recommend that you pay someone you like the high end of the local salary range. By law you are also required to pay your employees' social security, Christmas bonus, and possibly a few other small miscellaneous costs. These may add another 45 percent or so to your employees' pay. (See the Benefits section in the Employment chapter for specifics).

Employing household help in Mexico is very different than employing help in the United States. After your housekeeper or gardener has been with you for a while, you become their patron and have an unspoken responsibility not only to the person who works for you but also to their entire family. If one of your housekeeper's kids gets sick and the family can't afford medicine, you may offer to buy it for them. When a housekeeper's daughter gets married, if they have been with you for a while, you may be asked to pay for the ring or even the entire wedding. A friend recently did just that for her maid, who had become a friend and confidante after five years of service. The amount of time, energy, and money you devote to your housekeeper is entirely up to you. Strict laws protect the termination of domestic workers. For instance, when an employee leaves, he or she is legally entitled to severance pay based on a specific formula. Ask a Mexican lawyer for details.

Even if you pay your employees a great deal more than others might, if for any reason you insult them or cause them to lose face, you cannot count on them staying with you. To your employees, respect is far more important than money.

The differences in our two cultures are occasionally comically and curiously illustrated by money matters. For example, one day Barbara was buying some handmade trinkets as gifts. The price of each was 10 pesos. Assuming there would be a discount, she said, "If I take 10, then what will the price be?" The vendor looked at her for a few seconds and replied, "For 10 it will cost 150 pesos."

"But why?" she incredulously asked. "Can't I have a discount or at least pay the normal price for 10?"

"Because if you like them so much," replied the vendor with his own brand of logic, "you will pay more."

A friend once had a plant vendor come to her door in San Miguel de Allende with petunias. He quoted a reasonable price, and our friend said she'd buy the lot, all 20 of them. The man looked stricken. "But if you buy them all, what will I do for the rest of the day?" he asked. From then on, whenever he came to her door, he brought just a few plants and hid the rest in a doorway around the corner. He wasn't having his day ruined by this woman again!

Occasionally, foreigners may find they are charged more for certain things than local Mexicans are, especially services such as plumbing and electrical work. Even dentists and veterinarians sometimes charge us more than they do Mexicans. At the market, you may see a local Mexican buying fruit and vegetables for a few less pesos than you're paying. It's really up to you if you want to make an issue of this practice. Those who have lived here many years no longer pay attention to this. If they feel the price is high, they ask for a discount. Usually the vendor (or electrician) will grin and lower the price a fraction. Keep in mind that it is not just foreigners who are charged more than the locals. Mexican tourists or weekenders from the big city, with their shiny cars and expensive clothes, also pay higher prices. It's a question of what the market will bear. And, after all, most locals have many relatives and old family friends who automatically get a reduction. The system is fair enough.

Mexicans generally expect foreigners to have more money and are not at all upset about it. Their attitude for the most part is, "Such is life." I once heard a Mexican maid say, *"Dios les da el dinero a los ricos, porque si no lo tuvieran, se morirían de hambre"*—"God gives money to the wealthy because without it they would starve to death."

However, foreigners flaunting their money is offensive to every Mexican. But, then, it's offensive everywhere, so use common sense. If you run around spending as if pesos were play money, feeling like a millionaire, your budget will soon fall flat. Used wisely, your money will take you far and definitely give you a good life in Mexico. But don't be niggardly. Being closefisted is not politic in Mexico—in fact, it's downright alien to Mexicans. Mexicans tend to spend readily and usually with generosity when they have money, even poorer Mexicans. Money is not hoarded, even by rich Mexicans. If they have it, they spend it. *Mañana* will somehow bring more.

Many tourists visiting Mexico invariably feel that the peso is not real money. It is not unusual to hear a tourist ask a spouse, "How much is that in real money?" This feeling is understandable because prices are low, and Mexican money does look a little like play money, with the different denominations in different colors and some with gold sparkles. Some tourists throw Mexican bills around like they are playing Monopoly, happily overpaying and over-tipping waiters, vendors, and even taxi drivers (taxi drivers are usually not tipped in Mexico). Such behavior tends to increase prices in general for foreigners, whether or not they are tourists. Most foreigners are aware that they live in far more comfortable conditions than local Mexicans, and some feel uncomfortable about the difference. Nevertheless, no one likes being gouged.

Should you give money to beggars? That is entirely up to you. Many foreigners meet a beggar whom they like and decide to support. You may consider giving if the beggar appears genuinely in need or ill, and you have some coins in your pockets and are in the mood. If he or she is clearly a drunk or a fraud, it's best to ignore the person and walk past. The larger the city, the larger the scam. So be astute in deciding who is in genuine need.

Children from poor families may see you on the street and screech "Money! Money!," holding out their small hands. Again, it's up to you whether or not to give, but why not offer children food instead of money? They may take it or just give you a dirty look and turn away.

Banking

In recent years, huge international financial corporations have gobbled up all but one of Mexico's largest banks. Citibank owns Banamex;

HSBC, the Hong Kong and Shanghai Banking Corporation, bought Bital; Banco Bilbao Viscaya Argentaria owns Bancomer, and so on. One of the effects of new bank ownership has been an infusion of capital into the system. As a result, mortgage interest rates in Mexico have fallen to their lowest levels since the 1960s. One bank, Scotiabank Interlat, even introduced a single-digit interest rate for the first five years of a twenty-year mortgage. Most banks offer 13–15 percent rates paid over 15–20 years. These seem incredibly high to those of us from the States used to paying 5- and 6-percent rates, but for Mexicans this is exciting news.

Another of the effects of this conglomeration is improved services. For example, Wells Fargo Bank has announced a new, easier, and less expensive way for its clients in the States to transfer money to Mexico through its InterCuenta Express product. For a transfer fee of $6, Wells Fargo clients can transfer up to $3000 per day directly into their Bancomer or HSBC accounts in Mexico. For more information about this, call 800/556-0605, or check online at www.wellsfargo.com.

Most foreigners maintain a peso account in a major Mexican bank into which they transfer funds from the States (or another Mexican account) when they need more money.

Banamex has an interesting program—Programa Amistad (friendship). Foreign residents in Mexico open a checking account at Banamex's U.S. branch, California Commercial Bank (2029 Century Park East, 42nd Fl., Los Angeles, CA 90067, 310/203-3400). Their U.S. Social Security, pension, or other checks are deposited directly into the account. Banamex issues a checkbook and a debit card, which can be used to withdraw up to $300 at a time at any Banamex ATM in Mexico. Banamex says that the account can be opened only in person at their Los Angeles, San Francisco, or Guadalajara offices, but a friend opened an Amistad account in the San Miguel de Allende branch. New bank ownership now makes it possible to do transactions by fax, phone, and email, services that were provided in the past only by Operadoras de Fondos Lloyd, S.A.

Lloyd still remains the most popular "bank" among American and Canadian residents in towns where it has branches. Don't ask them to insure your good looks, though. This is not the Lloyd's of London that insured Betty Grable's legs and J.Lo's butt! Lloyd is a Mexican-owned organization, and, though it has many Mexican customers, it caters to the needs of foreign residents, offering high-interest investment accounts and other services, such as home and auto insurance.

Unlike the major Mexican banks, Lloyd is really an investment house. Money deposited with Lloyd is invested in one of six different standard plans. Each plan invests money into a different mix of Mexican stocks, bonds, and treasuries. Interest rates on returns vary according to the plan and the amount of money invested. As an investment house, Lloyd does not offer checking accounts or credit cards, but it has just begun offering debit cards to its account holders. Lloyd does offer some accounts from which you can withdraw funds as early as the day of deposit.

Lloyd provides the useful service of paying household bills when you are out of town, including utilities and employees' salaries. Lloyd has 10 branches in Mexico, most in areas with high concentrations of foreigners. (See the Investing section for Lloyd contact information). If you decide to open an account at Lloyd, it is best to develop a good personal relationship with one of their bankers.

Opening an account at Lloyd or any other bank in Mexico requires that you present your passport, FM3 or other entry document, and an electric or water bill with your name on it to prove that you have a permanent address in the country. Banks will provide you with checkbooks and debit cards for their ATM machines. It is best to keep your credit cards from the States, rather then apply for a Mexican credit card, which usually has a higher interest rate.

For those living in Mexico, handling common money transactions are relatively easy. Most foreigners maintain a peso account in a major Mexican bank into which they transfer funds from the States (or another Mexican account) when they need more money. This is usually more efficient than depositing a U.S. check, as some banks take as long as six weeks to clear a large check. Inquire about this before you open an account. Once you open the account, you can write checks or use the debit card provided by the bank to make withdrawals from ATM machines. All major banks have branches throughout the country. It is worth noting that only a few banks in Mexico have dollar accounts. For the most part, any money transferred to a Mexican bank account from a U.S. bank will be converted to pesos.

Some people who live in Mexico operate on a strictly cash basis. They do not have a Mexican bank account and never transfer money into the country. They have an arrangement with the local *casa de cambio* (money exchange house) to cash personal checks drawn on their U.S. bank account, and they use U.S. credit and debit cards at ATM machines.

Taxes

MEXICAN TAXES

The Fox administration has been diligently trying to change Mexico's dismal tax collection system, which takes in about 11 percent of Mexico's gross national product, less than half that of most developed Western nations. The Mexican congress passed a tax law, which became effective January 1, 2002. Among other things, it requires banks to report account transactions to SAT (formerly known as Hacienda—Mexico's IRS). This change will not affect most foreign residents, who are not required to file a Mexican tax return unless they earn interest of at least $100,000 per year.

As you travel and make purchases in Mexico, you will pay Mexico's 15 percent value added tax—*IVA* (VAT). Mexicans, as well as foreigners, pay VAT on a mystifying selection of goods and services. Hotels and restaurants in tourist areas will almost always charge VAT. Outside tourist areas, it is rarely charged. Also, there is still no VAT tax on medications or food. Anyone selling a home in Mexico will pay capital gains tax. (For information concerning capital gains tax on real estate see the Housing Considerations chapter; for information concerning self employment and other work-related taxes see the Employment chapter).

U.S. TAXES

The Internal Revenue Service in the States expects you to pay taxes on "earned" income anywhere on earth and undoubtedly from outer space as well. You are required to file a return if you earn more than $6,000 a year. If you file as a foreign resident, you are exempted from paying state income tax and you are allowed to put off filing your federal return until June 15, although tax owed is due from April 15.

If you run a business in Mexico and file a U.S. tax return, taxes you paid in Mexico will be an expense against other earnings. You are also expected to include the sale of your Mexican property on your U.S. tax return. Any Mexican tax you pay is considered by the IRS to be an expense, which will reduce your U.S. capital gain. Income tax benefits might apply if you meet certain requirements while living abroad. You may qualify to treat up to $72,000 of your income as not taxable by the United States. You may also be able to either deduct part of your housing expenses from your taxable income or treat a limited amount of income used for housing expenses as not taxable by the United States. These benefits are called the foreign-earned income exclusion and the foreign housing deduction and exclusion.

U.S. citizens or resident aliens living outside the United States are generally allowed the same exemptions, deductions, and credits as those living in the United States. However, if you choose to exclude foreign earned income or housing amounts, you cannot deduct or exclude any item or take credit for any item that is related to the amounts you exclude.

To qualify for either of the exclusions or the deduction, you must declare foreign residency as well as earn income in a foreign country.

Social security and other monthly federal benefit checks can be sent from the Department of the Treasury in the United States to a U.S. Embassy or Consulate in Mexico. However, it is probably safer to have your check deposited directly into your U.S. or Mexican bank account.

Investing

Any person who wishes to can buy stock in one of the companies listed on the Mexican Stock Exchange (Bolsa Mexicana de Valores). Individual shares of stock and Mexican government-issued bonds, known as Cetes (Federal Treasury Certificates), can be purchased through any of the major Mexican or U.S. brokerage firms. Commissions to Mexican brokerage houses range between 1 and 1.5 percent of the trade (buy/sell).

Mexican investment firms offer a wide variety of plans. As mentioned previously, many foreign residents have an account with Operadoras de Fondos Lloyd, S.A. (333/880-2000 in Guadalajara, lloyd@lloyd.com.mx). Lloyd offers several types of investment accounts with varying amounts of risk and return on investment, some long-term and others that provide quick access to your money. The rate of return on investments now ranges from 5.5 percent to more than 20 percent. Lloyd has offices in San Miguel, Ajijic, Chapala, Guadalajara, and Puerto Vallarta.

Another investment house with a fine reputation among foreign residents is Multivalores Casa de Bolsa (www.multivaloresgf.com.mx).

Mexican Stock Exchange

The *Bolsa Mexicana de Valores* (Mexican Stock Exchange), with only 40 listed companies, is not a large stock exchange by U.S. standards, but its companies are actively traded and have done very well. As a matter of fact, at the end of 2004, the Mexican stock exchange outperformed nearly all major markets, leaping nearly 50 percent in dollar terms. The four largest companies listed in the index were the telecommunications giant Teléfonos de México; América Móvil, Latin America's largest wireless company; WalMart de México; and Cemex, one of the world's largest cement companies. Together, they account for 47 percent of the index.

The Mexican Stock Exchange is a private institution governed by the Mexican Securities Market Act. Any person who wishes to can buy individual shares of stock and Mexican government–issued bonds, known as *Cetes* (Federal Treasury Certificates), through any of the major Mexican or U.S. brokerage firms. Securities can also be purchased through the acquisition of American Depository Receipts (ADRs) in the States. ADRs are negotiable receipts for the securities of a foreign company and are kept in the vaults of an American bank, allowing Americans to trade the foreign securities in the United States while accruing any dividends and capital gains. Commissions to Mexican brokerage houses range between 1 and 1.5 percent of the transaction amount. Some individual Mexican stocks and mutual funds, such as Cemex or Fondo Mexico, are currently listed in the NYSE.

Though nobody expects the Mexican stock market to boom in 2005 as it did in 2004, there is optimism that 2005 will be a very good year. For one, pension funds, known as *Afores* in Mexico, which have nearly $45 billion in assets, have been required by the Mexican government to invest in fixed-income securities. Starting in January of 2005, they began investing some of their funds in stock indexes in Mexico, the United States, Japan, and some European countries. This could net the *Bolsa* between $1 billion and $1.5 billion in fresh investment, an important sum for the relatively small market. Also, Mexico continues to be the leading Latin American recipient of U.S. investment in stocks and bonds.

They hold a seat on the Mexican stock exchange, offer a number of mutual funds of their own, and buy and sell individual Mexican stocks, bonds, and treasuries for their clients. They have offices in Mexico City, Ajijic, Monterrey, León, Guadalajara, Aguascalientes, and Zacatecas. Contact Laurie Clark at the Ajijic office at 376/766-0912.

One of the best investments in Mexico is real estate. In 2003 and 2004, real estate prices along the Mexican coasts and in the towns with the largest pockets of foreigners rose 25 percent, even more per year in some areas. New developments, condos, and time-shares marketed to retiring baby boomers are springing up throughout the country. Only the United States surpasses Mexico in the number of time-shares sold.

For those who own properties or have a substantial number of other assets in Mexico, it is a good idea to look into having a separate Mexican will drawn up. A U.S. will cannot cover a variety of assets in Mexico, and to avoid confusion and tax problems later, it is wise to have a Mexican will drawn up as well. This is not necessary if you own only one, or even a few properties in Mexico, as you can have your spouse and/or children named as owners or beneficiaries in the *escritora* (deed). In this way, you can cover yourself and avoid the extra expense of a Mexican will.

TAQUERIA
HNOS. MORENO
TACOS DE CABEZA DE RES Y DE CARNE ASADA. AGUAS FRESCAS

TAQUERIA "HNOS. MORENO"

TAQUERIA

TAQUERIA "HNOS

Communications

Even twenty years ago, Mexico was in the Dark Ages of communications. In large cities, private phones were rare. Local and long-distance calls were made at centrally located booths, often with long waiting lines. Believe it or not, this situation still exists in a few areas of the country—in sharp contrast to the rapid modernization of communications throughout the rest of Mexico. In many rural areas, there are no landlines, and it is not unthinkable to see a farmer bumping along on his burro or funky old pickup chatting away on his cell phone. In fact, because of the preponderance of cell phones it is very likely that landlines will never be installed in some of these areas.

Telephone Service

The Mexican dial-up telephone system—Telmex—was a government-owned monopoly until its privatization in the 1990s. Now it is owned

"Phone cards sold here."

mostly by Latin America's richest billionaire, Carlos Slim Helu. Telmex holds a virtual monopoly, although other phone companies like Alestra (a division of AT&T), Yahoo, and AOL have made small inroads into Mexico. Telmex and the few other providers of phone service charge fees of about 225 pesos ($20) a month, with no installation charges. Telmex also charges roughly $.15 per phone call after the first 100 calls in a calendar month. This may seem like a sufficient number of calls, but 100 calls can come and go quickly, and at 15 cents for each, the excess calls can really add up. If you have a dial-up modem, each *attempt* counts as a call!

In 2001, Mexico went through the trauma of changing every area code in the country. Phone numbers, which were typically of varying lengths from state to state (and often from city to city), were converted to ten-digit numbers, as per international standards. The problem is that many business cards, brochures, and even websites still list the former number. If you are in Mexico and run into this problem, call (or have a Spanish-speaking friend call) telephone information at 040 and ask for the new area code. Or find the correct area code by going to www.telmex.com. mx, clicking "English," then clicking "area code directory."

CELLULAR PHONES

Telcel, the cell phone subsidiary of Telmex has also managed to keep a stranglehold on the market. This means that if you have problems with the service, the line, the billing, etc., you can't jump ship and sign up with a competing company as you can in the States. On the positive side, Telcel has excellent coverage throughout Mexico. Cell phone rate packages are similar to those in the United States, including one- or two-year contracts.

If you are planning a shorter trip, don't have a permanent address, or do not want to receive a monthly bill, you can use Telcel's "Amigo" plan. The plan requires only that you purchase a cell phone from Telcel and a phone card. Cards come in various denominations up to 500 pesos (about $45). Punch the code from the card you purchase into the phone and you have your starting balance. The balance is reduced with each call you make or receive. When your balance is low, you buy a new card. This is worth considering if you are planning a long driving trip in Mexico. For international calls, use your "Amigo" phone and a call-back service (see the International Calls section) for a total of about $.25 a minute.

Surprisingly, given all the new, inexpensive options available for calling internationally, calls within Mexico are often more expensive. Barbara received a call on our cell phone from a friend in Mexico City to our home near Puerto Vallarta; they spoke for about 45 minutes and the call cost 300 pesos (about $27).

INTERNATIONAL CALLS

Direct international calling is expensive, so most foreigners living in Mexico use a call-back service, which involves calling a phone number in the States. After dialing the number, you let it ring once and then hang up so you are not charged for the call. The number you dialed connects to a computer, which automatically calls you back in Mexico with a U.S. dial tone. You then dial the number in the States that you want to reach. The per-minute charge is fixed (currently about $.19), regardless of time of day, for all calls including 800 numbers. Call-back services will call back to a landline or cell phone number.

Internet companies like vonage.com are now supplanting call-back services. Vonage.com allows you to have a dedicated phone in your home in Mexico to make and receive calls to and from the States. When you pick up the receiver, you have a dial tone in the States (specifically, in the city you chose when you registered for the service). You also have a U.S. phone number in that city. This allows friends in the States to make a domestic call to your U.S. number and talk to you in Mexico.

For this service, you pay a flat monthly fee of about $40 a month, which covers unlimited "local" calls within your city of choice. Long distance and international calls outside that city are billed as long-distance calls in the States. Vonage will also work with a high-speed Internet satellite system in some areas where there are no landlines.

An even less expensive way to speak to friends in the States is directly through your computer. This can be done with skype.com, iconnecthere.com, deltathree.com, and net2phone.com. These companies offer broadband phone and PC-to-phone service with calls from Mexico to the States costing about $.03 per minute. Or you can call free when you sign up for instant messaging with Yahoo, MSN, or one of their many competitors. Just look for the talk option on your instant message screen. Most newer computers have a built-in microphone, and that works just fine, although a dedicated mike or headset may be more comfortable. The cost of the call is $0. The downside is a slight delay between the end of sentences. Put a webcam on the computers at both ends of the call and you will be able to see as well as speak to the other party. Webcams are small, very portable, and some cost about $50 (but buy yours in the States if possible because prices are higher in Mexico for all electronic goods).

Another innovative new service is being offered from Verizon Wireless. They call it their "North America Choice" plan. For a minimum of $59/month, you can call with a cell phone, at a very low per-minute rate, between selected areas of Mexico and Canada, and most of the United States. If the person you are calling is also a Verizon customer, or if you are calling at night and on weekends, the call is essentially free because you get at least 1,000 minutes per month on the plan. Most of the larger cities in Mexico are covered under the plan. This would be especially useful for those planning to travel around Mexico. So far, there have been mixed reviews about how well this plan actually works for making calls from Mexico.

If all these other options seem expensive or too big a hassle to deal with, you can make your calls to the States, Mexico, or anywhere in the world for that matter with a Ladatel card. Ladatel cards can be purchased in most pharmacies, corner grocery stores, general stores, and in gas, bus, and train stations. Just look for signs that say, "Vende Ladatel Aquí." Cards come in 20- ($1.80), 30- ($2.70), 50- ($4.50), and 100-peso ($9.00) denominations. Ladatel phones look like normal pay phones and are found on almost every street corner, as well as in bus stations and airports. The card is placed in the slot on the phone and during your call the value of the card is reduced until it reaches zero. You then insert a new card. These calls cost about $1 per minute to the States and about $.06 a minute within Mexico. Ladatel cards are useful for calling the States when traveling in remote areas of Mexico where there is no cell-phone signal.

Internet Access

The many millions of Mexicans who cannot afford computers of their own rely on cyber cafés, found on almost every corner of Mexico, for Internet access. At last count, there were at least 50 Internet cafés in Puerto Vallarta alone. In Mexico, you will come across a storefront in the smallest villages with a sign announcing Internet access. In large cities, some bars offer email-checking service free with your drink. These "Internet cafés" (most are not cafés at all) make connecting to the Internet convenient for travelers, although in smaller towns the connection can be fairly slow. In larger cities, almost all Internet cafés have high-speed Internet access for about 10–15 pesos an hour ($.90–1.35). Cyber space has become so popular in Mexico that many Internet cafés are packed with kids during after-school hours, which makes checking your mail early in the day or at night a more tranquil experience.

In Mexico, you will come across a storefront in the smallest villages with a sign announcing Internet access.

Broadband, in the form of DSL and cable, is quickly growing more available and affordable throughout the country. DSL access is offered through Telmex in cooperation with Prodigy. Speeds range from 256kbps to 2Mbps, with monthly rates ranging from 550 pesos ($50) to 2,500 pesos ($135) per month depending on speed. Cablevision provides 256kbps service for 500 pesos ($45) monthly in some areas of Mexico City. AT&T is offering high-speed wireless connections with speeds from 128kbps to 512kbps for prices ranging from $40 to $90 monthly.

The largest national Internet provider in Mexico is prodigy.net.mx, which has an exclusive arrangement with the Mexican telephone company Telmex. Prodigy covers the entire country, so hooking up with them gives you access almost anywhere in Mexico. On the other hand, many foreign residents complain about Prodigy's poor customer service and prefer using a local ISP. A list of local providers can be found in the Communications section of the Resources chapter.

One other note about the Internet: Barbara and I live in a remote area and connect through a high-speed satellite Internet system in our home (there are no landlines where we live). Our "Direcway," with connection provided by Hughes Electronics, is fast and reliable and we are extremely happy with it. The system costs about $1,700, including installation. It's well worth the price as it is our primary connection to the world, with a signal more reliable than that of our cell phone—except when the electricity goes out! Satellite Internet systems are becoming more popular in remote areas as the price of this technology comes down.

Post Office

The Mexican postal service has a reputation for not being either safe or reliable. Reportedly, many millions of dollars worth of checks sent from up north disappear from the postal system each year. The most frequent complaints about missing mail come from U.S. residents and Mexican citizens who receive U.S. Social Security checks.

This situation has prompted U.S. and Mexican authorities to promote methods of direct deposit for Social Security beneficiaries. However, the United States has been slow to implement these measures. In Michoacán, for example, as many as three-quarters of the 8,000 beneficiaries receive their money through the mail because they have no bank account. Authorities say investigations for lost or missing checks take between two and three months, and it may take even longer to receive a new check.

Packages also occasionally disappear. Nevertheless, many foreign residents maintain an *apartado* (Mexican post office box), which they use primarily for mail sent from within Mexico and for less valuable, low-priority mail from the States, like newspapers and magazines. Apart from the previously mentioned problems, very few foreigners have anything negative to say about the quality of service of the Mexican postal system. At the same time, many of these same people maintain a box at one of the private mail services, like Mail Boxes Etc. or La Conexion (in San Miguel de Allende).

These services, which operate in most large and medium-sized towns, provide patrons with a U.S. mailing address, from which mail is picked up daily and shipped via UPS to the recipient's Mexican hometown office, where it is then put in his/her private box. Letters from the States and Canada are delivered to the postal box in Mexico as few as five or six days after they are mailed. These postal service companies generally will send mail out of Mexico and offer overnight and second-day UPS or FedEx service. Many postal service offices do packing and shipping as well, and have fax and copy machines for customer use. The downside, however, is that basic charges can run about $200 per year for a mail box, on top of which some companies charge extra by weight for packages received, and customs duty on top of that.

In comparison, packages received through the Mexican post office are usually duty free. It is worthwhile to compare services and costs if there is more than one private postal service company where you live. Most people living in Mexico simply give letters to friends and visitors who are returning to the States. For this reason, it is important to have a supply of U.S. stamps on hand. Documents of value sent within Mexico are almost always safe if they are sent via the Mexican postal system by registered mail or Mexpost, or with one of the package-delivery services. Registered mail also arrives at its destination more quickly.

Those of you who are planning to tour around Mexico and want to receive mail during your travels can use general delivery, or *Lista de Correos* as it is known in Mexico. When friends send a letter or package to you c/o *Lista de Correos*, ask them not to add unnecessary formalities or embellishments to your name. Mexican names usually emphasize the middle name as the paternal one. Therefore, if the letter was addressed to "John Paul Getty," the post office may recognize it as being addressed to "John Paul G."

This is how the letter will be written on "The List," which will either be an actual piece of paper with names on it (a number next to the name indicates how many parcels are waiting to be picked up), or a verbal list. If you see your name written on the list, just point to it and ask for your mail. If there is no list, and your Spanish is not too good, you can write your name clearly on a piece of paper and hand it over to the employee. They may ask to see your tourist card, plus a picture ID as verification. The post office will not accept anything but Mexican pesos. Mail is generally held for two weeks. Unclaimed letters have an excellent chance of eventually making it back to the sender.

SHIPPING OPTIONS

There is no such thing as overnight shipping from the United States to Mexico. Federal Express, UPS, and DHL will each take at least 2–3 days to get a package anywhere in Mexico. It seems that every package entering Mexico lands first in Mexico City or Guadalajara and is then reshipped to more remote locations. Puerto Vallarta, Mérida, Oaxaca, etc., can take up to four or five days to receive a second-day package. The most reliable companies for express shipping to Mexico are UPS and DHL. At the moment, Federal Express seems to have dropped the ball in Mexico when it comes to any remote location and cannot be recommended here for that service. Expect to pay about $20–25 for delivery of a document-sized package. For quick shipping within Mexico, use Mexpost, a service of the Mexican postal service, or registered mail, both of which are very reliable. Many people recommend Estafeta, a Mexican equivalent of UPS. Shipping prices vary greatly, with the Mexican postal service being the least expensive.

Media

Communities with large English-speaking populations generally have a local weekly newspaper, or at least a brochure with a listing of local current events, in English. Many local newspapers have very little interesting editorial content and are dedicated primarily to social comings and goings, cultural events, class schedules, and reports on galas supporting local charities, what you would normally find in a small suburban weekly. The weekly *Guadalajara Reporter* has more depth of editorial coverage, with continually useful information on the ins and outs of living in Mexico, some political (both U.S. and Mexican) reporting, articles on traveling in and around Mexico, highlights of events in Mexico's history, as well as classified and display advertising. This paper is worth subscribing to no matter where you live in Mexico.

Newsstands in and around expat communities will usually carry the *International Herald Tribune* (the only national daily English-language newspaper published in Mexico), current editions of *Newsweek* and *Time*, *USA Today*, and one or two other U.S. newspapers, such as the *L.A. Times* or the *Houston Chronicle*. They may also carry an array of the most popular magazines, like those you would see in any airport newsstand.

The Hometown Paper

Those planning a long excursion into Mexico, or even a longer-term move, might consider subscribing to the local English-language newspaper, if there is one published in the town or city of your choice. Even if there is no newspaper, there is most likely an Internet equivalent. Following news from your chosen city regularly, months in advance of your trip, can begin vicariously involving you in the flow of the place. You will get the latest scuttlebutt about local gringo politics (of which there will be plenty), and Mexican local politics as well.

It could be handy to know, for instance, that the new faction that just took control of the library is planning to restrict the use of its community room to only one "authorized" theater group, thereby shattering your dreams of opening a children's theater company from that location. Or maybe the city has finally decided to construct that badly needed water-purification plant, but to your dismay, it will be built just next door to the lot you have your eyes on. These kinds of decisions and the poli-

tics around them could affect your move in ways you might otherwise know nothing about.

Your local gringo newspaper may even be one of the few that covers Mexican national politics, and international events as well. None of that may seem important from your living room in Wichita, but the paper may offer entirely independent and interesting points of view, unlike the ones in your hometown. Plus, once you live in Mexico, you may have a greater craving for international news of the States.

And then there is the matter of tracking the real estate and rental markets in advance. The deal you have been looking for may suddenly appear in the form of a realtor's ad staring back at you from the page of a local newspaper, with a handy phone number to call.

Worst case, you will find out what is happening in the social and cultural whirl of the foreign community, what volunteer organizations are having a benefit, and when flu shots will be available. Subscription rates are usually pretty reasonable, as well. Enjoy!

Not found on the newsstands are a number of harder-to-find specialized magazines on different aspects of Mexican culture. For instance, *Voices of Mexico* (www.unam.mx/voices/), published by the Center for Research on North America at UNAM (Autonomous University of Mexico), offers a well-balanced analysis of political, economic, and social issues facing Mexico. Some others include *Mexico Desconicido* (Hidden Mexico; www.mexicodesconocido.com.mx), which offers beautifully detailed descriptions and photographs of wonderful off-the-beaten-path spots; *MB, The Magazine of the NAFTA Marketplace*; and *Yates y Villas*.

Depending on where you live, local cable-TV companies offer a mix of Mexican and U.S. channels. Among them are several excellent Mexican movie and art channels featuring programs with English subtitles. This is especially true in tourist areas and where many Americans live. In most other towns, TV programming is entirely Mexican. Some cable companies carry Mexican versions of popular U.S. networks: Spanish Discovery Channel, A&E, Travel Channel, VH1, MTV, and many others. Of course, if you want U.S. television in Mexico, you can buy DirecTV or another satellite system and have the normal massive U.S. array of channels. For those of you trying to learn or improve your Spanish, it is handy to have a few Spanish channels. Many expatriates claim they learn more Spanish from watching *telenovelas* (soap operas) than by any other method.

Many expatriates claim they learn more Spanish from watching telenovelas *(soap operas) than by any other method.*

Radio in Mexico is not much different than most radio in the States—constantly blaring commercials and ranchero music. But it could be worth spending some time listening to this noise as a way to learn the language. To be fair, Mexico City, Monterrey, Guadalajara, Puerto Vallarta, and some of the other larger cities have good classical and jazz stations on FM. Once you are settled, order high-speed Internet and listen to *All Things Considered* or your favorite hometown station on your computer. Still, we do miss listening to NPR on our car radio on long drives.

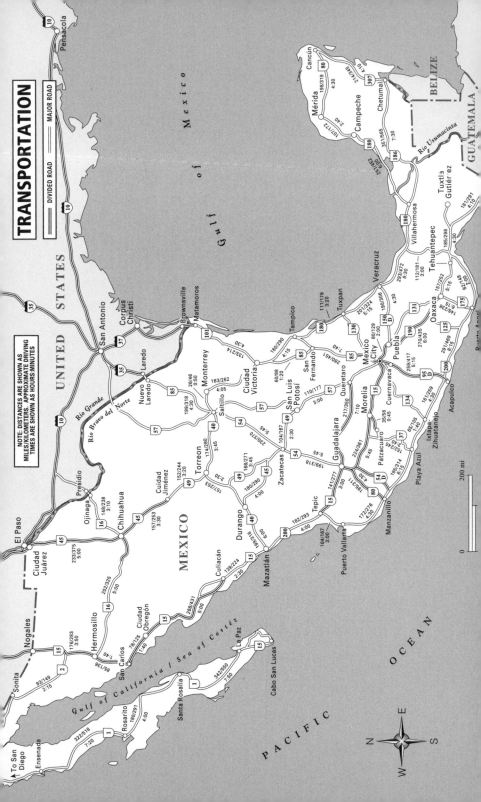

Travel and Transportation

O
ne of Mexico's greatest attractions is its proximity to the States, allowing you to fly to even the farthest corners of the country in just a few hours. Commercial and charter airlines offer direct flights into many of the most popular destinations, many at reasonable prices depending on the time of year. This is an important consideration for those living in Mexico who may need to return to the States quickly in an emergency.

For those people who are moving to Mexico or planning a longer stay and intend to drive, the trip from the border to any Mexican city can be completed in less than a week. For instance, the trip from Nogales, Arizona (south of Tucson) to Puerto Vallarta takes three days. From Laredo, Texas to Mexico City or Guadalajara, it takes only two days, and the drive from El Paso, Texas to Oaxaca can be done in four days.

Once you spend time in the country, it becomes apparent that Mexico is one of the most beautiful and culturally rich countries in which to travel. Spectacular natural and constructed wonders that would be crowded tourist attractions in the United States and other countries remain undeveloped and relatively unknown to Mexicans and visitors alike. Road trips to explore the countryside are safe and easy on Mexico's extensive, generally high-quality highway system, as long as some simple precautions are taken. And for those of you who prefer not to drive, Mexican buses travel to every corner of the country, and for a fraction of the cost of bus travel in the States.

> *Once you spend time in the country, it becomes apparent that Mexico is one of the most beautiful and culturally rich countries in which to travel.*

No matter how you arrange to travel in Mexico, it is important that you plan ahead by reading as many books as possible about the country. You will be more prepared and less likely to experience culture shock if you have a general understanding of Mexico's history, its culture, and its people. Go online to the websites of the cities you plan to visit, and study maps of the country in preparation for driving. To really ease your entry, take the time to learn at least a few Spanish words and phrases.

By Air

It seems that almost every week new flights are announced from the States and Europe to Mexican cities, even remote ones. It is now possible to fly directly into the city of Oaxaca from Houston, a trip that previously required a one-night layover in Mexico City. Along with the abundance of direct flights, there are occasionally low-priced ticket deals to be had. However, during the high season, December–Easter week, ticket prices usually go up. If you want to fly at that time of year and tickets are too high, check out one of the charter airlines, like Suntrips. They fly out of Seattle, San Francisco, Oakland, and Denver and offer low-priced tickets for Pacific coast cities, like Puerto Vallarta. Most charter airlines fly out of only one or two cities, so look on the Internet for charter companies in your area. One reason that tickets are so high is that all airport, departure, and other taxes are included in the price of your ticket.

Flying into Mexico is fairly hassle-free. You need only a picture ID—preferably a passport, but a driver's license or birth certificate will do. During the flight, you will be given both immigration and customs cards to fill out. At the airport in Mexico after you collect your bags, you will be asked to press the button at the base of a traffic light. If you get a green light, you continue out of the airport. With a red light, your bags get inspected by customs. It is supposedly a totally random system, and that seems to be the case. That's it. You do not need shots of any kind to enter Mexico.

Continental, United Airlines, American Airlines, Delta, America West, Frontier, and Alaska are among the major U.S. airlines carrying travelers to Mexico from the States. Mexicana and Aeromexico, the two major Mexican airlines, fly to a good number of U.S. cities. Both are affiliated with major U.S. airlines, so you may find yourself flying Mexicana on one leg and Delta on another.

Within Mexico, there are a number of domestic and regional airline companies. Some of them fly to one or two U.S. cities as well. For instance, Aeromar flies into San Antonio, and Aerolitoral flies into Pheonix and Houston. Aeromar has flights from Querétaro to Puerto Vallarta. The Querétaro airport is a small regional airport only 45 minutes away from San Miguel de Allende. It is a good idea to investigate the websites of these smaller national airlines as they often offer specials. Aeromar, for example, recently advertised a two-for-one special to Vallarta. The only requirement was that you book online between 11 P.M. and 7 A.M.! Their motto is "While Others Sleep, You Save."

There are more than 60 local airports in Mexico served by regional and Mexican national airlines. Even with all these airports and regional airlines, flying from point to point within the country often requires changing planes in Mexico City.

By Train

Passenger-train travel in Mexico, except for along a few tourist routes, is all but extinct. The only trains that carry passengers are the wonderful Copper Canyon railroad—operated by Ferrocarril Mexicano (www.ferromex.com.mx)—which runs from Chihuahua to Los Mochis; the Tequila Express (www.tequilaexpress.com.mx), which runs from Guadalajara to Tequila, complete with mariachi bands and, of course, tequila tasting; and the luxurious Expreso Maya (www.expresomaya. com), which connects archaeological sites in the Yucatán and offers two- to five-night packages. Tickets and schedules are available from several travel agencies listed on the Web. All other trains in the country are now carrying freight.

By Bus

Buses go everywhere throughout Mexico. They travel to every city and into every corner of the country. In most cases, more than one bus line will cover the same route, giving you a choice of schedules, prices, and quality. Buses are the most common form of transportation among Mexicans.

Long-distance buses in the United States seem shoddy in comparison to first-class Mexican buses. Surprised? Mexican *Lujo* (luxury—the best) and *Primera Clase* (first-class—next best) buses are no longer the overcrowded, broken-down contraptions—with chickens in cages precariously perched on the roofs—that you have seen in old Hollywood black-and-white flicks, like *Night of the Iguana*. The new top class of buses are ultra-modern, with plush seats (reserved in advance), plenty of leg room, no smoking, air-conditioning, clean bathrooms, movies, refreshments, and sometimes even cabin attendants.

> *Buses go everywhere throughout Mexico. They travel to every city and into every corner of the country.*

The movies are not always Oscar caliber, however. More often than not, they are shoot-em-ups starring Sylvester Stallone or Steven Seagal. Bring a portable CD player, a few good CDs, and a book for entertainment.

Any of the top-class buses is an inexpensive way to travel between distant cities—and it costs much less than a rental car. Of course, buses travel much more slowly than rental cars, but they usually leave and arrive on time. If you are feeling sociable, you can usually talk with a Mexican passenger en route, practice your Spanish, and learn something about the country. It is best to call ahead for reservations. A travel agent or your local hotel should be able to help you. If you can't book in advance, arrive at the station at least a half hour early to buy a ticket.

Second- and third-class buses operate between small towns, and are often old school buses or mini-vans. These are less comfortable than first-class buses. They generally run on time but can be very slow, making numerous scheduled stops as well as picking up anyone on the highway who flags them down. Two friends living in San Miguel de Allende regularly take a third-class bus four or five miles out of town, disembark when they spot an appealing dirt path, and hike off into the country for the day with a picnic lunch. They return to the highway in the afternoon to catch a bus back to town. Such buses are dirt cheap but would be back-breaking for long-distance travel.

Large cities have centralized bus terminals used by many bus lines. Mexico City has four such terminals: North, South, East, and West. Your destination determines which terminal to use. You may have to take a taxi from one terminal to another to switch bus lines and complete your trip. In smaller cities, each bus line generally has its own easy-to-find storefront terminal.

By Car

DRIVING

Driving in Mexico used to be quite a hair-raising experience. Every road was a narrow, two-lane blacktop with a surface like a potato grater. These days, it is a pleasure to drive on the modern, four-lane toll roads called *autopistas* or *maxipistas*. Though the tolls are very high, *autopistas* are the best way to travel long distances by car.

At points where an *autopista* has not been completed, you will be directed back to an old highway. Be cautious here. Even when straight, the old roads are dangerous. They are frequently used by slow-moving, overloaded trucks and buses. Occasionally, you'll see a pedestrian by the side of the road guiding livestock. When these roads curve over hills and mountains, they are even more hair-raising. Many Mexican drivers put their lives into God's hands and think nothing of passing just before the crest of a hill. Corkscrew mountain roads are rarely banked well and have few guard rails. Whether curvy or straight, none of the older roads have shoulders, and many have steep drops on both sides.

Fortunately, these days you can drive between most cities in Mexico on a four-lane highway. For shorter trips, drive on back roads. It will give you the opportunity to explore out-of-the-way villages and places of natural beauty.

typical *autopista* (toll road) rest stop

For maximum travel flexibility, it is worthwhile having a car in Mexico. But if you hate driving, the cost of occasional auto repairs and car insurance, parking problems, traffic tickets, and so on, take the bus. It will get you there.

Bringing a car into Mexico for the first time is less time-consuming if you prepare all your papers in advance. You will need your driver's license (a U.S. driver's license is accepted for driving in Mexico), a tourist card (available at the border or beforehand from AAA or the Mexican Consulate), a credit card, and your car's registration papers. Having a passport or proof of citizenship, like a birth certificate, is a good idea but not absolutely necessary for U.S. citizens. If the car is borrowed, a company car, leased, or owned by the bank, you will need a notarized letter from the owner giving permission for the car to enter Mexico. It may be worth stopping at a AAA office in the States near the border. They may have the necessary visa forms and can give you border-crossing advice.

With your papers in hand, you'll be able to get the permits necessary to import yourself and your car into Mexico. You may be stopped at the border to have your entry visa checked and your car searched by *aduana* (customs). This should not take long. Whether or not you are stopped, be sure to find out where you go to get a permit to legally import your car into Mexico. Usually this takes place at the immigration building on the Mexican side of the border. You must use a credit card to pay the permit fee of $11. Depending on the time of year, this can be a painfully slow process. Before Christmas, Easter, and other holidays, many thousands of Mexicans returning home will be standing in line for permits. Wait in line, follow the instructions, be patient. Eventually you will be given a sticker to put on your car's windshield.

If you bring a car into Mexico on a tourist visa, the sticker you get will be a temporary vehicle-importation permit, which allows your car to remain in the country for up to six months. When the permit expires, the car must leave—and you with it. The policy is intended to stop people from selling cars in Mexico. It is possible to have a vehicle permit and visa extended in Mexico, but it can be a real bureaucratic hassle. After you leave the border crossing, resist the urge to get out of town quickly. Border towns are notorious speed traps.

If you intend to live in Mexico with a car, it is best to have FM3 immigration status (see the Making the Move chapter). With an FM3, your car can remain in the country indefinitely. The law states that as long as your FM3 is current (renewed annually), your car can legally be in Mexico, even if its import papers have expired.

One word of caution: Be sure that the VIN numbers on your car match the VIN numbers on your car registration. A friend had two digits on his registration certificate reversed and was forced to return to the States to get the mix-up straightened out.

You should also stop at a bank or money-exchange booth on either side of the border and get at least enough pesos to get you to your destination. From El Paso to Mexico City, for instance, you'll need a minimum of 1,000 pesos for gas and tolls. Exchange rates at all points of entry into Mexico, including airports, are generally better than those in the interior. In addition, exchange booths near the border are open long hours, seven days a week. Farther into the country, booths may be closed on weekends and at night. In a bind, you can often, but not always, pay for gas and tolls in dollars, but you will get ripped off on the exchange rate. No toll booths or gas stations take plastic. Paying in pesos will make your trip far less complicated. Remember that most towns have ATMs.

Before crossing the border into Mexico, be sure to buy Mexican auto insurance. Your U.S. auto insurance policy will not cover you in Mexico. AAA sells it, as do many other reputable companies, like

Autopista Tolls

Autopistas (toll roads) in Mexico, are the safest, fastest, and most convenient way to travel by car from place to place in the country. These roads are clean, have a smooth surface, and offer fairly decent minimart-type restaurants along the way. Best of all, you have most *autopistas* almost to yourself. This is because most Mexicans cannot afford the high tolls. Here are a few *autopista* examples:

Puerto Vallarta–Guadalajara: Drive past maguey fields and over coastal mountains on this scenic 3.5-hour drive that covers a total of 222 miles (359 km); the current one-way toll is 225 pesos ($20).

Nogales–Mazatlán: This route touches the U.S. border, running south through Sonora state and into Sinaloa state. The route takes 14 hours and covers a total of 739 miles (1,192 km); the current one-way toll is 445 pesos ($17.50).

Mazatlán–Los Mochis: This busy corridor across the state of Sinaloa allows Copper Canyon visitors easy access to the beach resort of Mazatlán. The new highway covers 266 miles (429 km); the one-way toll is currently 232 pesos ($20.50). The drive takes four and a half hours

Mexico City–Acapulco: Now just a 3.5-hour drive (versus six previously), the route covers 213 miles (343 km) and the one-way toll is currently 423 pesos ($37).

Mexico City–Guadalajara: Drive time has been cut in half (from eight to four hours) via this new 307-mile (495-km) road. The one-way toll is currently 440 pesos ($39). The highway provides easier access to popular colonial-city destinations, such as Morelia and Guanajuato.

Mexico City–Oaxaca: This once-grueling 10-hour journey has been cut to a pleasant four hours; the route stretches 283 miles (456 km), and the current one-way toll is 258 pesos ($23).

Mérida–Cancún: What used to be a six-hour drive has been cut in half, thanks to this new route. The distance is 193 miles (315 km), and the current one-way toll is 240 pesos ($21). This route is also the fastest way to Chichén Itzá.

Lewis and Lewis Insurance (see the Resources chapter for a list). If you are in Mexico, inquire at any branch of Lloyd Bank for reliable auto insurance.

Several insurance companies also have travel clubs. Club membership usually costs extra, but you may find the services useful. The typical policy with full coverage (no club membership), depending on the value of your car, will run about US $250–450 for a year. RVs, boats, and motorcycles should also be covered.

As you approach the Mexican border, you will be barraged by signs offering insurance deals. If you haven't already bought insurance, drop into one of these places and buy enough to get you to your destination and a bit more—say six days' worth if you are traveling from Nogales to Puerto Vallarta. This will give you coverage until you find a rec-ommended, reliable local agent who can advise you about a longer-term policy. If you are traveling around and exploring the country, buy enough insurance for the entire trip.

About 15 miles (24 km) south of the border you will come to a check-point. Here your entry documents may be checked again by immigration and your car by customs. You will drive up to a traffic light. If the light turns green, drive straight on through and that's it. If it turns red, you will be asked to pull over and step out of your car so it can be searched. Be polite and patient, show your papers, and let the agents look. They may also ask to see papers for your pet. This should not delay you for more than a few minutes and you will be back on the road.

At several points farther down the road, you may arrive at check-points operated by the military. This is a cursory check for guns and drugs. Most often, you will be waved through, although they may, on rare occasions, pull you over and ask to search your car. Be polite and watch them like a hawk. They will not ask you for money.

Rules of the Road

The number-one auto safety rule in Mexico is *never drive at night.* You never know what you might encounter on the road at night. It could be a slow-moving or stopped vehicle, or one without back-up lights. At dusk, when it is especially hard to see, people walk home from the fields along narrow roadsides. Later in the night, livestock may wander into the road. In a few cases, "police cars" with lights flashing have pulled people over and robbed them. In the daytime, it would have been clear that these cars were not really police vehicles.

Toll highways are the safest and fastest roads in the country. Be-cause the tolls are expensive ($80 from Laredo, Texas to San Miguel de Allende; $25 from Puerto Vallarta to Guadalajara), the roads are used almost exclusively by foreign travelers and wealthier Mexicans. Thus, driving these roads is like having your own private highway. Most of the toll roads are in excellent condition, are well lit, and have emergency phones every few kilometers. Near the tollbooths, you'll find shiny new gas stations with clean bathrooms (some sinks and toilets work automatically, no less!) and nearby snack bars. These roads are much more pleasant to drive than crowded U.S. interstates. Speed limits are generally about 68–75 mph (110–120 km/h), but some macho Mexicans drive like they are trying to break the sound

A Mexican Motel

Touring in the States, you find that motels are ubiquitous along the highways and byways, especially on the outskirts of towns and cities. Not so in Mexico, although this is slowly changing. In Mexico, no matter how heavily traveled the highway is, motels are virtually nonexistent between towns and cities. This forces you to plan your trip so that you will arrive in a town or city toward the end of your driving day. In the past couple of years, motel chains like Holiday Inn Express have sprung up on the outskirts of some major cities and near airports.

For many decades, one type of motel has been present on the outskirts of almost every Mexican town. These "motels" are used for trysts and rented by the hour. Usually, they have beautiful grounds and are quite luxurious. They generally have names like Motel Roma, Motel Paradise, or The Sahara and they are adorned with a sexy, neon sign that displays only the name of the hotel. Nothing about air-conditioning, pools, TV, or restaurant, although almost all of them provide room service (with quite delicious food!). Your car is discreetly parked in a garage with direct access to the room.

One night, we were desperate after driving for many hours and knew we couldn't drive another kilometer. We noticed the lovely

barrier. Cars have sped by our car so fast that we felt like we were driving in reverse! It is recommended that you use these roads when you travel long distances.

Most other major Mexican highways are two- or four-lane blacktops. The four-lane highways are usually not too bad, although in some areas, truck and bus use is heavy, and you'll feel like you're driving in a monster roller derby. Two-lane highways, on the other hand, may be the most dangerous roads of all. Buses and trucks can clog these roads and play chicken as drivers try passing one another. These roads are narrow and without a shoulder. Many have potholes, washboard surfaces, and no centerline. There is not nearly the margin for error here as there is on a two-lane highway in the United States.

Even when traffic is light, these roads still offer their share of hazards. One of the most frightening hazards is the infamous Mexican left-turn signal. Often, the left-turn signal is used as a courtesy by a Mexican driver to tell the car behind that the road ahead is clear and that it is safe to pass (which may or may not be the case). Other times, drivers give a left-turn signal, then pull off to the right to wait for traffic to pass so they can turn left when the road is clear. On rare occasions, a driver will actually turn left after giving a left-turn signal. ¡*Caramba!*

"Palms Motel" on the other side of the highway. Barbara, at the wheel, hung a left. As she crossed over an unexpectedly high median strip, she accidentally shaved off the oil-pan clean-out bolt. In the office, we were told by the manager that we couldn't stay; it wasn't appropriate and we should go to the *motel familiar* (family motel) down the road. We had passed it, and it was a dump! When he realized our situation, seeing the large pool of oil under our car, he grudgingly agreed to let us rent the room for the entire night—for a reasonable price—and also offered to call a mechanic for us.

The mechanic, dressed in oil-soaked clothes, huge pot belly exposed in front, crack exposed in the rear, showed up promptly at 8 A.M. in a 40-year-old car. He was horrified that we had to spend the night in such a terrible place and said that we could have spent the night with him and his family! Barbara thanked him, sputtering something about having our dog, and by the way, we really enjoyed staying here!...That was it. From then on, every time he thought my back was turned, he would leer at Barbara, wink, and start a little bump and grind!

He very quickly had us on our way again, with a smile on our lips.

If traffic on a highway slows down quickly for any reason—a flagman, accident, detour, etc.—it is common courtesy for Mexican drivers to turn on their emergency blinkers. It is a good idea for you to also get into this habit.

Speed limits on all Mexican roads are clearly marked and are enforced by federal highway police, who seem to be honest. Be especially aware of hungry local police in cities, who will pull you over for the slightest infraction, real or imagined.

Generally, Mexican highways are well marked, although there are those occasional confusing intersections that drive you crazy—three or four roads with the same number all heading to different locations. Sometimes, there are no signs at all. Worse, signs might unexpectedly stop. This is especially true in Mexican cities, the easiest mazes on earth in which to get lost. You may follow signs through a complicated jumble of city streets just to have them disappear completely and leave you totally confused and stranded. Asking directions often doesn't help because many Mexicans don't drive and don't know how to get from place to place by car. But that *never* stops them from giving you detailed directions anyway! If you do get lost, hire a cab to lead you out of the maze.

Before arriving in a city, look for signs that say "*cuota*" (toll road), "*libramiento*" (truck route) and "*centro*." Following the first two signs will take you around the city, and following the third will take you into its heart. Another important highway sign says "*libre*" (free road). Always take the *cuota,* unless you are exploring back roads, heading for an out-of-the-way place, or broke.

Also, be on the lookout for *topes* (TOH-pays)—speed bumps—on two-lane country roads. These suckers often appear before you have time to react. Eventually, you will come to expect them before and after small towns, but not always. When you are lucky, you'll see a warning sign about 330 yards (500 meters) in advance of a *tope,* so you can slow down and take the bump with finesse. Some *topes* are not marked, however—if you hit them at full speed, they can shake your teeth loose, blow a tire, or do serious damage to your car. When driving these country roads, you'll need both caution and the protection of the saints of the Mexican highway.

But these are the roads you will use to explore Mexico's backcountry. On these roads, you'll pass through villages that haven't changed much in a hundred years and encounter areas of natural beauty that most tourists never get to see. If your timing is particularly good, you may find yourself participating in a small village fiesta or saint's days, complete with processions and musical celebrations.

Now a word about gas: All the gas stations in Mexico are part of the huge government gasoline monopoly called Pemex. As recently as 15 years ago, Pemex stations were few and far between, and running out of gas was a real concern. Recently, new stations have cropped up all over the country, so your chances of running out of gas now are nil. Nevertheless, when you are out in the boonies and see a Pemex station, fill up even if you still have half a tank left.

These days, almost all of the filthy gas stations of old have been torn down and replaced by spiffy new ones. If you are forced to pull into one of the few remaining older stations and you have to use the bathroom, hold your breath! Note that all the newer stations have spanking-clean bathrooms and American-style snack shops.

When you pull up for gas, you may be inundated by a flurry of activity around your car. While you are telling the attendant how much gas you want, some young kid may already be cleaning your windshield and a vendor or two may be trying to sell you a car seat cover or a bag of fruit. After a few fill-ups, you will get used to the activity and take it all very calmly.

Gas in Mexico has always cost more than in the States and that is still true, even with U.S. gas prices climbing in 2004 and 2005. Self-service has not yet hit Mexico. It is the custom to tip the attendant 2–5 pesos, especially if he or she has cleaned your windshield and checked your tires and oil. It is rare nowadays that a station will try and squeeze a few more pesos out of you by not resetting the pump to zero or by over-filling your tank, but be aware! Make sure the tank gauge has been reset before the attendant starts pumping (newer pumps are reset automatically), and when the nozzle clicks—signaling a full tank—tell the attendant to stop.

Generally, auto maintenance is much less expensive in Mexico than in the States. A complete tune-up can cost as little as $50, and a brake job about the same, plus parts. The problem you may run into most often is getting a needed part for your U.S.-model car. Mexican models of the same car often use different parts. In large cities, dealerships can help, but it is not unusual to have to wait for a part to be shipped down from the States.

Mexican mechanics are wizards at cannibalizing other cars and pieces of machinery to get repairs accomplished. Mechanics take pride in their creativity when parts are not available and they are forced to jury-rig devices to get a car back on the road. Still, this is a risk worth taking only if you are in a real fix. It is always best to wait for the part if you can. Don't be scared off by mechanics whose shops look like they came straight out of a Dickens novel. The mechanic may be a wizard! Funk is becoming rarer, though, as repair shops are modernizing to accommodate the newer cars being sold in Mexico. Almost all major car manufacturers now have dealerships in the big cities.

Perhaps Mexico's greatest gift to motorists are the *Angeles Verdes* (Green Angels). This government-sponsored, comprehensive highway-assistance program has been helping drivers free of charge for the last 35 years. The Green Angels are a fleet of almost 300 distinctive green radio trucks that patrol all the major highways in Mexico from 8 A. M. to 8 P.M. Green Angel personnel are trained mechanics who can get your car running if it breaks down. They carry gas, water, and oil, and will radio ahead to the nearest town if parts or a tow are needed. If you need a Green Angel, pull off the road, lift the hood, and get comfortable with a good book. You may have a bit of a wait, but a Green Angel will eventually arrive. If you are near a phone, call their 24-hour toll-free hotline within Mexico, 800/903-9200. Most Green

Angel drivers speak at least a little English. You will find it reassuring when a Green Angel passes you on the road. In an emergency, you can also call the Mexican Highway Patrol at 525/677-2227.

Before hitting the road to Mexico (or in Mexico) find a great road map of the country if you can. Many Mexican maps are not updated often enough to show new extensions of toll roads. Many maps are downright wrong. People have been known to follow maps deep into the backcountry, eventually finding themselves lost on roads that don't exist on the map.

Once, on a trip through the Sierra Gorda region in the state of Querétaro, Barbara and I ended up on a road that was three times removed from the last road marked on the map. Not surprisingly, this thrice-removed road went through lovely towns and forests and even passed a beautiful ex-hacienda hotel, where we stayed overnight. However, if we hadn't been with friends who knew the area well, we might still be lost in those mountains!

The best and easiest-to-use general map of the country seems to be the *Guía Roja,* a book of area maps in color. The AAA map is not bad. It will get you from big city to big city, but can be confusing and useless in the backcountry. For exploring, it is best to buy individual state maps, usually available in the state tourist office in large cities. Sanborn's, a large Mexican restaurant/store chain, carries a good selection of maps.

CAR RENTALS

Most U.S. rental car companies operate in Mexico. It is a good idea to reserve a car in advance, especially if you will be traveling during a holiday (including Mexican holidays). One-way rental cars are very expensive, so fly in and out of the same airport if you can. Here are a few numbers to call to reserve a car: Avis, 800/230-4898; Budget, 800/527-0700; Dollar, 800/800-3665; National, 800/CAR-RENT (800-227-7368).

Note that when a car is rented outside the airport (at your hotel, for instance), you can save the 15-percent tax airports add to all onsite rental cars. Often it is easier, less expensive, and more fun to hire a taxi (or private car and a driver) for the day. The driver may even take you to his Aunt Rosa's house for *comida!* To find one, simply go to the nearest *sitio* (taxi stand) and ask.

BUYING A CAR

A new car from a dealership may have a similar base price to that same car in the States, but it will cost more in Mexico. Added to the price will be ISAN (Mexico's new car tax), IVA (sales tax), and *tenencia* (car owner's tax, typically between 2 and 3 percent of the vehicle's original bill of sale price).

Used-car lots are ubiquitous, as are used-car ads in the local paper. Large cities often have auto *tianguis* (a huge auto flea market). For this experience, it is best to bring along a Spanish-speaking friend and a mechanic you trust. If you make a deal, they can help you get the car registered in your name. You will need to pay an annual *refrendo* (registration fee, about 300 pesos US$30 in 2004).

TAXIS

In Mexico, cab fares are fairly inexpensive. An average trip through San Miguel de Allende or Puerto Vallarta costs about 35 pesos ($3.50), and in Mexico City you may pay as little as 50 cents for a ride. Even though fares are set, it is a good idea to ask the price of a trip before getting into a cab. Taxi drivers are rarely tipped, but usually charge extra for handling luggage. Airports and some bus stations have a booth inside where you buy a fixed-price taxi ticket to your destination.

© Ken Luboff

Housing Considerations

You would be amazed at the number of people who come to San Miguel, Chapala, Puerto Vallarta, and other Mexican cities for the first time and grow so enamored with the place that within days they buy a piece of property. It takes a wonderful mixture of confidence, money, and impulsiveness to do such a thing. Some might also add foolishness, but surprisingly, many of these people are still very happily living in Mexico with no regrets. Those who return to the States for one reason or another generally do very well financially with real estate they bought in retirement and major tourist areas, most of which have appreciated nicely.

Nevertheless, no matter how much you love a town, it would be prudent to cool your jets and rent something, especially if this is your first foray into Mexico. Renting allows you time to explore the town both physically and spiritually and to ferret out the best deals.

Renting

Renting makes the most sense when you finally find the town or city you want to live in. You will have the time to get a feel for the local culture and to explore the various neighborhoods without taking on a long-term obligation. You will have the leisure to talk with long-time foreign residents and get the inside scoop on the best buys before tying up a large amount of money in real estate. Meanwhile, if you do find something you can't live without, you can buy it. If you have just sold a home or business in the States and are feeling flush for the first time in years, temporarily invest your money and rent a place while looking for the best buy. It is easy to find reasonable rents, but availability may be a problem during popular holidays like *Semana Santa* (Holy Week) and Christmas, and during the high season. If this is when you intend to rent, you should contact a rental agent well in advance to line up a place. If you have the time, arrive early (especially if it is a long-term rental) and check out your new home. If you are not happy with it, there may still be time to switch.

Unlike houses in the United States, traditional Mexican houses are more like family compounds, with many small rooms for parents, grandparents, brothers, sisters, and cousins, often surrounding a large courtyard.

There are a few downsides to renting, of course. You may have to live with steady increases in rent or wait forever to have a leak fixed. But in a disputes with the landlord, you will be protected by Mexican law, which favors the renter. For instance, if you should decide to withhold your rent, you cannot be evicted until the dispute is settled.

You find a house to rent in Mexico much like you would in the States. Check with realtors, many of whom also manage rental properties, and look through ads in the local newspaper for property-management companies. Towns and even larger cities have strategically placed bulletin boards, often papered with advertisements for everything from bicycles to boxer shorts. Here you are certain to find houses and apartments for rent. Often an owner will rent to you on a handshake. This usually works out fine. You are more likely to encounter a lease when you rent from a realtor or management company. Commonly, the lease will be in English and will have no surprises. Expect to pay more if you want to live in the most desirable parts of the most popular cities. As you move away from these areas, rental prices drop radically, especially in neighborhoods without large numbers of foreigners. Also, expect to pay more if you are planning to rent short-term in the high season. In most areas of the country, high season is November–March or April. Rentals in some cities during important festivals and holidays, like *Semana Santa* in San Miguel, and *Día de los Muertos* (Day of the Dead) in Pátzcuaro, are more costly. Usually, you get a better deal on a long-term rental, say six months or more. And good deals can still be found. A friend of ours got a wonderful bargain on a clean, four-bedroom, second-floor, furnished apartment with great views of the city. He took the apartment for a year and paid only $300 per month. It is just a few blocks out of one of San Miguel's ritziest areas.

Most rentals are furnished, especially apartments and houses intended for short-term rentals, as well as condos. Whether or not a property is furnished will not affect the price. You may actually prefer unfurnished if you are seeking to rent for a long term.

Rental prices vary in Mexican cities, as they do anywhere in the world, depending on size, area of town, condition, view, length of stay, furnished or unfurnished, whether it is a condo or a private home, etc. Go to the cities profiled in this book for more specific rental prices.

Unlike houses in the United States, traditional Mexican houses are more like family compounds, with many small rooms for parents, grandparents, brothers, sisters, and cousins, often surrounding a large courtyard.

Unless the house you are renting is out in the sticks, it will have city water and electricity. Trash will most likely be collected daily at a fixed time, and the propane gas truck will come by to fill your tank when needed. The water truck will regularly deliver five-gallon bottles of drinking water. If you want a telephone, be sure the house already has one. In some cities, it can take months to have a phone line installed.

Because labor costs are so low in Mexico, the majority of rental-property owners will have hired a housekeeper and gardener who will be included in the rental price. In this way, the owner can be assured that the property will be well cared for and secure from theft. The housekeeper may also be a great cook. If a housekeeper is not included, you should consider finding one. There is nothing quite like having someone on hand to do the cooking, cleaning, and laundry! For a good housekeeper, it is best to get a recommendation from a friend. For instance, their housekeeper may have a sister who is looking for work. Do not feel uncomfortable with the idea of having a full-time cook, housekeeper, and/or gardener. We Americans with our egalitarian and liberal ideas often forget how grateful people from other cultures are to have work of any kind, let alone a job that is clean and well paying (relatively, given what else is available).

The water pressure in your house or condo will be "compliments of gravity," unless you happen to rent a newer one with a water-pressure system. New or renovated houses may also have a water-purification system. Most amazing of all would be a house in a city with chilly winters that has central heating.

Buying

If you are more inclined to own a home and/or invest in real estate, this may be the perfect time to buy. In 2003, travelers from the States and Canada began returning to Mexico in large numbers. While most are coming to Mexico for short vacations, many are looking into retirement options, a change in lifestyle, or real-estate investment opportunities. This trend will only increase as more baby boomers look toward retirement. Real estate is appreciating rapidly in many areas of Mexico, including coastal areas around Puerto Vallarta, Zihuatanejo, Mazatlán, the Yucatán, and parts of Baja California. In inland towns, like San Miguel de Allende and Ajijic, real estate has taken off. Nevertheless, there are still many deals to be had.

Foreigners cannot hold direct title to any lands within 30 miles (48 km) of the coast or within 60 miles (97 km) of the border (known as the restricted zone).

Ownership laws were changed during the Salinas administration, making it easy and safe to buy a home in Mexico. Buying property almost anywhere in Mexico is generally a simple matter of hiring a *notario* (a real estate lawyer), paying your money, and transferring the title to your name, pretty much as it is in the States.

Buying property on the coast or along the borders of Mexico is done a little differently. The Mexican constitution of 1917 essentially gave common ownership of all beaches and borders to the Mexican people. Foreigners cannot hold direct title to any lands within 30 miles (48 km) of the coast or within 60 miles (97 km) of the border (known as the restricted zone). In 1994, amendments to the constitution allowed foreigners to buy land in the restricted zone for commercial purposes, but residential ownership is still restricted.

To develop tourism and encourage private ownership in the restricted zone while not violating the constitution, the government has created a trust arrangement known as a *fideicomiso*. Under this system, the coastal or border home (or lot) you want to buy will be placed in a trust with a Mexican bank as the trustee. The trustee, usually the trust department of the bank, is the owner of record of the property. But ownership rights belong to you, the purchaser of the property and the beneficiary of the trust. The trustee is prohibited by contract and by Mexican law from transferring the property or beneficiary rights without written permission of the beneficiary. For all practical purposes, a *fideicomiso* is the same as private-property ownership in the United States. You can develop the property, sell it, rent it, and pass it on to your heirs when you die. The *fideicomiso* has to be renewed every 50 years.

A 1993 law allows foreigners to obtain direct ownership rights to property on the coast by forming a Mexican corporation. The two required partners may be foreigners, but because the corporation is a Mexican entity, it can own land. The law limits ownership to commercial property but is unclear as to what constitutes commercial property. For instance, might a property in which one room is used as an office qualify? A minimum of 50,000 pesos (about $4,500) is required to start the corporation. Creating a Mexican corporation may be ideal for commercial real-estate deals, but a *fideicomiso* is simpler and easier for private homes.

Some newcomers to Mexico arrive with the expectation that they will find a hacienda in this "third world" country for a few thousand dollars. Forget it—unless you want to live in the middle of nowhere or buy a ruin. Real estate in Mexico works the same way it does in the United States. The most desirable areas are the most expensive. Once you move away from the highly sought-after areas, the cost of real estate plummets.

Mexican Homes

After you make the decision to stay in Mexico, most likely one of the first things you will learn is the difference between the modest home of an average Mexican citizen and that of a wealthy Mexican or a gringo. This will be especially apparent when you go house hunting.

The feeling of many modest Mexican homes may be different than what you are used to. For one, the home was most likely built 50–350 years ago, and probably has not been renovated since then. The rooms will usually be small and dark, loaded with heavy, dark wooden furniture, the couches and arm chairs about as comfortable as an electrocution seat. Kitchens will be old-fashioned, as will bathrooms, what there are of them. The walls may have some family photos, a cross or two, and a Virgin of Guadalupe. The home will be spotlessly clean.

This type of old-fashioned Mexican home can have a real charm about it. Many are L-shaped or square, built around a courtyard, often with an arrangement of beautiful plants and flowers and small wooden cages of colorful singing birds. Sometimes doors and windows are slightly out of square, offering a very homemade and warm feeling. If you are looking for a bargain, this is the type of home you want. It may take some work, but in the end, you will have something to be proud of.

Finding a real estate agent to show you property is easy, especially in tourist areas, large cities, and retirement communities. In all these places, real estate agents advertise heavily in local newspapers and magazines. Most have websites with listings and photos of available properties. If you know where you want to buy, you can start the search before you leave home. If you prefer to begin looking after you arrive in Mexico, you will easily find a well-marked real estate office, usually in a high-profile location. In downtown Ajijic, for instance, if you are not paying attention, you could easily bang your head on a real estate agent's sign. In Puerto Vallarta, Mazatlán, and other coastal cities, enthusiastic salesmen offer nights on the town and other freebies if you'll just take a look at the time-share condo they are pushing (check the Resources chapter for a list of Real Estate Agents).

Many of the real estate agents we have met in Mexico are American or Canadian expatriates who are riding the Mexican real estate wave. Some came to Mexico to make their fortunes, but many others retired here, got bored, and went into real estate to entertain themselves. Mexican realtors seem to keep a lower profile, but they are worth talking to. Many speak English and list properties owned by Mexicans that may not make it

A gringo or wealthier Mexican home is one that was either built from scratch or renovated by a "modern" Mexican, American, Canadian, or European. Generally, these are homes that most of you are familiar with. The previous buyers will have knocked a few walls down to create larger spaces, and they probably added several new windows. Most have modern kitchens, large shiny bathrooms, a modern clothes washer and dryer, and light-filled living and dining rooms. The furniture usually includes at least one soft, comfortable, stylish couch, a cushy chair or two, and king- or queen-size beds. There will usually be a newish big-screen TV, an interesting rug on the floor, and art covering the walls. Sometimes, the new owner has converted part of the courtyard into an outdoor dining or living room and may even have added a pool.

These homes cost quite a bit more money, but are worth it to those who do not want to deal with time-consuming and costly renovations.

An interesting note: A popular young Mexican architect recently said that, in general, you don't find large walk-in closets in the bedrooms of wealthy Mexicans. Why? Because they wouldn't be caught dead in last year's fashions and so they get rid of them. They only need space for the latest season.

onto the lists of American agents, as multiple listings are rare in Mexican cities. As in the States, real estate agents in Mexico generally work for a commission of 6 percent of the sale price, paid by the seller.

If you don't like dealing with real estate agents or you just want to try finding a house on your own, go to a part of town you like and ask people if they know of places for sale. The corner grocer or a woman sweeping the stoop may have a cousin who has a friend who knows a guy who wants to sell his house. This is exactly what happened to us in San Miguel de Allende.

Barbara and I were walking through the narrow streets of a Mexican *barrio* (neighborhood), just sort of looking around, when a very nice man came out of a *tienda* (shop) and asked if we would be interested in buying a house. We gave each other a quick look and simultaneously shook our heads yes. Why not look? The man's name was Carmelo, and he explained that the house belonged to a cousin who had gotten work in a beach resort town and was not planning to return to San Miguel. We liked the house and extracted a promise from Carmelo not to tell anyone else about it until we made up our minds. For the next two weeks, we almost lived in that house, redesigning it at least 100 times. Then, after some haggling with Carmelo, we bought it. The price was $25,000! Houses in that neighborhood have since gotten more expensive.

Another do-it-yourself method is to look for signs that say *Trato Directo* (direct deal)—the equivalent of For Sale by Owner. And keep in mind that many houses in Mexico are sold completely furnished.

The Mexican real estate scene is changing rapidly. Planned and gated developments are being built all over the country. Some of these developments are surprisingly well designed and constructed. Others are built quickly for a fast buck, with shoddy materials. Beware of the too-good deal.

Coastal property presents its own set of issues. Much of the property along the coast (and in other parts of the country) is still owned communally by *ejidos* (eh-HEE-dos). An *ejido* is a community of people, living together in an area or a town, who own the surrounding land in common. *Ejidos* were originally indigenous land collectives that disintegrated after La Reforma, the war to eject Emperor Maximilian from Mexico, which ended in 1861. It was not until after the revolution of 1910–1920 that *ejidos* were reformed as a way of redistributing land to the *campesinos* (the peasants). Until the law was changed in 1994, these lands could not be sold.

Under the new law, an *ejido* can meet and divide the land among its members. An individual member can then sell his or her parcel. Buyers must be certain that the land being sold has legally passed from the *ejido* to an individual owner, and that the owner has the right to transfer title—in the form of a *fideicomiso* (trust) if the property is near the coast. The buyer must hire a *notario publico* (a real estate lawyer with no resemblance in any way to a notary in the States) to determine the status of the property and draw up the necessary closing documents.

In the past, foreigners using a Mexican as the buyer have bought property on the Mexican coast directly from an *ejido*. In these cases, every member of the *ejido* signed a bill of sale, placing title to the property in the name of a Mexican citizen. This Mexican usually had a separate agreement with the foreign buyer (often a friend) to hold the property in his name until some later date. He was called a *prestanombre* (borrowed name). The *prestanombre* was generally paid a fee for this service.

Be aware that this arrangement can turn into a disaster. First, the sale to the *prestanombre* may not be legally recognized by the Mexican government. Secondly, any written agreement between a *prestanombre*

Luis Barragan

Luis Barragan is one of Mexico's most highly regarded architects. He was born in 1902 to wealthy, conservative parents and reared on the family's sprawling estate outside Guadalajara. He was drawn to engineering and graduated in Guadalajara with a degree in 1924. After school, he traveled extensively in Europe, where he is said to have been influenced by Moorish architecture in southern Spain as well as the art deco movement. Still, after he returned to Mexico, his designs of that time are considered pedestrian. In 1930, he befriended Mexican muralist Jose Clemente Orozco before making another trip to Europe, where he met the famous Swiss architect Le Corbusier and landscape architect Ferdinand Bac in Paris.

This time, when Barragan returned to Mexico and settled in Mexico City, he began developing a personal style. He reached back to Mexico's traditional enthusiasm for bright colors and combined them with large, flat geometric surfaces interrupted by small openings, thick walls, and other geometric surfaces to enhance variations of light and shadow. He added to these ideas the design element of water and a strong connection to gardens and landscapes. These became major stylistic themes in Barragan's architecture. Much of his work in Mexico City during the 1940s involved garden design. One of the finest examples of the combined use of Barragan's stylistic elements is the private Cuadra San Cristobal, built in 1968 at Los Clubes in the state of Mexico. Another is the incredible Francisco Gilardi house and outdoor pool in Mexico City, finished in 1978.

Barragan spent a good deal of the later part of his life broke and in relative obscurity. Then in 1975, the Museum of Modern Art in New York wrote to request staging a retrospective of his career. A few years later, Luis Barragan was awarded the Pritzker Prize, architecture's equivalent to the Nobel Prize. He is now considered one of the great architects of the 20th century and is probably Mexico's most well-known architect. Barragan died in 1988 in Mexico City.

and a foreigner has no legal standing. If the *prestanombre* forfeits, the buyer often winds up in a difficult court battle to keep the property.

Once you decide on the property you want to buy, hire a *notario publico* to research the deed and help you get a clear title. Your real estate agent can also help with this process. For the most part, the only difference between a Mexican and a U.S. real estate purchase is you will most likely pay cash in Mexico. Good-bye, mortgage payments—hello, clear home. The entire process usually takes from three to six weeks and can cost about $5,000, plus a title transfer fee of 2 percent of the declared purchase price.

Even if you don't have the cash, you may be still able to own a home or condo in Mexico. In the last few years, two or three U.S. and Canadian mortgage companies have begun offering mortgages on Mexican real estate. No doubt, in coming years the number of such companies will grow. Typically, mortgages are offered for up to 70 percent of the appraised value of the property, at about 2 percent above comparable U.S. rates. One realtor in Ajijic has been advertising that she will get 30-year mortgages on up to 40 percent of the value of the home you buy through her.

Mexican banks, mostly owned by U.S. and other foreign corporations, offer mortgages, but at rates too high to consider. Recently the Mexican bank Financiero Interlat was offering mortgages on Mexican properties under a plan called *Hogares Interlat*. Home buyers could apply for loans of up to 50 percent of the value of the property, but interest rates were high (about 20 percent) and loans had to be paid off within 12 years. One wonders how any but the wealthiest Mexicans can possibly afford to buy a home. On the other hand, this may work for you as a short-term cash-flow solution.

You may plan to be an absentee owner and not rent out your home. In this case, you need to take security precautions. Because there are very few home-security firms in Mexico, you should hire an honest and reliable full-time housekeeper, and a part- or full-time gardener. Having an employee work for you full-time builds loyalty to you personally and to the property. The house will be well cared for and less likely to be robbed, as there will appear to be activity in and around it. Your workers can leave lights on at night and even stop by and check occasionally after dark. Many larger Mexican properties are built with this in mind, with a small apartment on the property for a watchman and his (or her) family.

Those planning to rent their Mexican home either short or long term will want to hire a management company to look after the property and collect rents. For short-term rentals, you can sign up with one of the many effective vacation-home rental companies on the Web for about $100 a year. For long-term rentals, it is probably best to advertise in the local paper. The management company can help you with this and also tell you if they will provide housekeeping and security services or if it that is your responsibility.

BUILDING AND RESTORING

As in the States, or for that matter anywhere in the world, building a house can be a pleasant—though often frustrating—experience, or a nightmare. Those building in Mexico will most likely be very pleasantly surprised by the relatively low cost of construction. Your greatest savings will be in labor costs: The average Mexican laborer earns about $40 or $50 a week; a first-class foreman about $250 a week. Plumbers and electricians earn more because they charge by the piece, and they are reluctant to quote an entire job. When they do, they quote high. Material costs will be moderately low as long as the dollar remains strong against the peso and Mexico's inflation remains stable at about 5 percent. These factors help keep average building costs in the range of $70–100 per square foot in most parts of the country. High-end materials and expensive architects can increase costs.

Foreign residents who build in Mexico seem to fall into four categories. First are those who have lived in Mexico for some time, speak Spanish, and know the ropes. Often, they hire a crew and run the job themselves, achieving very low costs—as low as $50–60 a square foot. Then there are the newcomers who hire a reliable architect and builder to do the work for them. These people pay more, but usually have a relatively hassle-free experience. Next are the newcomers who design a house, hire a *maestro* (foreman) and crew, and begin building. They must seriously oversee costs and keep a watchful eye to be certain that materials don't walk away. If the owner has previous building experience and some good luck, this scenario can be satisfying. It is also a great way to learn Spanish and begin to understand the Mexican culture. Finally, there are those who get ripped off for a number of reasons: an unreliable and expensive architect, a builder who siphons off materials for his next job, or, worst of all, takes the money without completing the work. In each case, the key to a satisfactory outcome is close scrutiny of the relationship between the amount of money spent and the percent of work completed.

Barbara and I hired a Mexican architect/builder to help us renovate our old colonial house. She charged us 18 percent over the cost of materials for both design and construction. She also passed on to us discounts from suppliers (we were able to verify this by accompanying her to plumbing and electrical supply houses and lumber yards). The house was completed in record time with relatively few problems. Friends were amazed that we had such a smooth building experience.

Of course, it wasn't always painless. Almost every day, something would cause us to look at each other and say, "Unbelievable." It became our daily mantra. Usually, "unbelievable" referred to the lack of coordination among workers—like when one group putting in the patio was followed by another group digging up the patio to run electrical conduit. The architect occasionally forgot to order supplies and the crew would sit and wait. She would call early in the morning, frantic to have us run to the plumbing store to choose a bathtub because the plumber had unexpectedly decided to finish the bathroom that day. Of course, the tub we wanted would be sold out, and ordering one might take two months!

One of the most pleasant (or, depending on your point of view, frightening) aspects of building in Mexico is the lack of building codes anywhere in the country. This may seem wild and uncivilized, but, in fact, most contractors in Mexico build the way their fathers and their fathers before them built. The result is generally a more substantial brick and concrete building than would be found in most of the States, and without the additional delay of building inspectors. This puts the burden on you and your architect or builder to be certain that plumbing and electrical work and materials are excellent.

Building permits are obligatory everywhere in the country and usually require drawings. These can be supplied by the architect or by a draftsman hired by the owner or builder. Cities with historical zones, such as San Miguel de Allende, also require both new constructions and renovations to meet historical standards for the area.

FEES AND TAXES

All property transactions in Mexico are subject to taxes due to SAT (previously known as Hacienda). Here is a list of taxes due when buying and selling, as well as the approximate cost of other fees you may encounter. When buying property, you will pay an acquisition tax of 2 percent of the property's sale value, whether the property is sold to you, transferred, donated, placed into trust, split off, or merged. A fee goes to the *notario publico* (real estate lawyer) of about 1.5 percent of the transaction value for services rendered, plus the cost of the official appraisal. You will also pay a registry fee of 1.3 percent based on the value of the transaction, and a permit fee of about $150. A *fideicomiso* (bank trust) set-up fee of about $750 will need to be paid only if you are buying property within the restricted zone. There will also be an annual service charge of $300–500 for a *fideicomiso*. If possible, shop around as you may be able to find a lower annual fee at another bank.

You may also have survey costs and additional legal fees if you have to hire an *abogado* (lawyer) to handle legal matters having to do with the property. If you are buying a condominium or in a gated community, you will have to pay a monthly condo or association fee.

A title insurance policy, though not required, is recommended. Costs vary depending on the sale price of the property. Figure about $50–150.

When you sell a property, you will be required to pay a capital gains tax of the lesser of either 20 percent on the declared value of the transaction or 33 percent on the gain between the declared value of the property and the declared selling price. Commercial property is taxed at 33 percent. No tax is due if the home has been your main residence for at least the last two years. Be aware: Some may argue that if you have a *fideicomiso,* the bank is the legal owner and you must pay capital gains tax even if the home is your main residence. Many strongly disagree with this interpretation of the law.

If you use a real estate agent you will usually pay a 6-percent fee, plus sales tax on the fee.

Household Expenses

Expenses vary widely and wildly depending on where you live and how you live. A friend of ours who lives on the coast pays $10–20 a month for electricity. Other friends, who live in San Miguel de Allende, have had monthly electric bills as high as $500 (when they had winter renters who turned on every electric space heater and ran them all day every day). On average, San Miguelenses pay $45 per month. Propane costs the same no matter where you are. Most homes have a 300- or 500-liter tank, which is refilled when empty. The cost per liter is approximately $.40. Monthly water costs vary widely from rainy to desert areas.

Phone and Internet services are fairly standard throughout the country. With the onset of cable and DSL Internet connections and international phone services, like Vonage, many people use their phones only for local calls.

The salary of a full-time (40 hours a week) cook/housekeeper will set you back about $50. Many people opt to "share" a housekeeper with another household, having them come in three, rather than six, days a week. Very few people need full-time gardeners unless they have huge formal gardens. Gardeners on average get about $20 for three afternoons a week, about $2–3 per hour. It may take some time and a few tries to find compatible workers, but it is worth the effort. These folks, especially your housekeeper, will be sharing your space for a good part of the day.

Monthly entertainment and food costs vary by individual. Most restaurants are reasonably priced, as are movies (about $3.50 a ticket) and other diversions (theater tickets $6). Food costs vary depending on season and your location. Here are the latest prices in January 2005 at a supermarket in Ajijic: whole chicken, $.72/lb. (18 pesos/kg); ground sirloin, $2.27/lb. (54 pesos/kg); pork ribs, $1.97/lb. (49 pesos/kg); eggs, $1.12/dozen (19 pesos/kg); lettuce, $.28/lb. (7 pesos/kg); potatoes, $.44/lb. (11 pesos/kg); beets, $.36/lb. (9 pesos/kg); avocado, $.72/lb. (18 pesos/kg); onion, $.20/lb. (5 pesos/kg); limes, $.24/lb. (6 pesos/kg); bananas, $.28/lb. (7 pesos/kg); oranges, $.19/lb. (4 pesos/kg).

© Ken Luboff

Resources

Contacts

Consulates and Agencies

U.S. EMBASSY AND CONSULATES IN MEXICO

U.S. Embassy
Paseo de la Reforma 305
Colonia Cuauhtemoc, México City
tel.: 555/209-9100

Consulate Guadalajara
Progreso 175
44100 Guadalajara, Jalisco
tel.: 333/825-2998 or 333/825-2700
fax: 333/826-6549

Consulate Hermosillo
Calle Monterrey 141
Pte. 83260 Hermosillo, Sonora
tel.: 662/217-2375 or 662/217-2382
fax: 662/217-2578

Consulate Ciudad Juárez
Avenida Lopez Mateos 924-N
Chihuahua
tel.: 614/611-3000

Consulate Matamoros
Avenida Primera 2002 y Azaleas
87330 Matamoros, Tamaulipas
tel.: 868/812-4402
fax: 868/812-2171

Consulate Mérida
Paseo Montejo 453
97000 Mérida, Yucatán

tel.: 999/925-5011
fax: 999/925-6219

Consulate Monterrey
Avenida Constitución 411
Pte. 64000
tel.: 818/345-2120

Consulate Nuevo Laredo
Allende 3330
Col. Jard'n
88260 Nuevo Laredo, Tamaulipas
tel.: 867/714-0512
fax: 867/714-7984

Consulate General Tijuana
Tapachula 96
Col. Hipódromo
22420 Tijuana, Sonora
tel.: 664/681-7400
fax: 664/681-8016

U.S. CONSULAR AGENTS IN MEXICO

Acapulco
Joyce Anderson
Hotel Acapulco Continental
Costera M. Alemyn 121
Office 14
39580 Acapulco, Guerrero
tel.: 744/481-1699 or 744/469-0556
fax: 744/484-0300

Cabo San Lucas
David Greenberg

1 Blvd. Marina y Pedregal #3
Cabo San Lucas, Baja California Sur
tel./fax: 624/143-3566

Cancún
Carol Butler
Plaza Caracol Dos, Second Fl.
#320–323
Blvd. Kukulkan, Km. 8.5, Hotel
Zone
77500 Cancún, Quintana Roos
tel.: 998/883-0272
fax: 998/883-1373

Ixtapa
Elizabeth Williams
Office 9, Plaza Ambiente
40880 Ixtapa, Zihuatanejo
tel.: 755/553-1108
fax: 755/554-6276

Mazatlán
Gerianne Nelson Gallardo
Hotel Playa Mazatlán
Rodolfo T. Loaiza 202
Zona Dorada
82110 Mazatlán, Sinaloa
tel/fax: 669/916-5889 or 669/913-
4444, ext. 285

Oaxaca
Mark A. Leyes
Macedonio Alcaly 201, #206
68000 Oaxaca, Oaxaca
tel./fax: 951/514-3054

Puerto Vallarta
Laura A. Holmstrom
Vallarta Building

Plaza Zaragoza 160, Piso 2–18
48300 Puerto Vallarta, Jalisco
tel.: 322/222-0069
fax: 322/222-0074

San Luis Potosí
Carloyn Lazaro
Avenudida Venustiano Carranza
2076-41
78220 San Luis Potosí, San Luis Potosí
tel.:444/811-7802

San Miguel de Allende
Philip Maher
Hernandez Macias 72
37700 San Miguel de Allende,
Guanajuato
tel.: 415/152-2357
fax: 415/152-1588

MEXICAN EMBASSY AND CONSULATES IN THE UNITED STATES

Mexican Embassy
1911 Pennsylvania Ave. NW
Washington, D.C. 20006
tel.: 202/728-1600
fax: 202/728-1698

Arizona
135 Terrace Ave.
Nogales, AZ 85621
tel.: 602/287-2521

Saguaro Savings Bldg.
Ste. 150
700 E. Jefferson
Phoenix, AZ 85034
tel.: 602/242-7398

California
331 W. Second St.
Calexico, CA 92231
tel.: 619/357-3863

905 N. Fulton St.
Fresno, CA 93721
tel.: 209/233-3065

125 Paseo de la Plaza
Los Angeles, CA 90012
tel.: 213/624-3261

Transportation Center
201 E. Fourth St.
Oxnard, CA 93030
tel.: 805/483-4684

9812 Old Winery Place
Ste. 10
Sacramento, CA 95814
tel.: 916/363-3885

588 W. Sixth St.
San Bernardino, CA 92401
tel.: 714/889-9836

610 A St.
Ste. 100
San Diego, CA 92101
tel.: 619/231-8414

870 Market St.
Ste. 528
San Francisco, CA 94102
tel.: 312/392-5554

380 N. First St.
Ste. 102

San Jose, CA 95113
tel.: 408/294-3414

406 W. Fourth St.
Santa Ana, CA 92701
tel.: 714/835-3069

Colorado
707 Washington St.
Ste. A
Denver, CO 80203
tel.: 303/830-0601 or
   303/830-0607

Florida
780 N. LeJeune Rd.
Ste. 525
Miami, FL 33145
tel.: 305/441-8780

Georgia
3220 Peachtree Rd. NE
Atlanta, GA 30305
tel.: 404/266-2233

Illinois
300 N. Michigan Ave., Second Fl.
Chicago, IL 60601
tel.: 312/855-1380

Louisiana
World Trade Center
2 Canal St.
Ste. 840
New Orleans, LA 70130
tel.: 504/522-3596

Massachusetts
20 Park Plaza

Ste. 321
Boston, MA 02116
tel.: 617/426-8782

Michigan
1515 Bood Blvd. at W. Grand
River
Detroit, MI 48226
tel.: 313/965-1868

Missouri
1015 Locust St.
Ste. 922
St. Louis, MO 63101
tel.: 314/436-3233

New Mexico
Western Bank Building
401 Fifth St. NW
Albuquerque, NM 87102
tel.: 505/247-2139

New York
8 E. 41st St.
New York, NY 10017
tel.: 212/689-0456

Pennsylvania
575 Philadelphia Bourse Bldg.
21 S. Fifth St.
Philadelphia, PA 19106
tel.: 215/922-4262

Texas
200 E. Sixth St.
Ste. 200
Austin, TX 78701
tel.: 512/478-2866

724 Elizabeth and Seventh Sts.
Brownsville, TX 78520
tel.: 210/541-7061

410 North Tower
800 N. Shoreline
Corpus Christi, TX 78401
tel.: 512/882-3375

1349 Empire Central
Ste. 100
Dallas, TX 75247
tel.: 214/630-7341 or 214/630-7343

1010 S. Main St.
Del Rio, TX 78840
tel.: 210/774-5031

140 Adams St.
Eagle Pass, TX 78852
tel.: 210/773-9255

910 E. San Antonio St.
El Paso, TX 79901
tel.: 915/533-3644

4200 Montrose Blvd.
Ste. 120
Houston, TX 77006
tel.: 713/524-2300

1612 Farragut St.
Laredo, TX 78040
tel.: 210/723-6360

1418 Beech St.
Ste. 102–104
McAllen, TX 78501
tel.: 210/686-0243

511 W. Ohio
Ste. 121
Midland, TX 79701
tel.: 915/687-2334

127 Navarro St.
San Antonio, TX 78205
tel.: 210/227-9145

Utah
182 S. 600 E
Ste. 202
Salt Lake City, UT 84102
tel.: 801/521-8502

Washington
2132 Third Ave.
Seattle, WA 98121
tel.: 206/448-3526

Making the Move

NEWSLETTERS AND MAGAZINES

Adventures in Mexico
Apdo 31–70
45050 Guadalajara, Jalisco

Background Notes
Published by the U.S. Department of State about countries around the world.
Superintendent of Documents
U.S. Government Printing Office
Washington, D.C.
tel.: 202/512-1800 or 202/647-5225

The Mexico File
www.mexicofile.com

Retiring in Guadalajara
www.mexweb.com/g-retire.htm

International Travel News
A wonderfully informative small magazine covering the entire world.

P.O. Box 189490
Sacramento, CA 95818-9490
tel.: 800/486-4968
itn@ns.net
www.intltravelnews.com

Mexico Desconicido (**Hidden Mexico**)
A fine National Geographic–style magazine.
www.mexicodesconicido.com

MB, The Magazine of the NAFTA Marketplace
A slick four-color monthly magazine.
tel.: 281/261-2581
www.mexicobusiness.com

Puerto Vallarta Lifestyles
A four-color English-language quarterly.
tel.: 322/226-1543
jgyserpr@zonavirtual.com.mx
www.virtualvallarta.com/vallarta/
   lifestyles/

Xcaret
A full-color magazine in English
and Spanish on Cancún
and the Yucatán Peninsula.
tel.: 998/883-1539 or 998/883-0623
www.cancuncd.com/cancun-
brochures.php

Yates y Villas
A four-color magazine in both
English and Spanish; photos of
coastal locations.

tel.: 954/463-9040
revistas@mexmags.com

GENERAL INFORMATION
www.mexicodesconicido.com
www.mexconnect.com
www.sanborns.com.mx
www.peoplesguide.com
www.cia.gov
www.livingabroadin.com
www.travel.state.gov

Language and Education

LANGUAGE SCHOOLS

Cuernavaca

Center for Bilingual Multicul-
tural Studies at Universidad
Internacional
tel.: 777/317-1087
www.uninter.com.mx/spanish

Cuernavaca Language School
tel.: 777/317-5151
www.cuernavacalanguageschool.
 com

Tlahuica Spanish Learning
Center
tel.: 800/746-8335

Universal Centro de Lengua y
Comunicación Social
tel.: 777/318-2904 or 777/312-4902

Encuentros
tel.: 777-312-5088

encuentros@learnspanishinmexico.
 com
www.learnspanishinmexico.com

Guadalajara
IMAC Spanish School
www.spanish-school.com.mx

Guanajuato
Instituto Miguel de Cervantes
www.spanish-immersion.com

Academia Falcon
www.institutofalcon.com

Mazatlán
Centro de Idiomas
www.spanishlink.org

Oaxaca
Academia Vingulaza
tel.: 951/513-2763
director@vinigulaza.com
vingu@prodigy.net.mx
www.vingulaza.com

Instituto Amigos del Sol
tel.: 951/514-6076
Amisol@oaxacanews.com
amisol@prodigy.com.mx

Civilization Travel
www.civsite.com
bosworth@civsie.com

Becari Language School
tel.: 951/514-6076
Becarioax@prodigy.com.mx

Instituto Cultural Oaxaca
www.instculturaloax.com.mx/

Español Interactivo
www.mexonline.com/esp-interac-tivo.htm

San Miguel de Allende

Warren Hardy Spanish
tel.: 415/154-4017 or 415/152-4728
info@warrenhardy.com
www.warrenhardy.com

Americana Academia Hispano
tel.: 415/152-0349 or 415/152-4349
info@ahaspeakspanish.com
www.ahaspeakspanish.com

Instituto Habla Hispana
tel.: 415/152-0713
www.mexicospanish.com

Instituto Allende
tel.: 415/152-0190
www.instituto-allende.edu.mx

Centro Bilingue
tel.: 415/152-5400
www.geocities.com/centrobi-lingue/

Universidad Del Valle de Mexico
www.uvmnet.edu

PRIMARY SCHOOLS AND HIGH SCHOOLS

Mexico City

The American School Foundation
tel.: 555/227-4900
asf@www.asf.edu.mx

Greengate School
tel.: 555/373-0088/0089

Anglo-Montessori Kindergarten
Hacienda de Santana 15
Bosques de Echegaray
tel.: 555/560-7040
www.montessoriconnections.com/
    Schools/AngloMontessori/
    anglomontessori2.html

Eton School
Preschool:
Santa Lucia 220
Colonia Prado de la Montaña
555/520-0410

Elementary–High School:
Montes Alpes 605
Lomas Chapultepec
tel: 555/292-2294/95/96/97/99

El Colegio Britanico (The
Edron Academy)
Calzada Desierto de los Leones
5578
Colonia Olivar de los Padres
tel: 555/585-2847, 555/585-3154,
or 555/585-3049
fax: 555/585-2846
www.edron.edu.mx

Lomas Altas Primary School
Montañas Calizas 305
Lomas Chapultepec
tel.: 5520-5375
74751.2307@compuserv.com

Montessori Elementary
Segundo Cerrada de Duraznos 6
Colonia San Juan Totoltepec
Naucalpan
tel.: 5373-7732/7548
www.montessoriconnections.com/
Schools/AngloMontessori

Westhill Institute
Primary school:
Domingo Garcia Ramos 56
Colonia Prado de la Montaña

High school–University:
Monte Carpatos 940
Lomas Chapultepec
tel.: 555/282-4445 or 555/282-
4522
www.westhill.edu.com.mx

Cuernavaca
Colegio Williams de Cuernavaca
Luna 32
Col. Jardines de Cuernavaca
62360 Cuernavaca, Morelos

Pre-K–Grade 12
tel.: 777/316-0434, 777/316-0467,
or 777/316-0477
fax: 777/315-8298
www.williams-cuernavaca.edu.mx

Marymount College
Grades 7–12
Estrella del Norte #6
Colonia Rancho Tetela
Cuernavaca, Morelos
tel: 777/313-0077 or 777/313-1602
fax: 777/311-4277
www.portal-morelos.com/
regional/morelos/escuelasy
universidades.html

Instituto Suizo-American
Grades K–12
tel.: 777/316-0400
www.portal-morelos.com/
regional/morelos/escuelasy
universidades.html

Discovery School
Grades K–12
tel.: 777/318-5721, 777/318-
1133
www.portal-morelos.com/
regional/morelos/escuelasy
universidades.html

Centro Educativo Bilingue
Grades K–12
tel.: 777/313-0911 or 777/313-0011
www.portal-morelos.com/regional/morelos/escuelasy universidades.html

Colegio Porter
Grades K–6
tel.: 777/313-4070

Guadalajara/Lake Chapala

Cologio La Paz School
Guadalajara, Jalistco
http://ie3global.oregonstate.edu/guada3.html

American School Foundation of Guadalajara
Grades K–8, Junior and High School, Secondary and Preparatory
Colomos No. 2110
Col. Providencia
tel.: 333/817-3377
fax: 333/817-3356
www.asfg.mx/

Lincoln School
Grades Pre-school–10
Circunvalacion Sur No. 62
Col. Las Fuentes
tel.: 333/631-3032
www.usembassy-mexico.gov/gua-dalajara/GeSchools.htm

Roosevelt School
Grades K–6, Secondary
Prolongacion Americas No. 1506

Col. Country Club
tel.: 333/817-3296
fax: 333/817-2508
www.usembassy-mexico.gov/guadalajara/GeSchools.htm

Puerto Vallarta

The American School of Puerto Vallarta
Apartado Postal 275-B
Puerto Vallarta, Jalisco
48300 Mexico
tel.: 322/221-1525
fax.: 322/221-2373
http://aspv.edu.mx/puerto-vallarta/index.htm

Mazatlán

Instituto Anglo Moderno
www.anglomoderno.edu.mx

San Miguel de Allende

Colegio Atabal
tel: 415/152-8855

Jose Vasconcelos Bilingual School
Grades 1–9
APDO 74
Calle de Obraje No. 11
San Miguel de Allende, Gto.
tel: 415/152-1869
Escjosev@prodigy.net.mx,

Colegio Los Charcos Waldoft School
Rancho Los Charcos s/n
Apto. 1149

San Miguel de Allende,
Guanajuato
37700 Mexico
fax: 415/154-8780
loscharcos@hotmail.com
www.waldorfsanmiguel.com

COLLEGES AND UNIVERSITIES

Cuernavaca

Marymount College
Estrella del Norte #6
Colonia Rancho Tetela
Cuernavaca, Morelos
tel: 777/313-0077 or 777/313-1602
fax: 777/311-4277
www.marymount.edu

Mexico City

Alliant International University
Alvaro Obregón No. 110
Colonia Roma
06700 Mexico D.F.
tel: 555/264-2187
fax: 555/5264-2188
admissions3@alliant.edu
www.alliant.edu

Endicott College
Campuses in Mexico City and
Beverly, MA
Aristoteles 80
Colonia Polanco.
tel.: 555/531-0793 or 555/203-4514
fax: 555/254-1241
Endicottmex@hotmail.com

UNAM—Center for Foreign Students
San Juan Totoltepec and Av.
Alcanfores
Colonia San Mateo
tel: 555/623-1521, 555/623-1510,
or 555/623-1511

Anahuac University
Apdo. Postal 10–844
11000 Mexico DF
tel.: 555/627-0210, ext. 8297
fax: 555/596-1938
anahuac@anahuac.mx
www.anahuac.mx

Universidad De Las Americas
Puebla 223
Colonia Roma.
tel: 555/525-4633/34/35
fax: 555/511-6040

Universidad Iberoamericana
Prolongación Paseo de la Reforma
880
Santa Fe.
tel: 555/661-5827, 555/661-0079,
or 555/267-4200
International Division: 555/292-1883
fax: 555/292-1266

Universidad Nacional Autonoma de México (UNAM)
Apartado Postal 70–391
Av. Universidad 3002
Ciudad Universitaria
tel: 555/550-5172
fax: 555/548-9939
www.unam.mx

Westhill University
Domingo Garcia Ramos 56
Colonia Prados de la Monta

tel: 555/292-1729 or 555/292-2380
fax: 555/202-3277 or 555/520-2683
www.westhill.edu.mx

Health

INSURANCE

Sanborn's,
tel.: 800/222-0158
www.sanbornsinsurance.com

Solutions Abroad
www.solutionsabroad.com

Seguros Insurance
www.seguros-insurance.net

Lloyd's Bank
Lloyd@lloyd.com.mx

American Society in Guadalajara
tel.: 333/121-2395

Stephen M. Patton
tel. 800/001-9200 (toll-free within
  Mexico) or 555/533-1620
stephen@patton.mexis.com

Instituto Mexicano del Seguro
Social
www.imss.gob.mx

Employment

MEXICAN TRADE COMMISSION OFFICES IN THE UNITED STATES

California
World Trade Center
350 South Figueroa St., Ste. 296
Los Angeles, CA 90071
tel.: 213/628-1220

Florida
New World Tower, Ste. 1601
100 N. Biscayne Blvd.
Miami, FL 33132
tel.: 305/372-9929

Georgia
Cain Tower
229 Peachtree St. NE, Ste. 917
Atlanta, GA 30303
tel.: 404/522-5373

Illinois
225 N. Michigan Ave., Ste. 708
Chicago, IL 60601
tel.: 312/856-0316

New York
150 E. 58th St., 17th Fl.
New York, NY 10155
tel.: 212/826-2916

Texas
2777 Stemmons Fwy., Ste. 1622
Dallas, TX 75207
tel.: 214/688-4096

1100 N.W. Loop 410, Ste. 409
San Antonio, TX 78213
tel.: 512/525-0748

Finance

Contact the IRS for publication number 54, Tax Guide for U.S. Citizens and Resident Aliens Living Abroad, at tel. 800/829-3676 or www.irs.gov.

Financial Advisors

Operadoras de Fondos Lloyd, S.A.
tel.: 333/880-2000
http://lloyd@lloyd.com.mx

Multivalores Casa de Bolsa
tel.: 376/766-0912
www.multivaloresgf.com.mx.

Publications

El Financiero
A weekly national financial newspaper.
tel.: 525/227-7600 (Mexico City), 800/433-4872 and 213/747-7547 (in the United States)
www.elfinanciero.com.mx

Communications

INTERNET SERVICE PROVIDERS

Countrywide

www.prodigy.net.mx

Cancún

www.rce.com.mx
www.cancun.com.mx

Mexico City

www.data.net.mx
www.adetel.net
www.alestra.net.mx (AT&T)
www.aventel.com.mx (MCI)
www.axtel.com.mx

www.internet.com.mx
www.metrored.com.mx

Guadalajara

www.arbinet.com.mx
www.vinet.net.mx

Mérida

tel.: 999/942-2213
www.site.dyred.com.mx

Guanajuato

www.redes.int.com.mx

Puerto Vallarta

tel.: 322/223-1127
www.pvnet.com.mx

San Miguel de Allende

www.unisono@unisono.net.mx
www.mpsnet.com.mx

Ajijic

www.lagunanet.net.mx

Mazatlán

www.red2000com.mx
www.mazcity.com.mx
www.maztravel.com
moytoy@Mazatlan.com.mx
moytoy@red2000.com.mx

Two other local Internet servers are Noroeste Net and AcNet, both of which have the same email address, ventasmzt@acnet.net.

Cuernavaca

www.jabanetworks.us
tel.: 800/999-5222 in United States

Infosel Cuernavaca in Chapultepec
tel.: 777/322-7300 or 777/322-7300

PHONE COMPANIES

www.telmex.com.mx
www.vonage.com
www.net2phone.com
www.iconnecthere.com
www.deltathree.com

MEDIA

Chapala Area Publications

Guadalajara Reporter
A weekly newspaper in the Gua-

dalajara and Lake Chapala area, with Puerto Vallarta and Manzanillo supplements.
tel.: 333/615-2177
fax: 333/616-9432
www.guadalajarareporter.com

The Bargain Hunter
A free monthly advertising paper in the Lake Chapala area.
tel./fax: 376/762-0403

El Ojo Del Lago
A monthly newspaper containing general information about lakeside.
tel.: 376/765-2877 or 376/765-3676.
www.chapala.com

Puerto Vallarta Publications

Vallarta Today
Vallarta's daily English-language newspaper
tel.: 322/224-2829 or 322/226-1543
fax: 322/226-1544
jgyserpr@zonavirtual.com.mx

San Miguel De Allende Publications

Atencion San Miguel
A weekly newspaper in San Miguel de Allende.
tel/fax: 415/152-3770
atencion@unisono.net.mx

Oaxaca Publications

Oaxaca Times
A small local newspaper in English and Spanish.

tel.: 951/515-8764
www.oaxacatimes.com

Mazatlán Publications
Pacific Pearl
The only English-language
newspaper, with stories and information.
tel.: 669/913-0117
tel./fax: 669/913-4411
www.yooper@red2000.com.mx

Cuernavaca
La Union de Morelos
A local daily newspaper that has
an English-language international news section.
www.launion.com.mx

Mexico City
Herald Tribune
mexcittm@infosel.net.mx

Travel and Transportation

MEXICAN AUTO INSURANCE

Lewis and Lewis Insurance
tel.: 800/966-6830, 310/657-1112
www.mexicanautoinsurance.com

Solutions Abroad
www.solutionsabroad.com

Mexico Adventure
www.mexadventure.com

Sanborns
www.sanbornsinsurance.com

Lloyd
www.lloyd@lloyd.com.mx

Green Angels
Published by the Secretaría de
Turismo de Mexico, a description
and listing of all the Green Angel
locations throughout the country.
tel.: 800/929-4555 (in the

United States) or 525/203-0519
(in Mexico)

MEXICAN GOVERNMENT TOURIST OFFICES IN THE UNITED STATES

California
10100 Santa Monica Blvd., Ste. 224
Los Angeles, CA 90067
tel.: 310/203-8191
fax: 310/203-8316

Florida
2333 Ponce de León Blvd., Ste. 710
Coral Gables, FL 33134
tel.: 305/443-9160
fax: 305/443-1186

Illinois
70 E. Lake St., Ste. 1413
Chicago, IL 60601
tel.: 312/565-2778
fax: 312/606-9012

New York
450 Park Ave., Ste. 1401
New York, NY 10022
tel.: 212/755-7261
fax: 212/755-2874

Texas
2707 North Loop West, Ste. 450
Houston, TX 77008

tel.: 713/880-5153
fax: 713/880-1833

Washington, D.C.
1911 Pennsylvania Ave. NW
Washington, D.C. 20006
tel.: 202/728-1750
fax: 202/728-1758

Housing Considerations

Mexico Real Estate and Travel
tel.: 800/501-0319 (in the United States)

REAL ESTATE AGENTS

Mexico City

Century 21 Kasa
tel.: 555/264-5499

Century 21 Lomax
tel.: 555/520-5282

HIR
tel.: 555/525-3286

P&P Real Estate Consultants
tel.: 555/280-7474

ReMax Plus
tel.: 555/281-3881

Rojkind Real Estate
tel.: 555/344-1111

San Miguel de Allende

Dotty Vidargas Real Estate
tel.: 415/152-0286 or 415/152-5731
fax: 415/152-2347
Vidargas@unisono.net.mx

Real Estate San Miguel
tel.: 415/152-2284 or 415/152-6510
fax: 415/152-7377
resmig@unisono.net.mx
www.unisono.net.mx/realestatesm

ReMax
tel.: 415/152-7363 or 415/152-7365
mail@realestate-sma.com

Zavala Garay
tel.: 415/152-5389
zavala27@prodigy,net.mx
www.portalsanmiguel.com/zavgar

Lake Chapala

Century 21
Km. 4 Carretera Chapala-Jocotepec
Frac. Chula Vista

Chapala, Jalisco 45900
tel.: 376/765-2529; 367/765-3612

Lloyd Grupo Inmobiliario
Fco. I. Madero No. 232
Chapala, Jalisco 45900
tel.: 376/765-4042

Lake Chapala Area

Ajijic Real Estate
tel.: 376/766-2077
fax: 376/766-2331
email@ajijic.com
www.ajijic.com

Coldwell Banker Chapala
Realty
tel.: 376/765-2877
chapala@infosel.net.mx
www.chapala.com

Eager & Associates
tel.: 376/766-1917 or 376/766-1918

Laguna Real Estate
tel.: 376/766-1174 or 376/766-1186
laguna@laguna.com.mx

ReMax Fenix
tel.: 376/766-1776
remax-fenix@laguna.com.mx
www.ajijic-chapala.com

Applegate Realtors
tel.: 322/221-5434
www.applegaterealtors.com

Bill Taylor Real Estate
tel.: 322/221-0923
www.tristarrentals.com

San Francisco and Suyalita, Nayarit

F.L. Feibel Y Asociados
tel./fax: 322/258-4041
www.flfeibel.com
fred@flfeibel.com

PV Realty
tel.: 322/222-4288
www.pvre.com

Timothy Fuller & Associates
tel.: 322/222-1535
www.timothyfuller.com

Cuernavaca

Grupo Sys/Freeman Real Estate
Calle Jojutla No.3
Col. Vista Hermosa
C.P. 62290 Cuernavaca, Morelos
tel./fax: 777/312-5425
alavi@grupo-sys.net
arik_lavi@yahoo.com
www.grupo-sys.net
www.freeman-realestate.com

Century 21 CuernaMax
tel.: 777/322-5252 or 777/322-4981

Esquerro & Associates
tel.: 777/326-0128 or 777/324-1003

Mazatlán

Pacific Properties
tel.: 669/913-0117 or 669/913-4411

RealtyMex
tel.: 669/914-5323 or 669/914-4001
fax: 669/914-5328
realtytour@acnet.net
www.realtymex.com.mx

Guadalajara

Century 21
Av. Mexico No. 2497
Sector Hidalgo
Guadalajara, Jalisco
tel.: 333/615-1552
fax: 333/616-9669

Corona & Orozco
tel.: 333/616-5120

Frava Grupo Inmobiliaro
tel.: 333/678-0333

Lloyd Investments and Real Estate
Lloyd Grupo Inmobiliario
Av. Mariano Otero No. 1915-D
Guadalajara, Jalisco 44560
tel.: 333/647-5047 or 333/647-5056
fax: 333/647-50-56
lloyd@lloyd.com.mx

Promociones PIM, S.A.
Circ. Agustin Yañez No. 2422 - 2
Guadalajara, Jalisco
tel.: 333/615-4733, 333/615-0357, or 333/615-1427

Oaxaca
Bienes Raices Arlette Escobar Olie
tel.: 951/515-4737

Century 21 Grupo
tel.: 951/516-0323, 951/516-0347, or 951/516-0367

Manzanillo
Real Estate Lomelin
tel.: 314/334-0340
fax: 314/333-0783

Guanajuato
Carlos Ordaz Chico
tel.: 473/732-1222

Pátzcuaro
Century 21 Rodriguez Voirol
tel.: 434/314-9800 or 434/314-2381

Yucatán
Estudio Mérida
www.Méridahomes.com

Mexico International
www.mexico-international.com

Tierra Maya
www.jensyucatan.com

Spanish Phrasebook

Your Mexico adventure will be more fun if you use a little Spanish. Mexican folks, although they may smile at your funny accent, will appreciate your halting efforts to break the ice and transform yourself from a foreigner into a potential friend.

Spanish commonly uses 30 letters—the familiar English 26, plus four straightforward additions: ch, ll, ñ, and rr, which are explained in the Consonants section.

PRONUNCIATION

Once you learn them, Spanish pronunciation rules—in contrast to English rules—don't change. Spanish vowels generally sound softer than English vowels. (Note: The capitalized syllables below receive stronger accents.)

Vowels

a—like ah, as in "hah": *agua* AH-gooah (water), *pan* PAHN (bread), and *casa* CAH-sah (house)

e—like ay, as in "may:" *mesa* MAY-sah (table), *tela* TAY-lah (cloth), and *de* DAY (of, from)

i—like ee, as in "need": *diez* dee-AYZ (ten), *comida* ko-MEE-dah (meal), and *fin* FEEN (end)

o—like oh, as in "go": *peso* PAY-soh (weight), *ocho* OH-choh (eight), and *poco* POH-koh (a bit)

u—like oo, as in "cool": *uno* OO-noh (one), *cuarto* KOO-AHR-toh (room), and *usted* oos-TAYD (you); when it follows a "q" the **u** is silent; when it follows an "h" or has an umlaut, it's pronounced like "w."

Consonants

b, d, f, k, l, m, n, p, q, s, t, v, w, x, y, z, and **ch**—pronounced almost as in English; **h** occurs, but is silent.

c—like k, as in "keep": *cuarto* KOOAR-toh (room), Tepic tay-PEEK (capital of Nayarit state); when it precedes "e" or "i," **c** is pronounced like s, as in "sit": *cerveza* sayr-VAY-sah (beer), *encima* ayn-SEE-mah (atop).

g—like g, as in "gift" when it precedes "a," "o," "u," or a consonant: *gato* GAH-toh (cat), *hago* AH-goh (I do, make); otherwise, pronounce **g** like h, as in "hat": *giro* HEE-roh (money order), *gente* HAYN-tay (people).

j—like h, as in "has": *Jueves* HOOAY-vays (Thursday), *mejor* may-HOR (better)

ll—like y, as in "yes": *toalla* toh-AH-yah (towel), *ellos* AY-yohs (they, them)

ñ—like ny, as in "canyon": *año* AH-nyo (year), *señor* SAY-nyor (mister, sir)

r—lightly trilled, with tongue at the roof of your mouth like a very light English d, as in "ready": *pero* PAY-doh (but), *tres* TDAYS (three), *cuatro* KOOAH-tdoh (four).

rr—like a Spanish r, but with much more emphasis and trill. Let your tongue flap. Practice with *burro* (donkey), *carretera* (highway), and Carrillo (proper name), then really let go with *ferrocarril* (railroad).

Note: The single small but common exception to all of the above is the pronunciation of Spanish **y** when it's being used as the Spanish word for "and," as in "Ron y Kathy." In such cases, pronounce it like the English ee, as in "keep": Ron EE Kathy (Ron and Kathy).

Accent

The rule for accent, the relative stress given to syllables within a given word, is straightforward. If a word ends in a vowel, an n, or an s, accent the next-to-last syllable; if not, accent the last syllable.

Pronounce *gracias* GRAH-see-ahs (thank you), *orden* OHR-dayn (order), and *carretera* kah-ray-TAY-rah (highway) with stress on the next-to-last syllable.

Otherwise, accent the last syllable: *venir* vay NEER (to come), *ferrocarril* fay-roh-cah-REEL (railroad), and *edad* ay-DAHD (age).

Exceptions to the accent rule are always marked with an accent sign: (á, é, í, ó, or ú), such as *teléfono* tay-LAY-foh-noh (telephone), *jabón* hah-BON (soap), and *rápido* RAH-pee-doh (rapid).

BASIC AND COURTEOUS EXPRESSIONS

Most Spanish-speaking people consider formalities important. Whenever approaching anyone for information or some other reason, do not forget the appropriate salutation—good morning, good evening, etc. Standing alone, the greeting *hola* (hello) can sound brusque.

Hello.—*Hola.*
Good morning.—*Buenos días.*
Good afternoon.—*Buenas tardes.*
Good evening.—*Buenas noches.*
How are you?—*¿Cómo está usted?*
Very well, thank you.—*Muy bien, gracias.*
Okay; good.—*Bien.*
Not okay; bad.—*Mal* or *feo.*
So-so.—*Más o menos.*
And you?—*¿Y usted?*
Thank you.—*Gracias.*

Thank you very much.—*Muchas gracias.*
You're very kind.—*Muy amable.*
You're welcome.—*De nada.*
Goodbye.—*Adios.*
See you later.—*Hasta luego.*
please—*por favor*
yes—*sí*
no—*no*
I don't know.—*No sé.*
Just a moment, please.—*Momentito, por favor.*
Excuse me, please (when you're trying to get attention).—*Disculpe* or *Con permiso.*
Excuse me (when you've made a boo-boo).—*Lo siento.*
Pleased to meet you.—*Mucho gusto.*
How do you say... in Spanish?—*¿Cómo se dice... en español?*
What is your name?—*¿Cómo se llama usted?*
My name is...—*Me llamo...*
Do you speak English?—*¿Habla usted inglés?*
Is English spoken here? (Does anyone here speak English?)—*¿Se habla inglés?*
I don't speak Spanish well.—*No hablo bien el español.*
I don't understand.—*No entiendo.*
Would you like... ?—*¿Quisiera usted...?*
Let's go to...—*Vamos a...*

TERMS OF ADDRESS

When in doubt, use the formal *usted* (you) as a form of address.

I—*yo*
you (formal)—*usted*
you (familiar)—*tu*
he/him—*él*
she/her—*ella*
we/us—*nosotros*
you (plural)—*ustedes*
they/them—*ellos* (all males or mixed gender); *ellas* (all females)
Mr., sir—*señor*
Mrs., madam—*señora*
miss, young lady—*señorita*
wife—*esposa*
husband—*esposo*
friend—*amigo* (male); *amiga* (female)
sweetheart—*novio* (male); *novia* (female)
son; daughter—*hijo; hija*
brother; sister—*hermano; hermana*
father; mother—*padre; madre*
grandfather; grandmother—*abuelo; abuela*

TRANSPORTATION

Where is... ?—*¿Dónde está... ?*
How far is it to... ?—*¿A cuánto está... ?*
from... to...—*de... a...*
How many blocks?—*¿Cuántas cuadras?*
Where (Which) is the way to... ?—*¿Dónde está el camino a... ?*
the bus station—*la terminal de autobuses*

the bus stop—*la parada de autobuses*

Where is this bus going?—*¿Adónde va este autobús?*

the taxi stand—*la parada de taxis*

the train station—*la estación de ferrocarril*

the boat—*el barco*

the airport—*el aeropuerto*

I'd like a ticket to...—*Quisiera un boleto a...*

first (second) class—*primera (segunda) clase*

roundtrip—*ida y vuelta*

reservation—*reservación*

baggage—*equipaje*

Stop here, please.—*Pare aquí, por favor.*

the entrance—*la entrada*

the exit—*la salida*

the ticket office—*la oficina de boletos*

(very) near; far—*(muy) cerca; lejos*

to; toward—*a*

by; through—*por*

from—*de*

the right—*la derecha*

the left—*la izquierda*

straight ahead—*derecho; directo*

in front—*en frente*

beside—*al lado*

behind—*atrás*

the corner—*la esquina*

the stoplight—*el semáforo*

a turn—*una vuelta*

right here—*aquí*

somewhere around here—*por acá*

right there—*allí*

somewhere around there—*por allá*

street; boulevard—*calle; bulevar*

highway—*carretera*

bridge; toll—*puente; cuota*

address—*dirección*

north; south—*norte; sur*

east; west—*oriente (este); poniente (oeste)*

ACCOMMODATIONS

hotel—*hotel*

Is there a room?—*¿Hay cuarto?*

May I (may we) see it?—*¿Puedo (podemos) verlo?*

What is the rate?—*¿Cuál es el precio?*

Is that your best rate?—*¿Es su mejor precio?*

Is there something cheaper?—*¿Hay algo más económico?*

a single room—*un cuarto sencillo*

a double room—*un cuarto doble*

double bed—*cama matrimonial*

twin beds—*camas gemelas*

with private bath—*con baño*

hot water—*agua caliente*

shower—*ducha*

towels—*toallas*

soap—*jabón*

toilet paper—*papel higiénico*

blanket—*frazada; manta*

sheets—*sábanas*

air-conditioned—*aire acondicionado*

fan—*abanico; ventilador*

key—*llave*

manager—*gerente*

FOOD

I'm hungry—*Tengo hambre.*
I'm thirsty.—*Tengo sed.*
menu—*lista; menú*
order—*orden*
glass—*vaso*
fork—*tenedor*
knife—*cuchillo*
spoon—*cuchara*
napkin—*servilleta*
soft drink—*refresco*
coffee—*café*
tea—*té*
drinking water—*agua pura; agua potable*
bottled carbonated water—*agua mineral*
bottled uncarbonated water—*agua sin gas*
beer—*cerveza*
wine—*vino*
milk—*leche*
juice—*jugo*
cream—*crema*
sugar—*azúcar*
cheese—*queso*
snack—*antojo; botana*
breakfast—*desayuno*
lunch—*almuerzo*
daily lunch special—*comida corrida* (or *el menú del día,* depending on region)
dinner—*comida* (often eaten in late afternoon); *cena* (a late-night snack)
the check—*la cuenta*
eggs—*huevos*
bread—*pan*
salad—*ensalada*

fruit—*fruta*
mango—*mango*
watermelon—*sandía*
papaya—*papaya*
banana—*plátano*
apple—*manzana*
orange—*naranja*
lime—*limón*
fish—*pescado*
shellfish—*mariscos*
shrimp—*camarones*
(without) meat—*(sin) carne*
chicken—*pollo*
pork—*puerco*
beef; steak—*res; bistec*
bacon; ham—*tocino; jamón*
fried—*frito*
roasted—*asada*
barbecue; barbecued—*barbacoa; al carbón*

SHOPPING

money—*dinero*
money-exchange bureau—*casa de cambio*
I would like to exchange traveler's checks.—*Quisiera cambiar cheques de viajero.*
What is the exchange rate?—*¿Cuál es el tipo de cambio?*
How much is the commission?—*¿Cuánto cuesta la comisión?*
Do you accept credit cards?—*¿Aceptan tarjetas de crédito?*
How much does it cost?—*¿Cuánto cuesta?*
What is your final price?—*¿Cuál es su último precio?*
expensive—*caro*

cheap—*barato; económico*
more—*más*
less—*menos*
a little—*un poco*
too much—*demasiado*

HEALTH

Help me, please.—*Ayúdeme, por favor.*
I am ill.—*Estoy enfermo.*
Call a doctor.—*Llame un doctor.*
Take me to...—*Lléveme a...*
hospital—*hospital; sanatorio*
drugstore—*farmacia*
pain—*dolor*
fever—*fiebre*
headache—*dolor de cabeza*
stomach ache—*dolor de estómago*
burn—*quemadura*
cramp—*calambre*
nausea—*náusea*
vomiting—*vomitar*
medicine—*medicina*
antibiotic—*antibiótico*
pill; tablet—*pastilla*
aspirin—*aspirina*
ointment; cream—*pomada; crema*
bandage—*venda*
cotton—*algodón*
sanitary napkins—use brand name, e.g., Kotex
birth control pills—*pastillas anticonceptivas*
contraceptive foam—*espuma anticonceptiva*
condoms—*preservativos; condones*
toothbrush—*cepilla dental*
dental floss—*hilo dental*
toothpaste—*crema dental*
dentist—*dentista*
toothache—*dolor de muelas*

POST OFFICE AND COMMUNICATIONS

long-distance telephone—*teléfono larga distancia*
I would like to call...—*Quisiera llamar a...*
collect—*por cobrar*
station to station—*a quién contesta*
person to person—*persona a persona*
credit card—*tarjeta de crédito*
post office—*correo*
general delivery—*lista de correo*
letter—*carta*
stamp—*estampilla, timbre*
postcard—*tarjeta*
aerogram—*aerograma*
air mail—*correo aereo*
registered—*registrado*
money order—*giro*
package; box—*paquete; caja*
string; tape—*cuerda; cinta*

AT THE BORDER

border—*frontera*
customs—*aduana*
immigration—*migración*
tourist card—*tarjeta de turista*
inspection—*inspección; revisión*
passport—*pasaporte*
profession—*profesión*
marital status—*estado civil*
single—*soltero*
married; divorced—*casado; divorciado*

widowed—*viudado*
insurance—*seguros*
title—*título*
driver's license—*licencia de manejar*

AT THE GAS STATION

gas station—*gasolinera*
gasoline—*gasolina*
unleaded—*sin plomo*
full, please—*lleno, por favor*
tire—*llanta*
tire repair shop—*vulcanizadora*
air—*aire*
water—*agua*
oil (change)—*aceite (cambio)*
grease—*grasa*
My...doesn't work.—*Mi...no sirve.*

battery—*batería*
radiator—*radiador*
alternator—*alternador*
generator—*generador*
tow truck—*grúa*
repair shop—*taller mecánico*
tune-up—*afinación*
auto parts store—*refaccionería*

VERBS

Verbs are the key to getting along in Spanish. They employ mostly predictable forms and come in three classes, which end in *ar, er,* and *ir,* respectively.

to buy—*comprar*
I buy, you (he, she, it) buys—*compro, compra*

we buy, you (they) buy—*compramos, compran*

to eat—*comer*
I eat, you (he, she, it) eats—*como, come*
we eat, you (they) eat—*comemos, comen*

to climb—*subir*
I climb, you (he, she, it) climbs—*subo, sube*
we climb, you (they) climb—*subimos, suben*

Got the idea? Here are more (with irregularities marked in **bold**).

to do or make—*hacer*
I do or make, you (he she, it) does or makes—***hago**, hace*
we do or make, you (they) do or make—*hacemos, hacen*

to go—*ir*
I go, you (he, she, it) goes—***voy, va***
we go, you (they) go—***vamos, van***

to go (walk)—*andar*
to love—*amar*
to work—*trabajar*
to want—*desear, querer*
to need—*necesitar*
to read—*leer*
to write—*escribir*
to repair—*reparar*
to stop—*parar*

to get off (the bus)—*bajar*
to arrive—*llegar*
to stay (remain)—*quedar*
to stay (lodge)—*hospedar*
to leave—*salir* (regular except for I leave—***salgo***)
to look at—*mirar*
to look for—*buscar*
to give—*dar* (regular except for I give—***doy***)
to carry—*llevar*
to have—*tener* (irregular but important: ***tengo, tiene,*** *tenemos,* ***tienen***)
to come—*venir* (similarly irregular: ***vengo, viene, venimos, vienen***)

Spanish has two forms of "to be." Use *estar* when speaking of location or a temporary state of being: "I am at home." *"**Estoy en casa.**"* "I'm sick." *"**Estoy enfermo.**"* Use *ser* for a permanent state of being: "I am a doctor." *"**Soy doctora.**"*
Estar is regular except for I am—***estoy***. *Ser* is very irregular:

to be—*ser*
I am, you (he, she, it) is—***soy, es***
we are, you (they) are—***somos, son***

NUMBERS

zero—*cero*
one—*uno*
two—*dos*
three—*tres*
four—*cuatro*
five—*cinco*
six—*seis*
seven—*siete*
eight—*ocho*
nine—*nueve*
10—*diez*
11—*once*
12—*doce*
13—*trece*
14—*catorce*
15—*quince*
16—*dieciseis*
17—*diecisiete*
18—*dieciocho*
19—*diecinueve*
20—*veinte*
21—*veinte y uno* or *veintiuno*
30—*treinta*
40—*cuarenta*
50—*cincuenta*
60—*sesenta*
70—*setenta*
80—*ochenta*
90—*noventa*
100—*ciento*
101—*ciento y uno* or *cientiuno*
200—*doscientos*
500—*quinientos*
1,000—*mil*
10,000—*diez mil*
100,000—*cien mil*
1,000,000—*millón*
one half—*medio*
one third—*un tercio*
one fourth—*un cuarto*

TIME

What time is it?—*¿Qué hora es?*
It's one o'clock.—*Es la una.*

It's three in the afternoon.—*Son las tres de la tarde.*
It's 4 A.M.—*Son las cuatro de la mañana.*
six-thirty—*seis y media*
a quarter till eleven—*un cuarto para las once*
a quarter past five—*las cinco y cuarto*
an hour—*una hora*

DAYS AND MONTHS

Monday—*lunes*
Tuesday—*martes*
Wednesday—*miércoles*
Thursday—*jueves*
Friday—*viernes*
Saturday—*sábado*
Sunday—*domingo*
today—*hoy*
tomorrow—*mañana*

yesterday—*ayer*
January—*enero*
February—*febrero*
March—*marzo*
April—*abril*
May—*mayo*
June—*junio*
July—*julio*
August—*agosto*
September—*septiembre*
October—*octubre*
November—*noviembre*
December—*diciembre*
a week—*una semana*
a month—*un mes*
after—*después*
before—*antes*

Courtesy of Bruce Whipperman, author of *Moon Handbooks Pacific Mexico.*

Glossary

agua: water or water-based fruit drink

aguinaldo: Christmas bonus

Angeles Verdes: Green Angels, a government-sponsored highway-assistance program

autopista or maxipista: toll highway

avena: oatmeal

baluartes: forts

barrancas: canyons

biblioteca: library

bolillos: crusty French bread–style Mexican rolls

bruja: witch

cabrito: baby goat

café de olla: home-brewed coffee made with cinnamon

calesa: a horse-drawn buggy

camarones a la diabla: shrimp smothered in a hot sauce

campesinos: farmers and country folk; peasants

centro: downtown

charreada: Mexican rodeo

chiles en nogada: green chile stuffed with ground beef and smothered in a tamarind-walnut cream sauce with pomegranate seeds sprinkled on top

chipotle: a smoky, not-too-hot chile

colonias: neighborhoods

conchero: an Aztec style of dancing

cuota: toll road

curanderos: healers

ejido: a community of people, living together in an area or a town, who own the surrounding land in common

en punto: on the dot

escritora: deed

espiritualista: medium

fraccionamiento: subdivision

huitlacoche: a black fungus that grows on corn, often served in crepes

iglesia: church

jardín: main plaza

libramiento: truck route

libre: free or free road

licuado: a smoothie with any combination of fruits and water or milk

Lista de Correos: general delivery

maestro: teacher; also, foreman

magna sin: regular unleaded gas

malecón: jetty or breakwater

mal puesto: illnesses caused by witchcraft

mapaches: small raccoon-like mammals

menudo: tripe

mirador: observation deck

mordida: bribe; literally, bite

motel familiar: family motel

notario: a particular classification of lawyer

palacio municipal: town hall

palapa: a palm-frond shack with no flooring

parada: stop

pesera: a minibus, normally a VW van

posada: Advent celebration; inn

premium: super unleaded gas

prima vacaciona: vacation bonus

privadas: private, secure streets

sala: living room

sarandeado: a style of barbecuing fish in the state of Nayarit

sitio: official taxi stand

Sopa Azteca: Aztec soup, usually a clear tomato- or chicken-based broth with crisp tortilla strips, avocado, onions, cheese, chipotle chile, and chicken

sueldo minimo: minimum wage

Tapatios: people from Guadalajara

te de manzanilla: chamomile tea

telenovelas: soap operas

te negro: black tea

tianguis: outdoor arts-and-crafts markets

topes: speed bumps

Trato Directo: direct deal; equivalent of "For Sale by Owner"

tuna: cactus fruit

zócalo: public square

Suggested Reading

Nonfiction

AAA. *Mexico Travel Book*. San Francisco, California: American Automobile Association, 1999.

American Chamber of Commerce. *Guide to Mexico for Business*. Copies can be obtained from the American Chamber of Commerce in Mexico.

American Chamber of Commerce. *Relocating to Mexico*. Copies can be obtained from the American Chamber of Commerce in Mexico.

Box, Ben and Sarah Cameron. *Footprint Mexico & Central America Handbook 2000*. Lincolnwood, Illinois: Passport Books, 2000.

Bryant, Jean and John D. *Mexico Living and Travel*. Mexico Retirement & Travel, 1994.

Church, Mike and Terri Church. *Traveler's Guide to Mexican Camping*. Kirkland, Washington: Rolling Homes Press, 2001.

Coe, Andrew and Kal Muller. *Mexico City*. Hong Kong: Odyssey Publications, 1999.

Cohan, Tony. *On Mexican Time: A New Life in San Miguel*. New York: Broadway Books, 2001.

Consumer Guide Editors. *Best Rated Retirement Cities and Towns*. New American Library, 1988.

Cummings, Joe. *Moon Handbooks Baja, Tijuana to Cabo San Lucas. 6th Edition*. Emeryville, California: Avalon Travel Publishing, 2004.

Davis, L. Irby. *A Field Guide to the Birds of Mexico and Central America*. Austin, Texas: University of Texas Press, 1972.

Fisher, Richard D. *Mexico's Copper Canyon*. Tucson, Arizona: Sunracer Publications, 2003.

Franz, Carl, Steve Rogers, and Lorena Havens. *The People's Guide to Mexico*. Emeryville, California: Avalon Travel Publishing, 2002.

Gordon, Gus and Thurmon Williams. *Doing Business in Mexico: A Practical Guide*. Better Business Books, 2002.

Horn, James J. *Cuernavaca: A Guide for Students & Tourists*. Self-published by author, 1984.

Howells, John and Don Merwin. *Choose Mexico for Retirement*. Guilford, Connecticut: Globe Pequot Press, 2005.

Insight Guides. *Insight Guides: Mexico*. London, England: Insight Guides, 1999.

Kendrick, Teresa A. *Mexico's Lake Chapala and Ajijic: The Insider's Guide to the Northshore for International Travelers*. Self-published by author, updated yearly.

Lambdin, Griffith D. *Odyssey to Guadalajara*. Packrat Press, 1987.

Mader, Ron. *Adventures in Nature Mexico*. Emeryville, California: Avalon Travel Publishing, 1998.

Nelson, "Mexico" Mike. *Live Better South of the Border in Mexico*. Golden, Colorado: Fulcrum Publishing, 2000.

Nelson, "Mexico" Mike. *Spas & Hot Springs of Mexico*. Mission, Texas: Roads Scholar Press, 1997.

Newman, Gary and Anna Szterenfed. *Guide to Doing Business in Mexico*. New York: McGraw-Hill, 1995.

O'Reilly, James and Larry Habegger, eds. *Travelers' Tales Mexico*. Palo Alto, California: Travelers' Tales Guides, 2001.

Rogers, Steve and Tina Rosa. *The Shopper's Guide to Mexico*. California: John Muir Publications, 1989.

Schlundt, Hayes C. and Philip H. Hersey. *Living Easy in Mexico*. United Research Publishers, 1998.

Simon, Kate. *Mexico, Places and Pleasures*. New York: HarperCollins, 1988.

Street-Porter, Tim. *Casa Mexicana: The Architecture, Design and Style of Mexico*. New York: Stewart, Tabori & Chang, 1989.

Thurburn, Lee. *Mexico: New Land of Opportunity: A Guide to Doing Business in Mexico*. Mexico Information Services, 1994.

Valle, Victor M. and Mary Lau Valle. *Recipe of Memory: Five Generations of Mexican Cuisine*.

New York: The New Press, 1997.

Vicars, Polly G., Hubert Vicars (photographer), and Wayne McLeod (photographer). *Tales of Retirement in Paradise*. America-Mexico Foundation, 1995.

Whipperman, Bruce. *Moon Handbooks Guadalajara*. Emeryville, California: Avalon Travel Publishing, 2005.

Whipperman, Bruce. *Moon Handbooks Oaxaca*. Emeryville, California: Avalon Travel Publishing, 2004.

Whipperman, Bruce. *Moon Handbooks Pacific Mexico*, Emeryville, California: Avalon Travel Publishing, 2005.

Whipperman, Bruce. *Moon Handbooks Puerto Vallarta*. Emeryville, California: Avalon Travel Publishing, 2005.

Winsor, Anita. *Complete Guide to Doing Business in Mexico*. Amacom Books, 1994.

Wise, Sidney Thomas. *Invest and Retire in Mexico*. Dolphin Books, 1973.

Fiction

Doerr, Harriet. *Stones for Ibarra*. New York: Penguin Group, 1988.

Esquivel, Laura. *Like Water for Chocolate*. New York: Anchor Books, 1995.

Jennings, Gary. *Aztec*. New York: Forge, 1997.

Michener, James A. *Mexico*. New York: Fawcett Books, 1994.

History

Meyer, Michael C. and William H. Beezley, eds. *The Oxford History of Mexico*. Oxford, England: Oxford University Press, 2000.

Meyer, Michael C., William L. Sherman, and Susan M. Deeds.

The Course of Mexican History. Oxford, England: Oxford University Press, 2002.

Miller, Robert Ryal *Mexico: A History*, Norman, Oklahoma: University of Oklahoma Press, 1989.

Index

Acknowledgments

Writing the book was never as much fun as when I was working closely with Barbara. She always provided her critical eye, effortless good humor, and an often much needed hug. Support, love, and advice came from many quarters. Here are a just a few of the people who were there to help me over the rough patches. I love you all.

Jan Ambrose, Steven Cary, Smadar Belkind, Rita Bray, Bruce Brigham, Kendal Dodge Butler, Maureen Earl, Fred Feibel, Stan Grey, Kent Edwards and Linda Brown, Jim Johnston, Sandy Leonard, Elizabeth McCue from Avalon Travel Publishing, Jill Nokes, Bill Reiner, Bob and Lee Story, Hector Ulloa, Trudy Woodcock. Special hugs to Liza.

U.S. ~ Metric Conversion

1 inch = 2.54 centimeters (cm)
1 foot = .304 meters (m)
1 yard = 0.914 meters
1 mile = 1.6093 kilometers (km)
1 km = .6214 miles
1 fathom = 1.8288 m
1 chain = 20.1168 m
1 furlong = 201.168 m
1 acre = .4047 hectares
1 sq km = 100 hectares
1 sq mile = 2.59 square km
1 ounce = 28.35 grams
1 pound = .4536 kilograms
1 short ton = .90718 metric ton
1 short ton = 2000 pounds
1 long ton = 1.016 metric tons
1 long ton = 2240 pounds
1 metric ton = 1000 kilograms
1 quart = .94635 liters
1 US gallon = 3.7854 liters
1 Imperial gallon = 4.5459 liters
1 nautical mile = 1.852 km

To compute Celsius temperatures, subtract 32 from Fahrenheit and divide by 1.8. To go the other way, multiply Celsius by 1.8 and add 32.

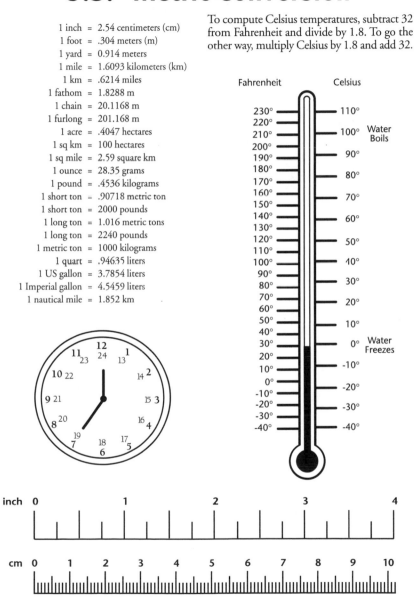

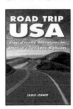